THE ROLLING STONES
COMPLETE RECORDING SESSIONS
1963 – 1989

THE ROLLING STONES

COMPLETE RECORDING SESSIONS
1963 – 1989

A Sessionography, Discography
and History of Recordings
from the Famous Chart-toppers
to the Infamous Rarities
January 1963 – November 1989

Martin Elliott

BLANDFORD

First published in the UK 1990 by Blandford
An imprint of
Cassell
Villiers House
41–47 Strand
London WC2N 5JE

Text and compilation copyright © Martin Elliott 1990

Reprinted 1990

Distributed in the United States by
Sterling Publishing Co. Inc
387 Park Avenue South, New York, NY 10016-8810

Distributed in Australia by
Capricorn Link (Australia) Pty Ltd
PO Box 665, Lane Cove, NSW 2066

British Library Cataloguing in Publication Data
Elliott, Martin
The Rolling Stones complete recording sessions 1963-1989.
1. Pop music. The Rolling Stones
I. Title
784.5'0092'2

ISBN 0-7137-2118-9 (Paperback)

Designed by Vaughan Allen
Typeset in Rockwell by Communitype Communications Limited, Leicester
Printed in Great Britain by the Bath Press

Contents

Acknowledgements

Thanks to the magnificent eight who made it all possible – a British institution.

Personal thanks to Wendy, for her support, encouragement and guidance – thanks for the typing. To Russell, without whom a lot more may have been achieved (and to Gregory latterly). To Jackie, who typed the original draft: you transformed the incoherent manuscript; so thanks (and you have a good surname!). To my father, Ronald Elliott, who edited the original draft. You made sense of the incoherence!

Thanks also to Chris Bartlett and Mike Carvalho for their advice.

The following books, magazines and musical papers have been very useful in my research and the majority are an invaluable read:

Mandy Aftel: *Death of a Rolling Stone*, Sidgwick & Jackson Ltd., 1982.

John Aldridge: *Satisfaction, the Story of Mick Jagger*, Proteus Books, 1984.

Stanley Booth: *The True Adventures of The Rolling Stones*, Sphere Books Ltd., 1986.

Roy Carr: *The Rolling Stones, An Illustrated Record*, New English Library Ltd., 1976.

Barbara Charone: *Keith Richards Illustrated*, Futura Publications, 1979.

David Dalton: *The Rolling Stones, The First Twenty Years*, Alfred A. Knopf, Inc., 1981.

David Dalton and Mick Farren: *In Their Own Words, The Rolling Stones*, Omnibus Press, 1985.

Miles: *Mick Jagger, In His Own Words*, Omnibus Press, 1982.

Philip Norman: *The Stones*, Elm Tree Books, 1984.

Anthony Scaduto: *Mick Jagger*, W.H. Allen & Co. Ltd., 1974.

Sue Weiner and Lisa Howard: *The Rolling Stones, A–Z*, Omnibus Press, 1984.

Record Collector, The New Musical Express, Melody Maker, Sounds, Q, and *Rolling Stone.*

Introduction

In my youth I wrote in large letters in the sand of a North Cornwall beach, 'The Rolling Stones — A British institution'. Such declarations, unless inscribed on tablets of stone, are temporary, and can be washed away with the tide. They do not begin to indicate the impact the Stones have made all around the world. Briefly, The Rolling Stones have influenced generations of youth culture. They are indigenous to the well-being of rock music and especially the form of music called the rhythm and blues.

I hope that this sessionography at least inspires an interest, and at best, an addiction, to the greatest rock and roll band in the world. The book is written from a 'fan's eye', but nevertheless does not gloss over the Stones' less inspiring moments.

It is nothing less than a chronological journey through the Stones' recorded works. It details many of their known and less well-known tracks. Inevitably a story unfolds, and the book may be used not only for reference purposes but also as an historical account of the Stones' story. Every effort has been made to ensure accuracy of data and events.

The text follows a numerical song-by-song format, based on the Stones' recording sessions. Where possible, every track has details of recording dates, the studio, the availability of the track, the song writers, the production team, and the musician personnel.

The following is a typical entry :

362. IT'S ONLY ROCK 'N' ROLL (BUT I LIKE IT) (Jagger, Richard)
March-April 1974: Musicland, Munich, West Germany. Producer: The Glimmer Twins. Engineer: Andy Johns, Keith Harwood. Assistant Engineers: Tapani Tapanainen, Rod Thear, Howard Kilgour, Mac 'Munich', George Chkiantz
UK Single: 26 July 1974: No. 10 – 7 weeks
USA Single: 26 July 1974: No. 16 – 7 weeks
UK LP IT'S ONLY ROCK 'N' ROLL: 18 October 1974: No. 2 – 9 weeks
USA LP IT'S ONLY ROCK 'N' ROLL: 18 October 1974: No. 1 – 11 weeks
UK Compilation LP MADE IN THE SHADE: 6 June 1975: No. 14 – 12 weeks

*USA Compilation LP MADE IN THE SHADE: 6 June 1975: No. **6** – 9
weeks
Rolling Stones with Ron Wood, Ray Cooper, Kenny Jones, Willy
Weeks, David Bowie*

A session number – here **362** – indicates the approximate sequence of recording. Since The Rolling Stones have recorded at a multitude of recording studios all around the world over a 26-year period, compilation of engineers' logs are impossible to obtain! The fact that the Stones ran many sessions themselves serves to complicate this even further. Therefore, the session number and recording dates are a rough guide to the actual dates.

The session number is followed by the song title. If known by another title, then an 'also known as (a.k.a.). . .' follows.

The song's composers and writers are placed in parentheses after the song title. Keith Richards is credited as 'Richard' until 1977, whereafter, following the Canada drug trial, he reverted to his original name 'Richards'. The songwriting team of Nanker, Phelge is an early band pseudonym.

Estimated recording dates are stated with the recording studio location. Producers, sound and mixing engineers are then accounted for. The production team of The Glimmer Twins is, in fact, Mick Jagger and Keith Richards.

The track's availability on single and album release is indicated. Where a chart position is applicable, the highest placing the song reached is quoted with the overall number of weeks that the single/album spent in the chart. Only the major UK and USA charts are mentioned.

Should the track never have had an official release, then the term 'bootleg only' is used. Not wishing to increase the notoriety of bootlegs, full details are not given!

Guest musicians are also credited. The use of the term 'Rolling Stones' is a broad one. It always includes the band members, Mick Jagger, Keith Richards, Bill Wyman, Charlie Watts, and Ian Stewart, plus either Brian Jones, Mick Taylor or Ron Wood (the latter three depend on the track's recording date). As a guide, from January 1963 to December 1968, Brian Jones was a credited member. Mick Taylor took over in May 1969 – he resigned in April 1974. Ron Wood took over the mantle of second guitarist in December 1974, but his position as a fully-fledged band member was not officially confirmed until December 1975.

It is impossible to separate the late Ian Stewart's contribution since he was always an integral band member. Quite simply, the band would not have existed without his enthusiasm. Ironically, his death in December 1985 also prompted the longest spell of Stones' inactivity until sessions resumed with the full band in April 1989.

'The sunshine bores the daylights out of me – the moon grows cold in memory.'

'First the sun and then the moon – one of them will be round soon'.

1

DIDDLEY DADDY – THE FATHER OF THEM ALL

JANUARY 1963 – FEBRUARY 1964

1. **DIDDLEY DADDY** (McDaniel)
28 January – 2 February 1963: Regent, IBC, London. Engineer: Glyn Johns.
Bootleg only.

At the end of January 1963 the line-up of The Rolling Stones was established. During 1962 Alexis Korner's band, Blues Incorporated, had provided a focal point for the future band members; Charlie Watts regularly played drums while Mick Jagger and Brian Jones guested or jammed on the rock and roll numbers. Brian Jones, keen to form his own band, recruited Ian Stewart, and after a gig Mick Jagger and Keith Richards decided to join the fold. The bass guitar and percussion positions were at that time filled by Dick Taylor and Mick Avory. When Dick Taylor returned to college, Bill Wyman stepped in (because he possessed his own amplifier, a rarity for those days), and Charlie was filched from Blues Incorporated. It was time for the Stones to book themselves into the IBC Studios. The outcome of the sessions are distinctly blues flavoured. *Diddley Daddy* is a Bo Diddley number and is performed in true rhythm and blues (R 'n' B) style. The song, although rough in texture, is guided by Mick Jagger's roots vocals and features two instrumental breaks: the first by Brian Jones on the harmonica and the second by Ian Stewart tinkering on the ivories to the fade out.

2. **ROAD RUNNER** (McDaniel)
28 January – 2 February 1963: Regent, IBC, London. Engineer: Glyn Johns.
Bootleg only.

Road Runner, another well-known Ellis McDaniel (a.k.a. Bo Diddley) number, was next on the list for the Stones treatment and is played in a hard-rocking, non-compromising style. The guitar is the main instrument, and sound-wise Brian Jones (or Elmo Lewis as he liked to be called in true blues tradition) had gained valuable experience by playing Duane Eddy-style numbers in the Cheltenham band, The Ramrods. It was a popular stage favourite at their Crawdaddy Club residency in Richmond and was a small concession in attempting to put across some of the more commercial material onto tape in order to secure a recording contract. Their musical upbringing was in jazz clubs where they were used to playing sedate blues. Andrew 'entrepreneur' Oldham, who was to become their manager, had his finger on the pulse of youth culture and knew that they had to stop sitting on the bar stools, jazz-style, and literally move with the music. They also had to make the music more accessible to the punter by playing more popular tunes. Ironically, on their first British tour as a support act they were to drop all Bo Diddley numbers in deference to the master himself – they found him also on the tour, second on the bill to the Everly Brothers.

3. **BRIGHT LIGHTS, BIG CITY** (Reed)
28 January – 2 February 1963: Regent, IBC, London. Engineer: Glyn Johns.
Bootleg only.

Mick Jagger, who was devoted to Jimmy Reed's music, had previously sent a rough tape to renowned musician Alexis Korner. The tape incorporated *Bright Lights, Big City* under the embarrassing band name of Little Boy Blue and The Blue Boys. His co-musicians at the time were Bob Beckwith, Allen Etherington and Dick Taylor. In 1960 Mick met Keith Richards on a train, the two having not seen each other since primary school days. They reminisced and then discovered music was their current common denominator – Jimmy Reed, Chuck Berry, Muddy Waters, etc. They were both playing in bands and also knew Dick Taylor (who later founded a successful mid-sixties R 'n' B band, The Pretty Things). The seeds were sown, the friendship renewed, and with the help of Alexis's Blues Incorporated they started to gain valuable club experience. This version of *Bright Lights* was literally a one-take at the end of a night session. The track, perhaps in its spontaneity, encapsulates the enthusiasm of the young band.

4. **I WANT TO BE LOVED** (Dixon)
28 January – 2 February 1963: Regent, IBC, London. Engineer: Glyn Johns.
Bootleg only.

This was later to be re–recorded for the B-side of the first single *Come On*. It is a leisurely mix indeed and again instrumentally Ian Stewart and Brian Jones are prominently featured. The song is an authentic Willie Dixon R 'n' B standard. Mick Jagger's vocals are meaningful and interpret the senior blues man's desires in a way that only the young are able – to the extent that the Crawdaddy Club (which met in a London hotel where the Stones had a residency) soon became a local phenomenon. The London 'hip squad' began to take notice, including the press, and membership escalated – dance improvization was rife on the hot sweaty dance floor. The word Craw-Daddy originated from a Bo Diddley-type dance number.

5. **CRACKIN' UP** (McDaniel)
28 January – 2 February 1963: Regent, IBC, London. Engineer: Glyn Johns.
Bootleg only.

Continuing the Bo Diddley theme, *Crackin' Up* was also recorded. Glyn Johns later denied that the recording was ever made! Despite this, original recordings can be found – a live version recorded in 1977 in Toronto being released on the LOVE YOU LIVE album. An earlier Stones' session recorded in October 1962 at Curly Clayton's Sound Studio is also much debated. Three tracks were recorded: *Soon Forgotten*, *Close Together* and *You Can't Judge A Book By Its Cover*. The tracks were recorded as a demo by a Stones line up which included Mick Jagger, Keith Richards, Brian Jones, Dick Taylor (bass guitar), Tony Chapman (on drums) and Ian Stewart – hence the reason for not giving the tracks full sessionography status. Only an EMI acetate remains of this historic recording. This was sold in April 1988 to a privileged collector.

6. **HONEY WHAT'S WRONG** (Reed, Reed)
28 January – 2 February 1963: Regent, IBC, London. Engineer: Glyn Johns.
Bootleg only.

This track wraps up the Stones' first recording session. The IBC sessions, although now famous and much sought after, were considered as a whole far too rough for a commercial release, much to the band's disappointment. *Honey (Baby) What's Wrong* is a meandering–type song and harmonies inspired by Keith Richards leave a lot to be desired. It is an example of the reason for rejection by EMI – sincerity was detected but the inferior studio quality outweighed the end product.

7. **COME ON** (Berry)
10 May 1963: Olympic, London. Producer: Andrew Oldham, Eric Easton. Engineer: Roger Savage.
*UK Single: 7 June 1963: No **21** – 14 weeks*
UK Compilation LP THANK YOUR LUCKY STARS VOL 2: September 1963
*UK Compilation LP READY STEADY GO!: January 1964: No **20** – 1 week*
*UK Compilation LP BIG HITS (HIGH TIDE AND GREEN GRASS): November 1966: No **4** – 43 weeks*

At the time there were only two major UK recording companies – EMI and Decca. Having been rejected by EMI, there was only one more door to knock on. Even the BBC had rejected a recording of the band for a possible radio broadcast in April 1963. The Decca artists and repertoire (A&R) man, Dick Rowe, who had previously turned down The Beatles in favour of Brian Poole and The Tremeloes, wanted to rectify this mistake and recover some standing in the music industry. Ironically, Dick Rowe was tipped off by George Harrison who, with The Beatles, had met the awe-inspired, tongue-tied Stones after a gig at the Crawdaddy Club. A month before, Andrew Oldham had convinced Eric Easton, who had a vast club circuit knowledge, that he was the ideal man to be their manager. Two days after seeing the Stones, Dick Rowe, anxious not to miss another talent, contacted Eric Easton and the uncommercial R 'n' B band were signed and contracted. Andrew Oldham negotiated a shrewd contract enabling the Stones to record independently and then sell the tapes back to Decca. Naturally, Decca wanted perfection and there were a lot of wasted tapes of *Come On.* At last Andrew Oldham relented and a satisfactory take was recorded in Decca's own studios, the outcome being a frenetic version of Chuck Berry's *Come On.* The band themselves were not too happy with the result created by 'no mix' producer Andrew Oldham and sound engineer Roger Savage. The speed of the record was significant – it was too fast to dance to. However, it entered the lower echelons of the UK charts on 25 July 1963 and became their first 'hit'. In the studio it is likely that they cut two further R 'n' B standards which have not subsequently been released: *Love Potion No 9* and *Pretty Thing. Come On* must have been chosen as the initial release because the Chuck Berry number was previously unknown in Britain and to the public it could have been construed as an original. The track was included on a THANK YOUR LUCKY STARS compilation of various artists released by Decca in September 1963.

8. **I WANT TO BE LOVED** (Dixon)
    10 May 1963: Olympic, London. Producer: Andrew Oldham, Eric Easton. Engineer: Roger Savage.
    UK B-side Come On: 7 June 1963

This song, which was previously recorded as a demo, now presented a problem to the signed six. IBC Studios retained the original recordings and after a tale of woe the unsuspecting IBC returned the tapes for a modest sum of £100. It was the first Stones' snatch – it is rumoured that they employed a band split/souvenir story to recover the tapes. This version of *I Want To Be Loved* is a faster guitar boogie than the original take and is also polished by a quality studio finish. The release of the single, of which this was the flipside, was coupled by an appearance on the acclaimed 'Thank Your Lucky Stars' TV show, where both sides were featured. As a result, a modest chart entry ensued. The TV recording is famous for the appealing chequered suits, an image they attempted hastily to reject. In order to project the Stones on camera, Andrew Oldham decided that Ian Stewart should not accompany the others in publicity features as he had a somewhat staid appearance. The Stones were starting to feel their way up the pop ladder by such compromises, whilst managing to retain their musical integrity.

9. **POISON IVY** (Leiber, Stoller)
    July/August 1963: Decca, London. Producer: Andrew Oldham, M. Barclay.
    UK Compilation LP SATURDAY CLUB: January 1964

The Stones were now eager to capitalize on their recent chart position with *Come On.* After a lot of internal conflict, they compromised and decided to record a Coasters' song; *I'm A Hog For You Baby* was considered but they settled for *Poison Ivy.* The song is a little rushed and suffers also from muffled studio problems. It was commercially viable but lacked the quality necessary to be a follow-up to *Come On*. Decca went as far as issuing a catalogue number of F11742 before the proposed single was scrapped. The Stones and Andrew Oldham were exasperated and Decca were positively fuming. Decca had attempted to use their own producer at the session, an idea which failed miserably. Andrew Oldham started to search frantically for a follow-up. He was aware that other popular groups, notably The Beatles, were recording their own songs and he pressurized Mick Jagger and Keith Richards to do the same.

10. **IT SHOULD BE YOU** (Jagger, Richard)
July/August 1963: Decca, London. Producer: Andrew Oldham.
Bootleg only.

The pressure from Andrew Oldham forced Mick Jagger and Keith Richards to attempt the art of songwriting. *It Should Be You* is their very first attempt and is clearly best forgotten. The song was given to another Decca artist, the late George Bean, but he was unable to bring any credibility to it, the lyrics being repetitive and the tune very basic. It was obvious that their creativity lay in R 'n' B and not contemporary pop songs. The ultimate aim, of course, was to mould the two.

11. **FORTUNE TELLER** (Neville)
July/August 1963: Decca, London. Producer: Andrew Oldham.
UK Compilation LP SATURDAY CLUB: January 1964

Fortune Teller was intended to be the B-side of *Poison Ivy*, but due to the non-release of this single, it was only made available to the public via a compilation album of the BBC's radio programme 'Saturday Club'. The song was put into the hands of an inexperienced engineer, and while naïvety in musicians can be turned into spontaneity, when producers and engineers are also inexperienced in pop technique, as in this case, the end result loses its potential. It was not as sweet as the American funk the Stones were attempting to imitate. However, it was not to be long before such problems were overcome.

12. **YOU BETTER MOVE ON** (Alexander)
14/15 September 1963: Kingsway, London. Producer: Eric Easton.
UK EP ROLLING STONES: 17 January 1964
*USA LP DECEMBER'S CHILDREN: November 1965: No **4** – 22 weeks*
UK Compilation LP THROUGH THE PAST DARKLY (BIG HITS VOL 2):
*12 September 1969: No **2** – 37 weeks*

Inspired by such luminaries as The Drifters, a song in a similar vein, written by Arthur Alexander, was recorded at the Kingsway Studios. Using acoustic guitars ballad-style, it became an instant Stones' classic and was lapped up by the fans. It soon became popular at their concerts and was released early in 1964. Plaintive and charged with emotion, the EP jumped into the UK Top Ten singles chart within a week of its release.

13. **BYE BYE JOHNNY** (Berry)
14/15 September 1963: Kingsway, London. Producer: Eric Easton.
UK EP ROLLING STONES: 17 January 1964

Keith Richards picks his fingers almost as nimbly through this song as did his hero Chuck Berry. He certainly copies the master's licks and the rest of the Stones rock along in fine style. It is a worthy contribution to their first EP and begins to show the potential of Mick Jagger's vocals. The release of this EP was mainly because the record company wanted to see if the group would be successful enough to merit a full twelve tracks of recording time. It proved the Stones' popularity and they were soon to enter a studio to record their first album.

14. **MONEY** (Gordy Junior, Bradford)
14/15 September 1963: Kingsway, London. Producer: Eric Easton.
UK EP ROLLING STONES: 17 January 1964

Mick Jagger remembered buying the 1960 American hit version by Barrett Strong and decided it could be worked upon for the English market. He was not the only one inspired by the song because the Beatles had recorded it in July for inclusion on their second LP, WITH THE BEATLES, which was subsequently released in November 1963. During the same month Bern Elliott and the Fenmen were at Number 14 in the UK charts with this Berry Gordy, Janice Bradford song and remained in the charts for 13 weeks. It emphasized the point that song-writers were few and far between at that juncture in pop culture. The Stones created a loose feel to the track but Brian Jones managed to hold it together by his excellent harmonica playing. Mick's vocals are a little undisciplined as though he needs some kind of restraint for his up-front voice. Considering it was only their second or third venture into a recording studio, The Rolling Stones were beginning to fuse into a tight unit.

15. **COME ON** (Berry)
5 October 1963: BBC Radio, London.
Bootleg only.

16. **MEMPHIS TENNESSEE** (Berry)
5 October 1963: BBC Radio, London.
Bootleg only.

17. **ROLL OVER BEETHOVEN** (Berry)
5 October 1963: BBC Radio, London.
Bootleg only.

18. **I JUST WANT TO MAKE LOVE TO YOU** (Dixon)
5 October 1963: BBC Radio, London.
Bootleg only.

Television and especially radio played an important part in broadcasting the early 'sixties rock-and-roll message. The above tracks are testimony to the Stones' affiliation with Chuck Berry and were recorded for a 'Saturday Club' radio broadcast on 26 October 1963. *Memphis Tennessee* and *Roll Over Beethoven* are notable as they have not been released on record. The Stones rock on all four numbers ... British beat music in the form of R 'n' B was ready to blossom and take over the 'boring' pop market! *Come On* is played at more of a relaxed pace and compares very favourably with the single version.

19. **I WANNA BE YOUR MAN** (Lennon, McCartney)
7 October 1963: Kingsway, London. Producer: Eric Easton.
UK Single: 1 November 1963: No **12** *– 16 weeks*
UK Compilation LP READY STEADY GO!: January 1964: No **20** *– 1 week*
USA B–side Not Fade Away. March 1964

The Stones, Andrew Oldham and Decca, having considered and refused the *Poison Ivy* single, sought a follow-up to *Come On*. In mid-September 1963, Andrew Oldham bumped into John Lennon and Paul McCartney and complained at the lack of suitable material for the Stones' second single release. John and Paul thought that they might be able to help. They were in the middle of recording their second album and had an unfinished R 'n' B song that was an instant hit! Andrew took them into Ken Colyer's club, Studio 51, where the band had a Sunday afternoon residency. The bass and electric guitars were handed over to the Liverpool duo and Charlie provided a back beat to the first verse and chorus. The Stones liked the feel of the song and so John and Paul disappeared into another room to finish it off. Much to everyone's surprise, they returned a few minutes later, with the finished product. Probably more than anything this song-writing adeptness inspired the Stones to write their own songs – the royalties would be helpful too! Two weeks later, after personalizing the song, the Stones entered Kingsway Studios. From the opening chords the song is pure high energy. Bill Wyman hits a hard-driving bass, and Keith Richards and Brian Jones deliver electrifying lead guitar with a tight, relaxed solo by Keith. The foundations had been laid for the Stones to establish their potential on the unassuming public by this gift from The Beatles and, indeed, the single reached Number 12 in the UK charts. On Wednesday, 1 January 1964, in a disused Manchester Church converted to a TV studio, the Stones (introduced by Jimmy Saville) promoted the single on the very first screening of a new BBC music programme, simply titled 'Top Of The Pops' – and so two musical legends were born. *I Wanna Be Your Man* was also released in the United States as their first single, but was quickly withdrawn due to a lack of sales. It was coupled with *Not Fade Away*.

20. **STONED** (a.k.a. **STONES**) (Nanker, Phelge)
7 October 1963: Kingsway, London. Producer: Eric Easton.
UK B-side I Wanna Be Your Man: 1 November 1963

Twelve bar improvization provided this so-called retake of Booker T and The MG's *Green Onions*. It is basically an instrumental with Mick Jagger occasionally uttering 'stoned' followed by 'outta my mind'. Well, it was the end of a hard session! It is the very first song, albeit plagiarized, written by the group to end up on a single, which meant royalties were split amongst the band. The writers of the track were stated as 'Nanker, Phelge' and this pseudonym was to be used for future group-written songs. The title originates from publicity shots where they put their fingers up their noses and pulled their eyelids down (a nanker) and Phelge, a friend, who had a dubious habit of wearing his stained under-pants on his head. The first few hundred copies of this single were entitled 'Stones' and copies of these are now collectors' items. An out-take can be obtained which features the piano work of Ian Stewart and echoed, stoned vocals.

21. POISON IVY (Leiber, Stoller)
November 1963: Kingsway, London. Producer: Eric Easton.
UK EP ROLLING STONES: 17 January 1964

The previous recorded version of this song was the track destined to be the second UK single but later cancelled because of the poor sound quality. The Stones were still insistent that they wanted to record a version of *Poison Ivy* and this track therefore ended up on the UK EP released in January 1964. It is taken at a more leisurely pace than the first recording and overall is far superior in texture; even the annoying washboard type ticking had been extracted and basic harmony vocals deployed at strategic places (Keith Richards' idea).

22. AIN'T THAT LOVIN' YOU BABY (Reed)
January/February 1964: Regent, IBC, London. Producer: Andrew Oldham. Engineer: Bill Farley.
Bootleg only.

The exact date and origin of this track is uncertain, but it has the makings of an early Regent Sound or BBC Radio session. It has a strong bass line, but lacks a positive approach, thereby confirming the feel that this Jimmy Reed composition is nothing more than a session warm-up accidentally recorded.

23. ROUTE 66 (Troup)
January/February 1964: Regent, IBC, London. Producer: Andrew Oldham. Engineer: Bill Farley.
UK LP THE ROLLING STONES: 26 April 1964: No 1 – 51 weeks
USA LP ENGLAND'S NEWEST HITMAKERS: May 1964: No 11 – 12 weeks
USA LP DECEMBER'S CHILDREN: November 1965: No 4 – 22 weeks
USA Compilation LP THE ROLLING STONES – PROMOTIONAL ALBUM: October 1969

In January 1964 the Stones started work on their first album simply titled THE ROLLING STONES, which featured on the cover a simple but effective David Bailey photograph of the five staring from a darkened background, plus the Decca logo. *Route 66* gets the album off to a rousing start. Keith Richards plays an excellent guitar with a tight clap-back track rhythm by Bill Wyman and Charlie Watts. It soon became a popular stage number. Later in June, on the same bill as Bobby Vee, The Chiffons, Bobby Goldsboro and Bobby Comstock, the Stones kicked off on the first date of their first American tour. The town was San Bernadino and the lyrics of *Route 66* mention San Bernadino, an unintentional way to win the fans over, who were jiving and bopping in the aisles. Security police, a feature of that tour, lined the stage and pushed over-exuberant fans back to their seats. A jaunty out-take version of this track is available on bootleg. Obviously unpolished, it still has the punch of the final take.

24. **I JUST WANT TO MAKE LOVE TO YOU** (Dixon)
January/February 1964: Regent, IBC, London. Producer: Andrew Oldham. Engineer: Bill Farley.
UK LP THE ROLLING STONES: 26 April 1964: No 1 – 51 weeks
USA LP ENGLAND'S NEWEST HIT MAKERS: May 1964: No 11 – 12 weeks
USA B-side Tell Me: 19 June 1964

The album is generally a mixture of American soul, Stones' R 'n' B and inspirational blues. *I Just Wanna Make Love To You* does not seem to fall into any category. Willie Dixon's delta blues song seems to have been misinterpreted and is driven home in a fast blues, Bo Diddley–type, rhythm manner. Mick Jagger is unable to bring feeling to the vocals at such a pace. Instrumentally, the song is fine, it just seems to be driven too close to the safety barriers. Producer Andrew 'Loog' (a publicity nickname) Oldham was an expert at pushing sensitivity to the limit. His sleeve notes on the reverse of the album cover show a certain controlled arrogance: 'The Rolling Stones are more than just a group – they are a way of life.'

25. **HONEST I DO** (Reed)
January/February 1964: Regent, IBC, London. Producer: Andrew Oldham. Engineer: Bill Farley.
UK LP THE ROLLING STONES: 26 April 1964: No 1 – 51 weeks
USA LP ENGLAND'S NEWEST HIT MAKERS: May 1964: No 11 – 12 weeks

Jimmy Reed was an artist who inspired the Stones to promote the blues gospel. This was their first public release of a Reed song although they had previously recorded the unreleased *Bright Lights, Big City*. They managed to do justice to the work and produced a song deep in feeling, laid back in approach and charged with atmosphere. The song plods forward positively and Brian Jones plays beautiful harp to accompany Mick Jagger's gutsy vocals.

26. **I NEED YOU BABY (MONA)** (McDaniel)
January/February 1964: Regent, IBC, London. Producer: Andrew Oldham. Engineer: Bill Farley.
UK LP THE ROLLING STONES: 26 April 1964: No 1 – 51 weeks

*USA LP THE ROLLING STONES NOW!: February 1965: No **5** – 29 weeks*

Otherwise known as *Mona*, this is yet another inspired copy of a Bo Diddley number where the shuffle beat runs rife throughout the song. The Stones were beginning to prove that they were not only marketing figure-heads, but also adequate musicians. Keith Richards was learning to improvise on every guitar lick in the R 'n' B catalogue and his understanding with Brian Jones created a tight rhythm. They often said that the reason for their success was the unique rhythm they were able to produce. They were both able to play lead if required, but could fall back into playing ensemble and then play licks off each other. *Mona* is such a number. The track was extracted from the American release of the album and replaced by *Not Fade Away*.

27. NOW I'VE GOT A WITNESS (LIKE UNCLE PHIL AND UNCLE GENE) (Phelge)
January/February 1964: Regent, IBC, London. Producer: Andrew Oldham. Engineer: Bill Farley.
*UK LP THE ROLLING STONES: 26 April 1964: No **1** – 51 weeks*
*USA LP ENGLAND'S NEWEST HIT MAKERS: 19 May 1964: No **11** – 12 weeks*
Rolling Stones with Phil Spector, Gene Pitney.

This is the first recording with featured guest artists. Phil Spector came along to offer his production expertise and Gene Pitney, who early in 1964 was to record a Jagger/Richards song *That Girl Belongs To Yesterday*, played on Ian Stewart's prized piano. The song is a basic re–working of *Can I Get a Witness*. It is said the inclusion of the track was to fill up the album, due to lack of authentic material. Ian Stewart, having given away the piano to Uncle Gene, plays very prominent organ with Brian Jones on outstanding harp complementing the prime drive of Ian. Keith Richards then sways into the song trading Chuck Berry chords whilst Mick Jagger hits the tambourine rhythmically on his gyrating hip; Bill Wyman and Charlie Watts create the basis for the jam.

28. I'M A KING BEE (Moore)
January/February 1964: Regent, IBC, London. Producer: Andrew Oldham. Engineer: Bill Farley.
*UK LP THE ROLLING STONES: 26 April 1964: No **1** – 51 weeks*
*USA LP ENGLAND'S NEWEST HIT MAKERS: May 1964: No **11** – 12 weeks*

I'm A King Bee was another straight copy. It surprised Mick Jagger that the public could listen to a pale imitation when the genuine Slim Harpo version was available. Modesty indeed. *King Bee* revolves around Mick's powerfully accentuated blues dialect. He spits out the sexual innuendoes and when the vocals turn to stinging around the honey hive, Keith Richards drags out a riff at the bottom of the fret board to deliver the shadowed message.

29. **CAROL** (Berry)
January/February 1964: Regent, IBC, London. Producer: Andrew Oldham. Engineer: Bill Farley.
UK LP THE ROLLING STONES: 26 April 1964: No 1 – 51 weeks
USA LP ENGLAND'S NEWEST HIT MAKERS: May 1964: No 11 – 12 weeks

The riff recasts Chuck Berry's original song and produces one of the album's barnstormers. Keith Richards had an unnerving ability continuously to improve his guitar virtuosity. It worried someone like Brian Jones, who, although extremely competent, tended to reach a peak on an instrument and then use his musical versatility quickly to master another. This is perhaps why the Stones fused together so well – their characters were diversified but as a unit their musical interpretation was superb. The Stones were all soloists in their own right, but first played for each other as a band. Such was the popularity of *Carol* as a live song that it resurfaced in 1970 on the Stones' first official live LP, GET YOUR YA YA'S OUT. An out-take of this song also exists on bootleg.

30. **TELL ME (YOU'RE COMING BACK)** (Jagger, Richard)
January/February 1964: Regent, IBC, London. Producer: Andrew Oldham. Engineer: Bill Farley.
UK LP THE ROLLING STONES: 26 April 1964: UK No 1 – 51 weeks
USA LP ENGLAND'S NEWEST HIT MAKERS: May 1964: No 11 – 12 weeks
USA Single: 19 June 1964: No 24 – 5 weeks
USA Compilation LP BIG HITS (HIGH TIDE AND GREEN GRASS): March 1966: No 3 – 35 weeks

The longest track on the album and the most controversial. It was the first Jagger, Richard composition to be released and is essentially an experimental song. The make up of the song was dub-based and it gradually built itself up on the eight-track to a cut that was passable for release. The influences on the song stemmed from commercial–type Beatles songs and their Merseyside counterparts. Surprisingly, it was later edited to become the Stones' second American single. Further, it sprang up to a commendable Number 24 in the USA Billboard charts. *Tell Me* plays on the same heart-strings as *You Better Move On* and manages to cross over into the pop mainstream.

31. **CAN I GET A WITNESS** (Holland, Dozier, Holland)
January/February 1964: Regent, IBC, London. Producer: Andrew Oldham. Engineer: Bill Farley.
UK LP THE ROLLING STONES: 26 April 1964: No 1 – 51 weeks
USA LP ENGLAND'S NEWEST HIT MAKERS: May 1964: No 11 – 12 weeks

Marvin Gaye had previously recorded this Motown classic and Andrew Oldham, keen to establish the band in a more pop-orientated mould, decided *Can I Get A Witness* was a suitable song for inclusion on the album. Consequently, Mick Jagger rushed down to the nearest music shop and bought the song sheet to the Holland, Dozier, Holland hit. Ian Stewart pounds out the basic chords and Mick Jagger contributes particularly up-front vocals.

32. **YOU CAN MAKE IT IF YOU TRY** (Jarrett)
January/February 1964: Regent, IBC, London. Producer: Andrew Oldham. Engineer: Bill Farley.
UK LP THE ROLLING STONES: 26 April 1964: No 1 – 51 weeks
USA LP ENGLAND'S NEWEST HIT MAKERS: May 1964: No 11 – 12 weeks

A slow, hollering blues song led by Mick Jagger's pleading vocals. Ian Stewart plays a gospel-type organ and Keith Richards and Brian Jones strum on acoustic guitars. The album as a whole was an immediate success and even knocked The Beatles off the top of the UK charts on 2 May 1964. It remained at the top for 12 weeks, only to be replaced by the release of the next Beatles album, A HARD DAYS NIGHT. Based on the 51 weeks in the charts, it was their most successful album ever. The blitz by the Stones had begun. While 1963 was the year of The Beatles, the Stones replaced them in the popularity polls in 1964. The British rock revolution had started.

33. **WALKING THE DOG** (Thomas)
January/February 1964: Regent, IBC, London. Producer: Andrew Oldham. Engineer: Bill Farley.
UK LP THE ROLLING STONES: 26 April 1964: No 1 – 51 weeks
USA LP ENGLAND'S NEWEST HIT MAKERS: May 1964: No 11 – 12 weeks
USA Compilation LP THE ROLLING STONES – PROMOTIONAL ALBUM: October 1969

The first Rolling Stones' album in Britain did not produce any single releases, but tracks released in other countries proved very popular. *Walking The Dog* was belatedly released in 1965 in Australia and jumped to the Number 3 position. The Number 1 and 2 positions were also held by the Stones, a feat rarely achieved even now by the most popular of the rock and roll fraternity. *Walking The Dog* is a humorous Rufus Thomas song, complete with dog call whistles. It is given the Stones' fast R 'n' B treatment and is a high point on the album. There is a controlled rowdiness under the surface, which is only once released when Keith Richards delivers a fine guitar solo. 'England's Greatest Hit Makers' were expressing their identities and at the same time the aforementioned title was used for the Stateside album release. A lacklustre version of *Walking The Dog* exists on bootleg.

34. **NOT FADE AWAY** (Petty, Hardin alias Norman Petty and Buddy Holly)
February 1964: Regent, IBC, London. Producer: Andrew Oldham. Engineer: Bill Farley.

*UK Single: 21 February 1964: No **3** – 15 weeks*
USA Single: March 1964
*USA LP ENGLAND'S NEWEST HIT MAKERS: May 1964: No **11** – 12 weeks*
*USA Compilation LP BIG HITS (HIGH TIDE AND GREEN GRASS): March 1966: No **3** – 35 weeks*
*UK Compilation LP BIG HITS (HIGH TIDE AND GREEN GRASS): November 1966: No **4** – 43 weeks*
Rolling Stones with Phil Spector, Gene Pitney, Allan Clarke, Graham Nash.

From the opening bars Keith Richards on his acoustic guitar gave the song its feel and instant appeal. Keith had been improvising on this Buddy Holly song at his Willesden flat which he shared with Mick Jagger and Andrew Oldham. Andrew recognised its potential and declared that he considered that the song's style was perfect for the Stones. Keith had conceived the sound and revamped the riff back to the rawness of the Bo Diddley rhythm which Buddy Holly had originally copied. The song had been turned upside down and at the end of February they returned to the studios to produce a Stones' classic. Originally, the session did not fare well – the first takes were just too fast. Andrew Oldham called in Gene Pitney who arrived at the studio with the obligatory bottles. The refreshments revived a flagging session. Two of the Hollies, Allan Clarke and Graham Nash, accompanied the Stones on backing vocals and Phil Spector, eager to help, grabbed Mick's maracas. From the all-important opening bars the atmosphere was right and within a breath-taking two minutes the basis of the track was complete. The harmonica playing of Brian Jones is full of energy and Phil Spector's 'manic maracas' create an exciting rhythm track. It was the logical extension to what they had previously attempted on *I Need You Baby (Mona)*. Phil Spector's presence obviously influenced Andrew Oldham's production and the sound quality was the best he had achieved so far. One wonders if Mick Jagger recalled, a few years previously, viewing with Dick Taylor an impressive performance by Buddy Holly of *Not Fade Away* at the Woolwich Granada?

35. LITTLE BY LITTLE (Phelge, Spector)
February 1964: Regent, IBC, London. Producer: Andrew Oldham. Engineer: Bill Farley.
UK B-side Not Fade Away: 21 February 1964
*UK LP THE ROLLING STONES: 26 April 1964: No **1** – 51 weeks*
*USA LP ENGLAND'S NEWEST HIT MAKERS: May 1964: No **11** – 12 weeks*
Rolling Stones with Phil Spector, Gene Pitney.

This was similar to *Now I've Got A Witness* for Phil Spector was there to add his prowess as a co-writer with the group (Phelge). While obviously a strong influence in the studio, production was firmly in the hands of Andrew Oldham (at least in name). Phil Spector created an ambience in the studio and a spirit, perhaps due to the empty bottles of cognac, which was hard to emulate. As a result, the Stones, with the maestro, tended to create a 'wall of noise' as opposed to the famed 'wall of sound' which Spector had created with the Crystals and Ronettes. *Little By Little* is a composition made up of selections from various parts of Jimmy Reed's *Shame, Shame, Shame*. It is essentially a jam session made after the successful recording of *Not Fade Away* the same night. But it is one which does not allow the looseness of the gathering to infiltrate the song, written by Phil Spector and Mick Jagger in the darkened corridors of the IBC Studios. Phil plays maracas with Ian Stewart and Gene Pitney on the piano.

36. **ANDREW'S BLUES** (a.k.a. **AND THE ROLLING STONES MET PHIL AND GENE, MR SPECTOR AND MR PITNEY CAME TOO** and **FUCKIN' ANDREW**) (Phelge, Spector)
February 1964: Regent, IBC, London. Producer: Andrew Oldham. Engineer: Bill Farley.
Bootleg only.
Rolling Stones with Phil Spector, Gene Pitney, Allan Clarke, Graham Nash.

The session must have been good because although this whimsical ditty was recorded, its lyrical content was a little too shocking for public release. This is the reason for it only being available on bootleg. It comprises of verses which generally describe Andrew Oldham's imagined sexual exploits with nursery-rhyme heroes Jack and Jill, and mimicry of the then Chairman of Decca Records. He describes Phil Spector, 'what a load of balls, Phil Spector is a load of shit' and Phil Spector, who cried, 'The Rolling Stones are a load of shit, but now that I've heard them, I *know* they're a load of shit!'. A load of fun and generally a good 'Mick-take'.

2

CHESS – FIRST MOVE TO THE TOP

MARCH 1964 – MARCH 1965

37. **COPS AND ROBBERS** (McDaniel)
19 March 1964: Camden Theatre, London.
Bootleg only.

38. **ROUTE 66** (Troup)

19 March 1964: Camden Theatre, London.
Bootleg only.

39. **YOU BETTER MOVE ON** (Alexander)
19 March 1964: Camden Theatre, London.
Bootleg only.

40. **MONA**, (a.k.a. **I NEED YOU BABY**) (McDaniel)
19 March 1964: Camden Theatre, London.
Bootleg only.

The Stones had been touring persistently since early January 1964 with such artistes as The Ronettes (hence Phil Spector, the Ronettes' handyman, being available for the Regent Studio sessions), The Swinging Blue Jeans, Marty Wilde and The Wildcats, Dave Berry and The Cruisers, Johnny Kidd and The Pirates, Jet Harris, Mike Berry, Bern Elliott and The Fenmen, and The Hollies. In all, they had played 40 gigs from 6 January to 7 March 1964 and recorded at least 14 tracks, including a Number 1 album and a Top 3 single. They were cruising from town to town, sleeping sometimes in Ian Stewart's van and occasionally grabbing a greasy egg and chips at a roadside café, as publicity photos testify. The four tracks detailed above were recorded just after their hectic touring schedule and were destined for a future BBC broadcast transmission on 9 May 1964. The transmission was innovatory because it featured mock stereo, the television being used as one channel while the radio broadcast another – a unique method of creating a stereo mix. *Cops And Robbers*, another strident Bo Diddley number, is of particular interest since it has not officially been made available.

41. **SURPRISE, SURPRISE** (Jagger, Richard)
May 1964: Regent, IBC, London. Producer: Andrew Oldham. Engineer: Bill Farley.
UK Compilation LP FOURTEEN: 21 May 1964
*USA LP THE ROLLING STONES NOW!: February 1965: No **5** – 29 weeks*
UK B-side Street Fighting Man: 20 July 1970.
UK Maxi-Single: 30 June 1972

The early attempts by Jagger, Richard to write popular songs were not successful. They seemed to have the Mersey sound too close to their hearts instead of what they knew best. They were aware of this problem and the fact that *Surprise, Surprise* was little more than a demo made it conveniently slot onto a Decca compilation album FOURTEEN, the royalties of which were donated to the Lord Taverners National Playing Fields Association. Lulu and the Luvvers believed the track had some standing, and they recorded it for single release in April 1965.

42. **GOOD TIMES, BAD TIMES** (Jagger, Richard)
May 1964: Regent, IBC, London. Producer: Andrew Oldham. Engineer: Bill Farley.

UK B-side It's All Over Now: 26 June 1964
USA B-side It's All Over Now: July 1964
USA LP 12 X 5: October 1964: No **3** *– 20 weeks*
USA Compilation LP BIG HITS (HIGH TIDE AND GREEN GRASS):
March 1966: No **3** *– 35 weeks*

A blues song fit for any Andrew Oldham 'anthology' compilation, it strides along purposefully. Mick Jagger spreads his lips and illustrates the need for placing more trust in the world. The writing duo were beginning to broaden their horizons. The group at that time were being forcefully led by Andrew Oldham's well-oiled publicity machine, which was laying the rock foundations and creating a group the exact antithesis of The Beatles. The Stones were the group the parents loved to hate. The Press acceded to Andrew Oldham's strategy with stories of a headmaster who had suspended pupils for imitating the Stones' unruly mops and requested that they had them styled neatly like The Beatles. The *Daily Mirror* headline read, 'Beatle Your Rolling Stone Hair'. The pressure was mounting, but still they played the blues and there were 'good times, bad times'.

43. **OFF THE HOOK** (Nanker, Phelge)
May 1964: Regent, IBC, London. Producer: Andrew Oldham. Engineer: Bill Farley.
UK B-side Little Red Rooster: 13 November 1964
UK LP ROLLING STONES NO 2: 30 January 1965: No **1** *– 37 weeks*
USA LP THE ROLLING STONES NOW!: February 1965: No **5** *– 29 weeks*
USA Compilation LP THE ROLLING STONES – PROMOTIONAL ALBUM: October 1969

The Stones were at last formulating a style which set them apart from other so-called English beat groups. *Off The Hook* is an example with a nifty repetitive hook line. It is a mid-tempo rocker controlled by a clean lead guitar sound. Keith Richards and Brian Jones had the happy knack of being able to play black American blues music with a popular feel, illustrated well on this particular track. The success of The Rolling Stones was in turn having a good effect on their blues idols, who were increasing in popularity due to the resurgence of the blues in Britain.

44. **CONGRATULATIONS** (Jagger, Richard)
May 1964: Regent, IBC, London. Producer: Andrew Oldham. Engineer: Bill Farley.
USA B-side Time Is On My Side: September 1964
USA LP 12 X 5: October 1964: No **3** *– 20 weeks*

This track is not available in the United Kingdom, but can be obtained on the reverse side of *Time Is On My Side*, the third American single, and second American album 12 × 5 (twelve tracks by five musicians). It is a Mick Jagger and Keith Richard composition, predictable and lacking direction. The initial releases in the United States were all of a slow tempo and *Congratulations* was probably added onto the *Time Is On My Side* single to continue the trend.

45. YOU CAN'T CATCH ME (Berry)

May 1964: Regent, IBC, London. Producer: Andrew Oldham. Engineer: Bill Farley.
UK LP ROLLING STONES NO 2: 30 January 1965: No **1** *– 37 weeks*
USA LP THE ROLLING STONES NOW!: February 1965: No **5** *– 29 weeks*

A wealth of material was being recorded in this period, but a lot of the chosen tracks were still predominantly cover versions. *You Can't Catch Me* was originally played by Chuck Berry and was Bill Wyman's first recollection of rock and roll, back in his National Service RAF days. This interpretation, destined for release on their second British and third American albums, is a real rocker. The rhythm section of Bill and Charlie Watts play 'fifties style, whilst Keith Richards quite effortlessly picks the song's rhythm out on his guitar. (It is rumoured that around this time Brian Jones was intending to record a solo single, but it is doubtful if a recording was ever made.)

46. TIME IS ON MY SIDE (Meade, Norman)

May 1964: Regent, IBC, London. Producer: Andrew Oldham. Engineer: Bill Farley.
USA Single: September 1964: No **6** *– 9 weeks*
USA LP 12 X 5: October 1964: No **3** *– 20 weeks*

This track, recorded in Britain, was destined to be an American single. Ironically the same song, recorded later in the year at the famed Chess Studios in Chicago, was set for inclusion on a British album – definitely a trans-Atlantic mix-up. The British outcome is slightly slower than Irma Thomas's USA hit version and is a worthy ballad, poignant in context, and given the full Stones' treatment. Ian Stewart supplies the gospel-type organ, helping the USA single released in September 1964 to peak later at an incredible number 6 position in November/December 1964. It was a major breakthrough into the American market. They had accomplished the feat of transposing the song into a Stones' original, just as they had cleverly done with *Not Fade Away*.

47. UNDER THE BOARDWALK (Resnick, Young)

May 1964: Regent, IBC, London. Producer: Andrew Oldham. Engineer: Bill Farley.
USA LP 12 X 5: October 1964: No **3** *– 20 weeks*
UK LP ROLLING STONES NO 2: 30 January 1965: No **1** *– 37 weeks*

The Stones' reworking of The Drifters' *Under The Boardwalk.* It is an example of their effort to produce some authentic soul-based work, but unfortunately seems to lack the Drifters' original feel. The Drifters' version charted in July 1964 reaching Number 4. The Stones' arrangement is not solid and gradually falls by the wayside. The soul, perhaps due to the acoustic guitar, is lacking. Despite this, it was later to stomp to the top of the Australian singles charts!

48. SUSIE Q (Hawkins, Lewis, Broadwater)
May 1964: Regent, IBC, London. Producer: Andrew Oldham. Engineer: Bill Farley.
USA LP 12 X 5: October 1964: No **3** *– 20 weeks*
UK LP THE ROLLING STONES NO 2: 30 January 1965: No **1** *– 37 weeks*
USA Compilation LP THE ROLLING STONES – PROMOTIONAL ALBUM: October 1969

From Charlie Watts' opening beat, this track is full of R 'n' B spirit. It seems to be a mod 'work out' featuring some particularly deranged guitar playing. Having made its point on the tail-end of the album, it quickly fades out, leaving you to wonder what would happen if they were left to improvise on a more inspiring rocker.

49. GROWN UP WRONG (Jagger, Richard)
May 1964: Regent, IBC, London. Producer: Andrew Oldham. Engineer: Bill Farley.
USA LP 12 X 5: October 1964: No **3** *– 20 weeks*
UK LP THE ROLLING STONES NO 2: 30 January 1965: No **1** *– 37 weeks*

Another abbreviated song which does not manage to fulfil itself. The production is lacking and despite Brian Jones trying to enliven the proceedings with his harmonica, it goes nowhere fast. Mick Jagger and Keith Richards were finding that the task of writing songs was not an easy one. However, it is clear that there was a dormant genius waiting to be unleashed. There had been a brief taster on *Off The Hook*, but the other self-penned songs seemed to lack inspiration.

50. NOT FADE AWAY (Petty, Hardin)
3 June 1964: Hollywood Palace TV Show, USA.
Bootleg only.

The Stones' first State-side adventure was to last just over three weeks. They arrived to a reception at J. F. Kennedy Airport, modest compared with the previous years' hysterical reception for The Beatles. The Stones sadly lacked hit material. Their first two American singles, *I Wanna Be Your Man* and *Not Fade Away* released in January and March 1964, respectively, failed to make an impression on the Billboard charts. They were trying to reimport the blues to America and it would be a severe test of their musical integrity. They handled their first TV interviews with Les Crane comfortably. Then the next day they flew to Los Angeles to record two tracks for television, *Not Fade Away* and *I Just Want To Make Love To You* – the latter being the B-side of the forthcoming American single *Tell Me*. The show was a compendium of clowns, cowboys and other doubtful entertainers and was hosted by Dean Martin. Mr Martin delighted American viewers with snide comments about Stones/Beatles hair-pulling contests and prior to a commercial break he announced 'Now don't go away, you wouldn't leave me with these Rolling Stones, would you?' The Stones were antagonized but performed their second number *Not Fade Away* with professional gusto in front of limited teen screamers. Dean Martin gave the Stones their first taste of American publicity and Andrew Oldham, the Stones' manager, loved every perverse minute.

51. **IF YOU NEED ME** (Pickett, Bateman, Sanders)
10/11 June 1964: Chess, Chicago. Producer: Andrew Oldham.
Engineer: Ron Malo.
UK EP FIVE BY FIVE: 14 August 1964
USA LP 12 X 5: October 1964: No **3** *– 20 weeks*
UK Compilation LP STONE AGE: 23 April 1971: No **4** *– 7 weeks*

For the previous six months, the Stones had been trying to emulate the American blues and soul sound. They were now to realize an ambition and actually record at the renowned Chess Studios, previously used by Muddy Waters and Chuck Berry. Keith Richards recalls the incongruous situation when they met Muddy Waters; he was assisting the up-keep of the Chess Studios by decorating the studio ceiling! The band were in their element with magic fingers Ron Malo at the controls and were not over-awed by the occasion. *If You Need Me* is a medium tempo ballad which creates a soul searching feel to the opening tracks of the British EP. It had been previously recorded by Wilson Pickett.

52. **EMPTY HEART** (Nanker, Phelge)
10/11 June 1964: Chess, Chicago. Producer: Andrew Oldham.
Engineer: Ron Malo.
UK EP FIVE BY FIVE: 14 August 1964
USA LP 12 X 5: October 1964: No **3** *– 20 weeks*

Mick Jagger and the boys were feeling their way into the Chicago Studio ambience. As their confidence bristled, they recorded a worthy band composition. Mick's vocals are powerful, backed by Keith Richards' distinctive voice. Brian Jones wails on the harmonica in the background and the track, which might have sounded pale captured in an English studio, seems to bloom with the undoubted enthusiasm of half-a-dozen blues devotees playing at the Chess 'blues Mecca'. It established a new era in the Stones' recordings.

53. **2120 SOUTH MICHIGAN AVENUE** (Nanker, Phelge)
10/11 June 1964: Chess, Chicago. Producer: Andrew Oldham.
Engineer: Ron Malo.
UK EP FIVE BY FIVE: 14 August 1964
USA LP 12 X 5: October 1964: No **3** *– 20 weeks*

This was essentially a studio jam session. Bill Wyman opens the instrumental track and Ian Stewart pumps his organ into overdrive. Each member of the band takes his turn on an instrumental break and the *South Michigan Avenue* escalates into a steam-rolling number. The final cut as released on the British EP is shortened and the reason is endlessly debated. Those who own the rare bootleg, extended by an additional one and a half minutes, believe that this was due to blues *aficionado* Muddy Waters joining in the jam, thereby causing contractual problems. The more technically orientated simply adhere to the fact that only so much time can be filled on an early 'sixties extended-play single. Andrew 'Loog' Oldham stated on the sleeve notes: 'This new EP was recorded in Chicago during the Stones' recent American tour and is yet another showcase for their exciting vocalising and unique instrumental sound. And by way of saying "thank you" to their friends and fans, we have included an extra track on this, their latest disc outing.' 2120 is the address of the Chess Studios!

54. CONFESSIN' THE BLUES (Brown, McShann)
10/11 June 1964: Chess, Chicago. Producer: Andrew Oldham.
Engineer: Ron Malo.
UK EP FIVE BY FIVE: 14 August 1964
*USA LP 12 X 5: October 1964: No **3** – 20 weeks*
*UK Compilation LP STONE AGE: 23 April 1971: No **4** – 7 weeks*

Inspired by the Chess Studios, Brian Jones and Keith Richards started to record all the old blues standards that they knew so well from their record collections. They both agreed later that Andrew Oldham did not seem to be into the blues scene and that the Chess sessions were held together by Ron Malo. *Confessin'*, an old Chuck Berry number, was slowed down and performed in true blue-bottle style. The song plods along with ease. The band knew that they had together accomplished a transformation from the type of tracks already laid down in England which were set for inclusion on the second album. An out-take of *Confessin' The Blues* is available on bootleg.

55. AROUND AND AROUND (Berry)
10/11 June 1964: Chess, Chicago. Producer: Andrew Oldham.
Engineer: Ron Malo.
UK EP FIVE BY FIVE: 14 August 1964
*USA LP 12 X 5: October 1964: No **3** – 20 weeks*
USA Compilation LP THE ROLLING STONES – PROMOTIONAL
ALBUM: October 1969
*UK Compilation LP STONE AGE: 23 April 1971: No **4** – 7 weeks*

Around And Around was an old Chuck Berry favourite. It was the first number Mick Jagger had sung live when he and Keith Richards had made an impromptu appearance in London with Blues Incorporated at the Ealing Club in 1962. It had also been included in the first demo tape sent by Mick Jagger to Alexis Korner. By now a degree of maturity had replaced the initial inexperience, and this version is nothing short of immaculate. Keith Richards, whose guitar playing is excellent, leads the song, rocking and rolling in a manner that would inspire any 'greased duck's quiff' and helps create an EP whose achievements have long since been copied but not emulated.

56. **STEWED AND KEEFED** (a.k.a. **BRIAN'S BLUES**) (Nanker, Phelge)
10/11 June 1964: Chess, Chicago. Producer: Andrew Oldham.
Engineer: Ron Malo.
Bootleg only.

The first Chicago session was to produce a number of unreleased tracks, of which this was one. This was not necessarily because the product was below standard, but perhaps due to the prolific output of a group who were on their first blues pilgrimage. It is an instrumental which features two duelling instrumentalists, bar room shuffling Ian Stewart and the lazy blues guitar of Keith Richards. Like the Mississippi, the track meanders inexorably to the blues delta. *Stewed And Keefed* is undoubtedly a worthy jam track, typical of the laid-back ambience achieved at Chess. Brian Jones was unwell and missed the session, hence his 'blues' in the alternative title.

57. **HIGH HEELED SNEEKERS** (Higgenbotham)
10/11 June 1964: Chess, Chicago. Producer: Andrew Oldham.
Engineer: Ron Malo.
Bootleg only.

It was not unusual during the two–day sessions at the Chess Studios for the bands' idols to drop by, carry in their gear, and chat to them in between takes. Muddy Waters, Willie Dixon and Buddy Guy were among those who genially gave them advice. Generally, all this gave the Chess sessions a distinct blues flavour, but this particular Tommy Tucker track falls into no-man's land. It lacks the band's usual positive drive, needing a faster pace. Despite Mick Jagger's insistent vocals and Brian Jones's harmonica playing which temporarily lifts the track, the take was not a success – the probable reason for it not being released.

58. **TELL ME BABY** (a.k.a. **HOW MANY TIMES?**) (Broonzy)
10/11 June 1964: Chess, Chicago. Producer: Andrew Oldham.
Engineer: Ron Malo.
Bootleg only.

This time the Stones latch on to an average Big Bill Broonzy song. They play a typical plodding blues with the obligatory wailing harmonica. It is certainly not a classic and has not officially been made available, either in the United States or the United Kingdom. In Germany, a 1983 boxed set of Stones' material included *Tell Me Baby* – a fact which may have disconcerted some Decca personnel! The basic attitude adopted at the Chess sessions was to have a good time and lay down as many tracks as possible, usually in just one take. *Tell Me Baby* catches the enthusiasm but not the skillful direction of other tracks.

59. **DOWN IN THE BOTTOM** (a.k.a. **FAT OLD MAN**) (Dixon)
10/11 June 1964: Chess, Chicago. Producer: Andrew Oldham.
Engineer: Ron Malo.
Bootleg only.

Possibly inspired by the presence of Willie Dixon himself, the band turn out an up-tempo number which streaks along. Keith Richards puts on his running shoes and gets to grips by laying down an atmospheric rhythm guitar. Ron Malo adds his studio expertise and helps to create a solid Stones performance. He was a famed Chess engineer who had previously recorded classics by Chuck Berry, Muddy Waters, Bo Diddley and Howlin' Wolf at the very same studios.

60. **DOWN THE ROAD APIECE** (Raye)
10/11 June 1964: Chess, Chicago. Producer: Andrew Oldham.
Engineer: Ron Malo.
UK LP ROLLING STONES NO 2: 30 January 1965: No 1 – 37 weeks
USA LP THE ROLLING STONES NOW!: February 1965: No 5 – 29 weeks

Keith Richards was particularly inspired by Chuck Berry. This Raye song had been performed and mastered by Berry, so the Stones were more than excited when Chuck Berry called into the studio and caught them in the middle of one of his classics. He commended the Stones on the performance, remarking that they were really getting it on. He was also impressed by the immaculate playing of the guitar player (Keith Richards) and no wonder – this track is a notable example of his skill as he swings and boogies in unique style. A practice studio run–through of this track is available on bootleg – was the master performing? *Reeling And A Rocking* was also recorded at the same time, but is not readily available on bootleg. It was probably played to show Chuck Berry that the Stones were out to get his R 'n' B crown!

61. **I CAN'T BE SATISFIED** (Waters)
10/11 June 1964: Chess, Chicago. Producer: Andrew Oldham.
Engineer: Ron Malo.
UK LP THE ROLLING STONES NO 2: 30 January 1965: No 1 – 37 weeks

This type of song was described as 'nigger music' by Muddy Waters (tongue firmly in cheek) and discredited by Murray the K (an American promoter) who reckoned the Stones were on a loser 'cos white kids didn't listen to Muddy Waters tunes and the rest of the blues fraternity. How wrong – the Stones create a song sentimental in approach with the controlled methodical rhythm unit of Bill Wyman and Charlie Watts hardly breaking into sweat. Brian Jones is the instrumentalist on this particular track, and he plays some inspirational bottleneck blues. Keith Richards stands in the background supporting the rhythm with upfront acoustic and lends a hand at the end trading blues licks with Brian. The guitar roles were temporarily reversed, but you cannot deny the sheer mastery of a skillful bottleneck player – and still only aged 22! *I Can't Be Satisfied* was not released in the States until the December 1972 MORE HOT ROCKS (BIG HITS AND FAZED COOKIES) muddled collection of B-sides, single hits and album tracks.

62. **DON'T LIE TO ME** (Berry)
10/11 June 1964: Chess, Chicago. Producer: Andrew Oldham.
Engineer: Ron Malo.
*UK Compilation LP METAMORPHIS: 6 June 1975: No **45** – 1 week*
*USA Compilation LP METAMORPHIS: 6 June 1975: No **8** – 8 weeks*

This is a substandard Chuck Berry rocker which was incorrectly credited to Jagger, Richards on initial copies of the album sleeve-work. Ian Stewart opens the song purposefully but the song lacks conviction and disintegrates into a studio work out, despite Keith Richards occasionally plunging in with his impetuous lead guitar. Mick Jagger tries to convince the band to charge on this medium-packed rock and roll tune but it did not fulfil the band's expectations. So it faltered only to resurface on an out-take compilation album in 1975.

63. **IT'S ALL OVER NOW** (B. and S. Womack)
10/11 June 1964: Chess, Chicago. Producer: Andrew Oldham.
Engineer: Ron Malo.
*UK Single: 26 June 1964: No **1** – 15 weeks*
*USA Single: July 1964: No **26** – 6 weeks*
*USA LP 12 X 5: October 1964: No **3** – 20 weeks*
USA Compilation LP BIG HITS (HIGH TIDE AND GREEN GRASS):
*March 1966: No **3** – 35 weeks*
UK Compilation LP BIG HITS (HIGH TIDE AND GREEN GRASS):
*November 1966: No **4** – 43 weeks*
*UK Compilation LP STONE AGE: 23 April 1971: No **4** – 7 weeks*

Murray the K, a popular American disc jockey, turned the Stones on to this Valentinos' song. The Stones decided to record it and with Ron Malo's engineering technique a Chess soul classic was created. It went straight to Number 1 in Britain – Jagger nonchalantly admitted it was great that it had reached that position but he was looking for a worldwide hit with far more copies sold. His thoughts were probably of the States, where it only achieved a Number 26 position, despite 8 weeks of promotional work and a brief tour of the northern states. On *It's All Over Now* Ron Malo blends Keith Richards' reverberating earthy guitar with a country rhythm plucked by Brian Jones. Bobby Womack, the Valentinos' lead singer and songwriter, had ignored the abrasive edge of the lyrics, which Jagger intuitively saw. Bobby Womack at the time was an established soul artiste and was rather annoyed that the Stones should improvise on his song. Despite this, *It's All Over Now* is a landmark in the Stones' recording history and is typical of the creative influence of the Chess Studios. An out-take of this song exists on bootleg, the difference being a slower guitar approach. Little were they to know that 20 years later Bobby Womack would guest on the 1986 DIRTY WORK album.

64. LOOK WHAT YOU'VE DONE (Morganfield)
10/11 June 1964: Chess, Chicago. Producer: Andrew Oldham.
Engineer: Ron Malo.
*USA LP DECEMBER'S CHILDREN: November 1965: No **4** – 22 weeks*
*UK Compilation LP STONE AGE: 23 April 1971: No **4** – 7 weeks*

Yet another track recorded in the two-day Chicago visit. There was such a wealth of recording material that it was suggested a Chicago LP should be made but unfortunately this was not done. It would certainly have made an interesting album. Indeed a compilation album of Chess songs was put together in Japan. Instead an EP and a single were released which still left a lot of tracks on the shelf. Some such as *Look What You've Done* resurfaced on compilations (a 1971 album released by Decca, titled STONE AGE) and others on bootlegs. *Look What You've Done* is a slow blues featuring Ian Stewart on the ivories and Brian Jones's wailing harmonica. Ron Malo uses a subtle echo on Brian's harp. The song plods along and the five instrumental breaks by Ian Stewart and Brian Jones are restricted by the song's indirection.

65. BYE BYE JOHNNY (Berry)
10/11 June 1964: Chess, Chicago. Producer: Andrew Oldham.
Engineer: Ron Malo.
Bootleg only.

A fun run-through of an old Chuck Berry favourite... its pace is faster than the original released British EP track; as ever the lead guitar wheels the song down the highway in the fast lane. Chuck Berry must have been quaking in his winkle-pickers!

66. AS TIME GOES BY (a.k.a. AS TEARS GO BY) (Jagger, Richard, Oldham)
11 July 1964: Kingsway, London.
Bootleg only.

The Stones returned from the States in late June 1964 and, prior to setting off on a British tour, briefly revisited the Kingsway Studio. The outcome was a demo for Marianne Faithfull, titled *As Time Goes By*. With just Mick Jagger and Keith Richards in attendance, Andrew Oldham assisted the song-writing process. The song is an acoustic ballad, and with revamped lyrics and title (*As Tears Go By*) Marianne Faithfull obtained her first hit with it in August 1964, reaching Number 9 in Britain. In the States, in early 1965, it flirted with a Top 30 position at Number 22.

67. DA DOO RON RON (Spector, Greenwich, Barry)
July 1964: Kingsway, London. Producer: Andrew Oldham, John Paul Jones.
UK LP 16 HIP HITS: Andrew Loog Oldham Orchestra and Chorus: 2 October 1964

Again, it is unlikely that all the Stones were in attendance for this run through of a Phil Spector classic, although it is evident that Mick Jagger is the vocalist on this Crystals' cover. Andrew Oldham seemed to be determined to construct a British mirror-image of the Phil Spector success story. Recording cover versions of Spector songs was not a subtle way of achieving this!

68. MEMPHIS TENNESSEE (Berry)
July 1964: Kingsway, London. Producer: Andrew Oldham, John Paul Jones.
UK LP 16 HIP HITS: Andrew Loog Oldham Orchestra and Chorus: 2 October 1964

Andrew Oldham would neither deny nor confirm that the Stones contributed to the 16 HIP HITS album. He knew that the very possibility of their inclusion would prosper his sales on an odd compilation of cover material and Andrew Oldham originals. *Memphis*, a Chuck Berry cover performed without vocals, has a hint of the Keith Richards/Brian Jones guitar work. John Paul Jones, then only a young session player, assisted Andrew Oldham in the production work.

69. HEART OF STONE (Jagger, Richard)
July 1964: Kingsway, London. Producer: Andrew Oldham.
*UK Compilation LP METAMORPHIS: 6 June 1975: No **45** – 1 week*
*USA Compilation LP METAMORPHIS: 6 June 1975: No **8** – 8 weeks*
Rolling Stones with Jimmy Page.

This version was more than likely recorded in Britain. However, it is difficult to pinpoint a recording date, but it is likely to have been tried and tested before the Hollywood '64 sessions. It features a choral voice back-drop and possibly guest session musician, Jimmy Page. The feel is Country and Western with 'electric' steel guitar solos. An unusual version, it was probably pulled together by Andrew Oldham, hence its availability on the 1975 compilation out-take album METAMORPHIS. Keith Richards credits Jimmy Page, acknowledging that he copied Jimmy's guitar licks for the RCA version.

70. SOME THINGS JUST STICK IN YOUR MIND (Jagger, Richard)
July 1964: Kingsway, London. Producer: Andrew Oldham.
*UK Compilation LP METAMORPHIS: 6 June 1975: No **45** – 1 week*

Probably recorded at the same time as the Jimmy Page version of *Heart Of Stone*, due to its country flavours. Session musicians including John McLaughlin were possibly incorporated in this Andrew Oldham production. Pedestrian in approach, it allows Mick Jagger to twist his tongue around a western movie sound-track. *Some Things Just Stick In Your Mind* emphasizes the two-way struggle between attempting to write commercial pop songs and R 'n' B rockers.

71. SLEEPY CITY (Jagger, Richard)
July 1964: Kingsway, London. Producer: Andrew Oldham.
*UK Compilation LP METAMORPHIS: 6 June 1975: No **45** – 1 week*

Another experimental Jagger, Richard composition which was given to a British group The Mighty Avengers; predictably it flopped. Andrew Oldham's idea of capitalizing on the Stones' success by issuing these tracks to unsuspecting artistes was a mistake. The version by the Stones is ruined by being over-produced; simplicity, as they would soon learn, was the key to success.

72. **AROUND AND AROUND** (Berry)
25 October 1964: Ed Sullivan TV Show, USA.
Bootleg only.

Four months had passed since the Chess recording sessions in June. The months of August, September and early October were spent touring Britain. They performed in the Channel Islands, throughout England (including the National Jazz and Blues Festival at Richmond) and also Northern Ireland and Scotland. They were even guest panelists on the infamous 'Juke Box Jury' BBC 'hit or miss' TV show where they created public controversy by their non-committal off-hand comments. They were now self-proclaimed celebrities and in late October 1964 they returned to the States for their second tour. The ultimate TV media show in the USA was the Ed Sullivan Show and on Friday 23 October they started rehearsals for their appearance. Mass hysteria from armies of fans enveloped the studios for three days. *Around And Around*, a genuine rock and roller, further inflamed the atmosphere, and the Stones responded accordingly. Keith especially was in fine form. After the show, Ed Sullivan said that he had received hundreds of letters from parents complaining about the long-haired Stones' performance. But he also received thousands of letters from excited teenagers who were more than into this British rock phenomenon.

73. **TIME IS ON MY SIDE** (Meade, Norman)
25 October 1964: Ed Sullivan TV Show, USA.
Bootleg only.

Time Is On My Side was the second song performed on the show. It is a slow number, but due to the excitement of the crowd was speeded up as they screamed at every available lull in the proceedings. Adult American TV viewers were alarmed at this seeming riot in their own homes and gradually the pressure mounted. Ed Sullivan, anxious to reaffirm his prestige, denied responsibility that he had anything to do with the booking of the Stones. He was shocked by the performance and vowed to cancel all future rock and roll acts. He claimed that his show had been built up over 17 years and he did not want it broken up by such unruly behaviour. They were not like that other British act, The Dave Clark Five – such nice gentlemen!

74. **DOWN HOME GIRL** (Leiber, Butler)
27 October 1964: RCA, Hollywood. Producer: Andrew Oldham.
Engineer: Dave Hassinger.

*UK LP THE ROLLING STONES NO 2: 30 January 1965: No 1 – 37
weeks
USA LP THE ROLLING STONES NOW!: February 1965: No 5 – 29
weeks
Rolling Stones with Jack Nitzsche.*

Following the publicity coup on the Ed Sullivan Show they settled into the RCA Studios in Hollywood. *Down Home Girl* is a blues which typifies the 'at home' approach to recording. The Stones were now competent musicians and recording artistes. Their astounding success was assured by two other factors – Andrew Oldham's hype and their own self-confidence. *Down Home Girl* does not explore new land, but it does reiterate their blues status.

75. EVERYBODY NEEDS SOMEBODY TO LOVE (UK Version) (Russell, Burke, Wexler)
*27 October 1964: RCA, Hollywood. Producer: Andrew Oldham.
Engineer: Dave Hassinger.
UK LP THE ROLLING STONES NO 2: 30 January 1965: No 1 – 37
weeks
USA Compilation LP THE ROLLING STONES – PROMOTIONAL
ALBUM: October 1969
UK Maxi-Single: 30 June 1972*

76. EVERYBODY NEEDS SOMEBODY TO LOVE (USA Version) (Russell, Burke, Wexler)
*27 October 1964: RCA, Hollywood. Producer: Andrew Oldham.
Engineer: Dave Hassinger.
USA LP THE ROLLING STONES NOW!: February 1965: No 5 – 29
weeks*

The Stones turned this Solomon Burke composition into an R 'n' B mini epic. Solomon Burke released *Everybody* as a single in 1964 but despite previous hits in the States it did not chart on that occasion. The Stones' version was an impressive opening to the album, lasting almost five minutes. There are several versions, with the British released track apparently being the official one, although there are other abridged copies of the song. The track is progressive in nature and does not rely on the typical three-minute pop formula. It almost reaches a standstill at one stage, until Jagger lurches the 'jam' forward again. The American version (claimed to be put on THE ROLLING STONES NOW! album in error) is completely different. It lacks the R 'n' B panache of the British original. The beat is generally faster and the harmony arrangements of the vocals serve to emphasize the difference.

77. PAIN IN MY HEART (Redding, Walden)
*27 October 1964: RCA, Hollywood. Producer: Andrew Oldham.
Engineer: Dave Hassinger.
UK LP THE ROLLING STONES NO 2: 30 January 1965: No 1 – 37
weeks*

*USA LP THE ROLLING STONES NOW!: February 1965: No **5** – 29 weeks*

Through Phil Spector the Stones had met Jack Nitzsche, who recommended the Hollywood Studios. They arrived on Sunset Boulevard intent on enjoying the image and were amazed at the glamour of the RCA Studios and the size of the limos. Even Dave Hassinger, the studio engineer, had one. When they bopped in on 27 October 1964, the place ground to a halt as the Studio hands stared open-mouthed at the unique appearance of this English band. Dave Hassinger was impressed by their uncanny method of recording as they transformed tempos of songs in order to get the perfect cut. Mick Jagger and Keith Richards gave Dave Hassinger the Stones' approval and yet another track was in the can. *Pain In My Heart* tugs at the heart-strings in typical Jaggeresque fashion.

78. **HEART OF STONE** (Jagger, Richard)
27 October 1964: RCA, Hollywood. Producer: Andrew Oldham.
Engineer: Dave Hassinger.
*USA Single: December 1964: No **19** – 5 weeks*
*USA LP THE ROLLING STONES NOW!: February 1965 No **5** – 29 weeks*
*UK LP OUT OF OUR HEADS: 6 September 1965: No **2** – 24 weeks*
*USA Compilation LP BIG HITS (HIGH TIDE AND GREEN GRASS): March 1966: No **3** – 35 weeks*
*UK Compilation LP BIG HITS (HIGH TIDE AND GREEN GRASS): November 1966: No **4** – 43 weeks*
*UK Compilation LP METAMORPHIS: 6 June 1975: No **45** – 1 week*
*USA Compilation LP METAMORPHIS: 6 June 1975: No **8** – 8 weeks*

This track was not released in Britain for a further 10 months but it was a natural for the American market. Released as a single containing the slow Stateside mould, it is a well-managed Jagger, Richard composition in the blues tradition. The song lived up to the macho bad-boy image of grabbing girls as a typical boys pursuit ... although attracted she would never break the heart of stone! The guitar work is neat and captured well by Dave Hassinger, who claims he only helped the lads out. He knew when to keep his mouth shut and allowed the positiveness of the group to dictate the session.

79. **HITCH HIKE** (Gaye, Stevenson, Paul)
27 October 1964: RCA, Hollywood. Producer: Andrew Oldham.
Engineer: Dave Hassinger.
*USA LP OUT OF OUR HEADS: July 1965: No **1** – 35 weeks*
*UK LP OUT OF OUR HEADS: 6 September 1965: No **2** – 24 weeks*

Hitch Hike was Marvin Gaye's first single and became a small success for him early in 1963. The Stones' version is led by a full guitar entrance but the song plods in an indifferent manner. There is an intermittent slow guitar solo which stands out from the rest of the song. *Hitch Hike* is only an album filler.

80. **OH, BABY (WE GOT A GOOD THING GOING)** (Ozen)
27 October 1964: RCA, Hollywood. Producer: Andrew Oldham.
Engineer: Dave Hassinger.
*USA LP THE ROLLING STONES NOW!: February 1965: No **5** – 29*
weeks
*UK LP OUT OF OUR HEADS: 6 September 1965: No **2** – 24 weeks*

This is supposed to be a song learned by playing the original Otis Redding single over and over. The slow blues is converted to a roaring R 'n' B track, led by Mick Jagger's exasperated vocals. A short track which has an out-take version available on bootleg.

81. **AROUND AND AROUND** (Berry)
28/29 October 1964: Santa Monica Civic Auditorium, USA.
Bootleg only.

82. **OFF THE HOOK** (Nanker, Phelge)
28/29 October 1964: Santa Monica Civic Auditorium, USA.
Bootleg only.

83. **TIME IS ON MY SIDE** (Meade, Norman)
28/29 October 1964: Santa Monica Civic Auditorium, USA.
Bootleg only.

84. **IT'S ALL OVER NOW** (B. and S. Womack)
28/29 October 1964: Santa Monica Civic Auditorium, USA.
Bootleg only.

85. **I'M ALRIGHT** (Nanker, Phelge)
28/29 October 1964: Santa Monica Civic Auditorium, USA.
Bootleg only.

The Santa Monica Civic Auditorium played host to the 1964 Teen Awards Music International (T.A.M.I.). Recordings for television broadcast were made of the principal teen stars and the Stones, the only British act, closed the concert, which included formidable performances by James Brown, Chuck Berry and The Beach Boys. The Stones lived up to expectations and produced a set full of gusto, even upstaging the great soul performer James Brown.

86. **WHAT A SHAME** (Jagger, Richard)
5/6/8 November 1964: Chess, Chicago. Producer: Andrew Oldham.
Engineer: Ron Malo.
*UK LP THE ROLLING STONES NO 2: 30 January 1965: No **1** – 37*
weeks
USA B-side Heart Of Stone: December 1964
*USA LP THE ROLLING STONES NOW!: February 1965: No **5** – 29*
weeks

What A Shame featuring Ian Stewart on piano and Brian Jones on harmonica, and released as a flip side to the American single *Heart Of Stone*, lacks excitement and careers blindly along, not pausing to allow some R 'n' B venom to slip out. The Stones' song-writing team were up and down; this was certainly a 'down'.

87. I'D MUCH RATHER BE WITH THE BOYS (Oldham, Richard)
November 1964: Chess, Chicago. Producer: Andrew Oldham.
*UK Compilation LP METAMORPHIS: 6 June 1975: No **45** – 1 week*
*USA Compilation LP METAMORPHIS: 6 June 1975: No **8** – 8 weeks*

Another demo, but unusual since the songwriters are Andrew Oldham and Keith Richards. It was written and recorded for the Toggery Five whose version was released in February 1965. The song tends to be stilted, and the country guitars generally lack inspiration. It ends in a rather embarrassing crescendo which leaves Mick Jagger entirely baffled. Bill Wyman humorously chose this track for inclusion on a proposed mid-'seventies compilation album THE BLACK BOX. Decca ignored the idea but this track eventually ended up on their own compilation album METAMORPHIS.

88. WE'RE WASTIN' TIME (Jagger, Richard)
November 1964: Chess, Chicago. Producer: Andrew Oldham.
*UK Compilation LP METAMORPHIS: 6 June 1975: No **45** – 1 week*

This particular track, another demo, was not released on the American album version of METAMORPHIS. Session musicians were probably used and again there is a country feel to the song. Jimmy Tarbuck, by profession a comedian, had the dubious honour of recording this track and issuing it as a single.

89. EACH AND EVERY DAY OF THE YEAR (Jagger, Richard)
November 1964: Chess, Chicago. Producer: Andrew Oldham.
*UK Compilation LP METAMORPHIS: 6 June 1975: No **45** – 1 week*
*USA Compilation LP METAMORPHIS: 6 June 1975: No **8** – 8 weeks*

Written for another British combo The Thee, and recorded as a demo for them. They subsequently released it as a single in May 1965. It is an orchestrated track featuring horns and is reminiscent of a Spanish fiesta song, or rather a siesta song *zzzzzzz* .....

90. LITTLE RED ROOSTER (Dixon)
5/6/8 November 1964: Chess, Chicago. Producer: Andrew Oldham.
Engineer: Ron Malo.
*UK Single: 13 November 1964: No **1** – 12 weeks.*
*USA LP THE ROLLING STONES NOW!: February 1965: No **5** – 29 weeks*
*UK Compilation LP BIG HITS (HIGH TIDE AND GREEN GRASS): November 1966: No **4** – 43 weeks*

This single was back to mainstream blues and had advance orders of over 200,000 copies in the UK, subsequently securing the group's second British Number 1 single. It was a particularly audacious move to record the song in the Chicago Studios with the original composer (Willie Dixon) looking on. The Stones obviously needed to consolidate the foundations they had already laid and many critics believed this slice of unadulterated blues was risky in a commercial sense. Andrew Oldham agreed, but the Stones insisted on its release. Brian Jones later described it as his favourite Stones' track. No wonder, since he plays incredible slide guitar. They had succeeded in taking a pure blues song to the top of the charts, a feat that has never been repeated.

91. **TIME IS ON MY SIDE** (Meade, Norman)
5/6/8 November 1964: Chess, Chicago. Producer: Andrew Oldham.
Engineer: Ron Malo.
UK LP THE ROLLING STONES NO 2: 30 January 1965: No 1 – 37
weeks
USA Compilation LP BIG HITS (HIGH TIDE AND GREEN GRASS):
March 1966: No 3 – 35 weeks
UK Compilation LP BIG HITS (HIGH TIDE AND GREEN GRASS):
November 1966: No 4 – 43 weeks

Recorded in America and released only in Britain, this is the second version, featuring lead guitar with gentle organ. It seemed as though it was necessary to re-record the song in order to liven it up for the British market. It became a popular live song, even if the screams tended to drown this rousing ballad.

92. **YOU CAN MAKE IT IF YOU TRY** (Jarrett)
December 1964: BBC Radio, London.
Bootleg only.

93. **DOWN IN THE BOTTOM** (a.k.a. **FAT OLD MAN**) (Dixon)
December 1964: BBC Radio, London.
Bootleg only.

94. **BEAUTIFUL DELILAH** (Berry)
December 1964: BBC Radio, London.
Bootleg only.

95. **HIGH HEELED SNEEKERS** (Higgenbotham)
December 1964: BBC Radio, London.
Bootleg only.

A further excursion into the BBC radio 'Saturday Club' studios produced four live tracks available only on bootleg. The session closed a successful year and produced a tasty product for collectors. The tracks are an adequate performance led by a slow rocker into a track which was recorded earlier in the year in Chicago, but not subsequently released. *Down In The Bottom* swings along, driven by Bill Wyman's hard-driving bass. *Beautiful Delilah* is the notable performance, and stresses the importance of delivering live as well as in the studio. The track rocks and Keith Richards delivers a nimble solo (or two).

96. **THE LAST TIME** (Jagger, Richard)
10/11 January and 17/18 February 1965: RCA, Hollywood. Producer: Andrew Oldham. Engineer: Dave Hassinger.
UK Single: 26 February 1965: No **1** *– 13 weeks*
USA Single: March 1965: No **9** *– 8 weeks*
USA LP OUT OF OUR HEADS: July 1965: No **1** *– 35 weeks*
USA Compilation LP BIG HITS (HIGH TIDE AND GREEN GRASS):
March 1966: No **3** *– 35 weeks*
UK Compilation LP BIG HITS (HIGH TIDE AND GREEN GRASS):
November 1966: No **4** *– 43 weeks*
UK Compilation LP STONE AGE: 23 April 1971: No **4** *– 7 weeks*

The Last Time is the first self-penned single and it was nonchalantly recorded at the RCA Studios prior to dropping in on the Australasian continent for a 20-date tour which included such jet-set venues as Singapore and Hong Kong. Mick Jagger was not sufficiently happy with the vocals on the track and so they returned in February after the tour to re-do them. *The Last Time* signified a slight change in style – the sound was harder hitting, thriving on a repetitive guitar riff. This type of sound was later to evolve into the genre of rock music and was a small step to the mid-'sixties acceleration of different music forms. The recording instantly satisfied Keith Richards; he knew he had written and performed on an addictive driving song and that this feel could be developed on. Mick Jagger at that time was not fully part of the music-writing process, although he clearly played an important part with the lyrics and ideas. Brian Jones filled in on rhythm again, helping to create the notable 'wall of noise' electric charge. Phil Spector was also in the studio lending a significant hand. Out-takes exist which possibly contain the poor vocal takes.

97. **PLAY WITH FIRE** (Nanker, Phelge)
10/11 January 1965 and 17/18 February 1965: RCA, Hollywood.
Producer: Andrew Oldham. Engineer: Dave Hassinger.
UK B-side The Last Time: 26 February 1965
USA B-side The Last Time: March 1965
USA LP OUT OF OUR HEADS: July 1965: No **1** *– 35 weeks*
USA Compilation LP BIG HITS (HIGH TIDE AND GREEN GRASS):
March 1966: No **3** *– 35 weeks*
Rolling Stones with Phil Spector, Jack Nitzsche.

Probably two versions of this song were recorded, a more up-tempo number *Mess With Fire* and this the slower take. Chrissie Shrimpton, Mick Jagger's girlfriend, is rumoured to have delivered the wrong master to the studio and as a result the slower version featuring Phil Spector on acoustic guitar and Jack Nitzsche playing guitar and harpsichord was released. The rest of the Stones, apart from Mick and Keith, were apparently a little worse for the length of the session and were asleep on the studio couches. There is no proof of the faster version since the tape was destroyed. *Play With Fire*, although a flip-side, still generated interest. It was an atmospheric song, lyrically adventurous, reminiscent of Bob Dylan and seedy in approach.

98. EVERYBODY NEEDS SOMEBODY TO LOVE (Russell, Burke, Wexler)
5/16 March 1965: Edmonton Regal, Liverpool Empire, Manchester Palace, Greenford Granada. Producer: Andrew Oldham. Engineer: Glyn Johns.
UK EP GOT LIVE IF YOU WANT IT!: 11 June 1965

This live track, coupled with a dubious Nanker, Phelge composition *We Want The Stones* (a crowd chant) that cannot possibly be given its publishing royalty dues, kicks off a completely spontaneous recording of the band on their sixth British tour. Glyn Johns instigated the recording by dangling a few microphones over the balcony at selected gigs. The decision to release these sparse recordings was a brave one, but the record did not claim to be anything other than just a fair representation of the band at work. The rest of the tracks on the EP are the following 99 to 102.

99. PAIN IN MY HEART (Redding, Walden)
5/16 March 1965: Edmonton Regal, Liverpool Empire, Manchester Palace, Greenford Granada. Producer: Andrew Oldham. Engineer: Glyn Johns.
UK EP GOT LIVE IF YOU WANT IT!: 11 June 1965

A slow interpretation of the song, which permitted the screams to be properly heard!

100. ROUTE 66 (Troup)
5/16 March 1965: Edmonton Regal, Liverpool Empire, Manchester Palace, Greenford Granada. Producer: Andrew Oldham. Engineer: Glyn Johns.
UK EP GOT LIVE IF YOU WANT IT!: 11 June 1965.

A rabble rouser, in true 'peppermint twist' style.

101. I'M MOVING ON (Snow)
5/16 March 1965: Edmonton Regal, Liverpool Empire, Manchester Palace, Greenford Granada. Producer: Andrew Oldham. Engineer: Glyn Johns.
UK EP GOT LIVE IF YOU WANT IT!: 11 June 1965
*USA LP DECEMBER'S CHILDREN: November 1965: No **4** – 22 weeks*

This track was never attempted in the studio and so this is the only available recording. It was a Hank Snow country standard also made popular in the jazz clubs, and the Stones' R 'n' B approach warmly lifted the EP.

102. I'M ALRIGHT (Nanker, Phelge)
5/16 March 1965: Edmonton Regal, Liverpool Empire, Manchester Palace, Greenford Granada: Producer: Andrew Oldham. Engineer: Glyn Johns.
UK EP GOT LIVE IF YOU WANT IT!: 11 June 1965
USA LP OUT OF OUR HEADS: July 1965: No 1 – 35 weeks

An adequate Stones' (Nanker, Phelge) composition which ends the live EP in orgasmic screams. It is widely believed that a studio version of this song exists, but it is certainly not the filler track on the American OUT OF OUR HEADS album, that is also this live track. The EP in Britain reached Number 13 in the single charts. The EP cover displayed band members in white on black mod pose – the Stones were credited for arrangement!

3

SATISFACTION GUARANTEED
APRIL 1965 – SEPTEMBER 1966

103. EVERYBODY NEEDS SOMEBODY TO LOVE (Russell, Burke, Wexler)
17/18 April 1965: Olympia, Paris.
Bootleg only.

104. PLAY WITH FIRE (Nanker, Phelge)
17/18 April 1965: Olympia, Paris.
Bootleg only.

105. THE LAST TIME (Jagger, Richard)
17/18 April 1965: Olympia, Paris.
Bootleg only.

106. LITTLE RED ROOSTER (Dixon)
17/18 April 1965: Olympia, Paris.
Bootleg only.

107. HEY CRAWDADDY (McDaniel)
17/18 April 1965: Olympia, Paris.
Bootleg only.

A selection of tracks featuring their two latest singles which were recorded at a Paris concert on a quick promotional visit in April 1965 – the band's busiest year for world-wide concert promotions. Paris certainly erupted with Stones fever on this Easter holiday weekend. The performance culminated in an epic five-minute Bo Diddley number entitled *Hey Crawdaddy*. The track intensively builds up to a ritual climax. Jagger entices the crowd in a deep voice encouraging the 'Crawdaddy' chant. The atmosphere is intense and you can almost feel the sweat falling from the ceiling as the song stomped along to the end of a noteworthy set. *Hey Crawdaddy* is an essential collector's item.

108. THE UNDER ASSISTANT WEST COAST PROMOTION MAN
(Nanker, Phelge)
10/11 May 1965: Chess, Chicago. Producer: Andrew Oldham.
Engineer: Ron Malo.
USA B-side Satisfaction: May 1965
USA LP OUT OF OUR HEADS: July 1965: No 1 – 35 weeks
UK LP OUT OF OUR HEADS: 6 September 1965: No 2 – 24 weeks

Two versions of this track exist, the song being recorded predominantly for the American market. This version appeared on the flip-side of the American release of *Satisfaction* and the other on OUT OF OUR HEADS. Only true *aficionados* will be able to spot the difference between the two versions. The song is akin to *Off The Hook*. They are both Nanker, Phelge compositions and deserve more credit than just being placed on a single flip-side. *The Under Assistant West Coast Promotion Man* is an adventurous composition which gently pokes fun at George Sherlock who accompanied the band on the American tour as a representative of their American-based label, London Records. Did Andrew Oldham really have to resort to tongue-in-cheek jibes at the opposition?! This track has subsequently become an anthem for all aspiring promo men.

109. MERCY MERCY (Covay, Miller)
10/11 May 1965: Chess, Chicago. Producer: Andrew Oldham.
Engineer: Ron Malo.
USA LP OUT OF OUR HEADS: July 1965: No 1 – 35 weeks
UK LP OUT OF OUR HEADS: 6 September 1965: No 2 – 24 weeks

Another attempt at a soul standard made popular during 1964 by Don Covay and His Goodtimers. It is a satisfactory cover version suitable for Mick Jagger's vocals, although the harmony vocals appear a little stretched. Ron Malo places the guitar sound to the forefront of the track and he allows Keith Richards and Brian Jones to diversify from the usual clear note by using a more fulfilling valve sound, thereby making full use of the amplifiers. The sound is unique and punchy.

110. THAT'S HOW STRONG MY LOVE IS (Jamison)
10/11 May 1965: Chess, Chicago. Producer: Andrew Oldham.
Engineer: Ron Malo.
USA LP OUT OF OUR HEADS: July 1965: No 1 – 35 weeks
UK LP OUT OF OUR HEADS: 6 September 1965: No 2 – 24 weeks

This oddly abbreviated ballad is introduced by an acoustic guitar and almost certainly features Jack Nitzsche on organ and piano. Mick Jagger utters his normal explicit vocals from the bottom of his heart. Possibly sincere, but not a classic. Andrew Oldham's heady sleeve notes on the album cover were also possibly sincere; they certainly played to the American market in a sycophantic manner : 'In this world where minds have overtaken reason and every thought is potential treason the only message about this new ellpee is let's all live to enjoy it.' Bob Dylan would surely be proud!

111. FANNY MAE (Brown)
10/11 May 1965: Chess, Chicago. Producer: Andrew Oldham.
Engineer: Ron Malo.
Bootleg only.

The May '65 Chess sessions produced several tracks which were never released (despite Bill Wyman's attempts to allow several of them to be made 'official' in 1975 under the 'Black Box' title). *Fanny Mae* touched on old ground, a straight 1960 Buster Brown R 'n' B rocker featuring harmonica. It is certainly not sub-standard, but perhaps was not included on the OUT OF OUR HEADS album in order to concentrate on a more sophisticated, emerging Stones sound equivalent to their main rivals, The Beatles.

112. THE SPIDER AND THE FLY (Nanker, Phelge)
12/13 May 1965: RCA, Hollywood. Producer: Andrew Oldham.
Engineer: Dave Hassinger.
USA LP OUT OF OUR HEADS: July 1965: No 1 – 35 weeks
UK B-side (I Can't Get No) Satisfaction: 20 August 1965.
UK Compilation LP STONE AGE: 23 April 1971: No 4 – 7 weeks

A eulogy of life on the road, the song encapsulates the decision facing a young rock 'n' roller on tour – do I sleep with the groupie? It is a slow country blues which was thought just right for the British market, hence its UK release on the prestigious flip-side of *Satisfaction.* Mick Jagger relates the pitfalls awaiting a touring rock 'n' roll band with an image to live up to. It obviously has to be tongue in cheek! An out-take version of this track is available on bootleg. It is slightly heavier in approach and has a stronger boogie rhythm.

113. ONE MORE TRY (Jagger, Richard)
12/13 May 1965: RCA, Hollywood. Producer: Andrew Oldham.
Engineer: Dave Hassinger.
USA LP OUT OF OUR HEADS: July 1965: No 1 – 35 weeks
UK Compilation LP STONE AGE: 23 April 1971: No 4 – 7 weeks

A jaunty, discordant song which is emblematic of the distinct trial between producing R 'n' B songs in a rock vein and commercial songs incorporating a distinct vocal style. The vocals undoubtedly let this track down. Mick Jagger ushers the song forward at an awkward pace which completes the recording in record time!

114. MY GIRL (Robinson, White)
12/13 May 1965: RCA, Hollywood. Producer: Andrew Oldham.
Engineer: Dave Hassinger.
USA Compilation LP FLOWERS: June 1967: No **3** *–* 18 *weeks*
UK Compilation LP STONE AGE: 23 April 1971: No **4** *–* 7 *weeks*

A track made available by Decca in 1967 on a compilation album
FLOWERS. It is a soft ballad previously performed by The Temptations
who reached Number 1 with it in January 1965 in the States. At the mixing
desk, unobtrusive orchestral strings were added to the recorded track
by Andrew Oldham. He tried this on many other tracks in the hope that
they would then become more marketable. This time the result was not
totally absurd.

115. (I CAN'T GET NO) SATISFACTION (Jagger, Richard)
10/13 May 1965: Chess, Chicago on 10/11 May and RCA, Hollywood on
12/13 May. Producer: Andrew Oldham. Engineer: Chess, Ron Malo –
RCA, Dave Hassinger.
USA Single: May 1965: No **1** *–* 12 *weeks*
USA LP OUT OF OUR HEADS: July 1965: No **1** *–* 35 *weeks*
UK Single: 20 August 1965: No **1** *–* 12 *weeks*
UK Compilation LP BIG HITS (HIGH TIDE AND GREEN GRASS):
November 1966: No **4** *–* 43 *weeks*

This monster of rock was conceived by Keith Richards during the Spring
'65 American tour on one of the many routine overnight hotel stops. He
claims he pinched the opening riff from Martha and The Vandellas'
Dancing In The Street. The many implications of this recorded rock
anthem were obviously not realized at its inception. Keith wrote the
music and the lyrics in a folk mould and therefore never believed that it
could be other than a soft rock song. Mick Jagger was aware of the
possibilities of the anti-establishment lyrics, and after much persuasion
Keith permitted the switch to a rock 'n' roll beat. The decision was a
monumental stepping stone in their career. The lyrics were anarchic for
the time and were atypical of the mid-'sixties, speaking for a new generation. Keith was still reluctant to release the end product; he felt the riff
was over-simplified, for he intended that it would have been played by
brass instruments rather like the February 1966 Otis Redding version.
Bill Wyman recalls that *Satisfaction* was eventually released following a
democratic band vote which included Ian Stewart. Ironically, the two
who voted against release were Keith Richards and Mick Jagger. The
mammoth recording programme began in Chicago at midday on 10 May,
finishing at 5.00 am on 11 May. After a quick break and a detour to
Hollywood, recording resumed on May 12 and finished late evening May
13. Both engineers recorded in stereo but mixed and ultimately released
the final cut in mono. The outcome therefore features acoustic sounds on
one track and a heavier electric sound using fuzz-box techniques on the
other. Out-takes of *Satisfaction* exist which demonstrate some of the
different mixes. On one out-take, the acoustic guitar and tambourine taps
vanish and the released vocal track is also missing. The final version

fades out, whereas the out-take abruptly finishes after the last chorus. The released version features an outstanding Charlie Watts backing track. Andrew Oldham decided that the vocals should be submerged in the over-all sound. This may have been a deliberate play to avoid the *double entendre* critics who were eager to ban any subversive aggression. The combination of all these factors produced a synthesis of acoustic/electric sounds unique in style (although perhaps reminiscent of Bob Dylan) and helped to create a world-wide Number 1 hit even though British fans were upset by the late release of the single in the UK. It had already been Number 1 in the States for two months. The tardiness of the release, however, produced 250,000 advance orders and a guaranteed Number 1 hit.

116. GOOD TIMES (Cooke)
12/13 May 1965: RCA, Hollywood. Producer: Andrew Oldham.
Engineer: Dave Hassinger.
UK LP OUT OF OUR HEADS: 6 September 1965: No 2 – 24 weeks
USA LP OUT OF OUR HEADS: July 1965: No 1 – 35 weeks

The experiment with soul continued, this particular track being a cover of a song written by Sam Cooke. It was a Top 20 hit for him in June 1965, six months after he was tragically killed in a shooting incident. This tribute is a short sharp reminder of 'fifties soul employing Shirley and Lee's good time phrase 'Let The Good Times Roll'. The melody hooks the listener to this pleasant up-tempo song. It is a positive contribution to the OUT OF OUR HEADS album, but also emphasizes the disjointedness of the album's song styles.

117. CRY TO ME (Russell)
12/13 May 1965: RCA, Hollywood. Producer: Andrew Oldham.
Engineer: Dave Hassinger.
UK LP OUT OF OUR HEADS: 6 September 1965: No 2 – 24 weeks
USA LP OUT OF OUR HEADS: July 1965: No 1 – 35 weeks

Cry To Me reverts to the pleading soul songs so reverently included on the first and second albums. The guitar stings in painful tones and Mick Jagger's vocals try to comfort those who have thoughts of loneliness. The out-take version available on bootleg is played at the same pace and instead of fading out drifts along for a few seconds more before the band ends the sad ordeal. Coincidentally, another British R 'n' B band, The Pretty Things (which included Keith Richards' old mate Dick Taylor), had recorded the song and charted with it in July prior to the release of the Stones' British version in September.

118. SHE SAID YEAH (Roderick, Jackson, Christy)
12/13 May 1965: RCA, Hollywood. Producer: Andrew Oldham.
Engineer: Dave Hassinger.
UK LP OUT OF OUR HEADS: 6 September 1965: No 2 – 24 weeks
USA LP DECEMBER'S CHILDREN: November 1965: No 4 – 22 weeks

USA Compilation LP THE ROLLING STONES – PROMOTIONAL ALBUM: October 1969

She Said Yeah is a rousing number which noisily opens the British OUT OF OUR HEADS and the American DECEMBER'S CHILDREN albums. It portrayed the heavier beat/mod sound with which The Pretty Things, The Who and The Yardbirds were having so much success. The vocals are aggressive and slightly indistinct. The guitar sound is superb – imagine Keith Richards and Brian Jones fraternizing with feedback!

119. GOTTA GET AWAY (Jagger, Richard)
12/13 May 1965: RCA, Hollywood. Producer: Andrew Oldham. Engineer: Dave Hassinger.
UK LP OUT OF OUR HEADS: 6 September 1965: No 2 – 24 weeks
USA LP DECEMBER'S CHILDREN: November 1965: No 4 – 22 weeks
USA B-side As Tears Go By: December 1965

A Jagger, Richard composition which is just an album filler. The lyrics lack imagination and the tune never gets off the ground. It does an injustice to the hidden talent of the group. They were going through an industrious period and inevitably some tracks would not meet the fans' expectations or the band's potential.

120. I'VE BEEN LOVING YOU TOO LONG (Redding, Butler)
12/13 May 1965: RCA, Hollywood. Producer: Andrew Oldham. Engineer: Dave Hassinger.
Bootleg only.

This Otis Redding ballad was recorded just a month before Otis himself obtained a Number 21 hit with it in the American Billboard charts. Due to this coincidence, it is unlikely the Stones themselves wished the track to be released and although performed live, it never gained an official release – except on the aforementioned German 1983 collection of Stones material. The original recording, however, did serve a useful purpose and with screams overdubbed it was used to fill out the 1967 live album GOT LIVE IF YOU WANT IT. An unpopular ending to an other-wise satisfactory cover of an Otis Redding number. (Otis died aged 26 in a plane crash in December 1967 – he posthumously charted at Number 1 in February 1968 with the memorable *The Dock Of The Bay*.)

121. TALKIN' 'BOUT YOU (Berry)
12/13 May 1965: RCA, Hollywood. Producer: Andrew Oldham. Engineer: Dave Hassinger.
UK LP OUT OF OUR HEADS: 6 September 1965: No 2 – 24 weeks
USA LP DECEMBER'S CHILDREN: November 1965: No 4 – 22 weeks

Covering Chuck Berry tunes was a happy studio pastime. The decision actually to record them for release was a brave one, since they would always be compared to the master's original. The Stones, however, were progressing to their own inimitable style and when covering Chuck Berry songs the rhythm was usually the key to the success of the copy.

The Stones describe it as 'shuffle and eighths', as opposed to the more usual eight to the bar. *Talkin' 'Bout You* is played mid-tempo in a slow competent manner. It is not a classic Berry cover but is worthwhile due to its extempore nature.

122. I'M FREE (Jagger, Richard)
12/13 May 1965: RCA, Hollywood. Producer: Andrew Oldham. Engineer: Dave Hassinger.
*UK LP OUT OF OUR HEADS: 6 September 1965: No **2** – 24 weeks*
USA B-side Get Off My Cloud: September 1965
*USA LP DECEMBER'S CHILDREN: November 1965: No **4** – 22 weeks*
USA Compilation LP THE ROLLING STONES – PROMOTIONAL ALBUM: October 1969

The four days of sessions from 10–13 May 1965 were in the middle of the American tour and as such were unique. The recordings paved the foundations for two albums, more than a dozen tracks being recorded including the infamous *Satisfaction*. It was noticeable that the musical style was beginning to shift from the R 'n' B of the early 'sixties to a rock foundation; *I'm Free* typifies this approach. It is predictive of the recordings to follow and also has distinct Beatle touches. It was a stage favourite.

123. BLUE TURNS TO GREY (Jagger, Richard)
12/13 May 1965: RCA, Hollywood. Producer: Andrew Oldham. Engineer: Dave Hassinger.
*USA LP DECEMBER'S CHILDREN: November 1965: No **4** – 22 weeks*
*UK Compilation LP STONE AGE: 23 April 1971: No **4** – 7 weeks*

Cliff Richard popularized this track (a Top 20 hit) by releasing his version as a British single in early 1966. The Stones were obviously not impressed with the song since it was not featured on an authorized UK release. It did, however, re-surface on a dubious Decca compilation of Stones' 'so-called' rarities in 1971. The Stones were angry at the release just after the cessation of their contract with Decca. Indeed, they placed an advertisement in the British musical newspapers advising against purchase of inferior product! The track has weak foundations, relying on vocal harmonies which sounded very experimental. This was one area that needed a certain amount of work – the arranger could be excused on this occasion.

124. (I CAN'T GET NO) SATISFACTION (Jagger, Richard)
20 May 1965: Shindig TV Show, Hollywood.
Bootleg only.

The Last Time, the band's current single, was sliding down the charts, so *Satisfaction* was released in the States almost immediately. The remaining live performances of the tour and TV appearances ensured that it entered the Billboard Top 40 the following month. The first television appearance was on Jack Good's 'Shindig' and the nation-wide appeal of this show guaranteed a hit. The uncensored performance was repeated on future 'Shindig' shows, since Jack Good was proud to claim his coup: 'Here's the Number 1 national hit song that was heard for the first time in the World right here on 'Shindig'.' It had been a busy time for the group. A few days earlier they had shared the bill with Chuck Berry on the 'Hollywood A Go Go' TV show and had narrowly escaped being crushed by fan hysteria when their limousine was literally swamped by over-enthusiastic followers. The roof of the car had been dangerously close to cracking.

125. MERCY MERCY (Covay, Miller)
30 August 1965: BBC Radio, London.
Bootleg only.

126. CRY TO ME (Russell, Burke, Wexler)
30 August 1965: BBC Radio, London.
Bootleg only.

127. EVERYBODY NEEDS SOMEBODY TO LOVE (Russell, Burke, Wexler)
30 August 1965: BBC Radio, London.
Bootleg only.

128. (I CAN'T GET NO) SATISFACTION (Jagger, Richard)
30 August 1965: BBC Radio, London.
Bootleg only.

129. THE LAST TIME (Jagger, Richard)
30 August 1965: BBC Radio, London.
Bootleg only.

130. FANNY MAE (Brown)
30 August 1965: BBC Radio, London.
Bootleg only.

131. DOWN THE ROAD APIECE (Raye)
30 August 1965: BBC Radio, London.
Bootleg only.

Back from the States, and after a brief tour of Scotland and Scandinavia in June 1965, the band welcomed the apparent calm and rest of Britain. It was unfortunate the peace was shattered by an innocuous garage uri-nation scene which guaranteed public outrage. The event was repre-sentative of the kind of trouble that encircled the Stones. The subsequent court appearances and fines for three members of the Stones helped to take up the month of July. It is likely that the Stones needed this early summer recess to recharge their batteries, play one-off gigs and also to enter the BBC Studios again. The preceding titles were recorded for use on the BBC Radio shows 'Yeah, Yeah' and 'Saturday Club' and were the Stones' final BBC Radio broadcasts. Sessions became an unnecessary means of publicity while the Number 1 hits rolled in. The tracks were played very much in the same style of the originals recorded that summer in the States, but are also important to collectors because they do not feature the obvious studio polish of the finished product and lack fade-outs of any kind.

132. GET OFF MY CLOUD (Jagger, Richard)
6/7 September 1965: RCA, Hollywood. Producer: Andrew Oldham.
Engineer: Dave Hassinger.
USA Single: September 1965: No **1** *– 11 weeks*
UK Single: 22 October 1965: No **1** *– 12 weeks*
USA LP DECEMBER'S CHILDREN: November 1965: No **4** *– 22 weeks*
USA Compilation LP BIG HITS (HIGH TIDE AND GREEN GRASS):
March 1966: No **3** *– 35 weeks*
UK Compilation LP BIG HITS (HIGH TIDE AND GREEN GRASS):
November 1966: No **4** *– 43 weeks*

Returning to the States the trilogy of 1965 UK and USA hit singles continued with this track which was again criticized by Keith Richards. He felt the production let it down. However, it became the first simultaneous Number 1 in the States and the UK and the band's fifth consecutive Number 1 hit in Britain, an achievement which had only been previously matched a year before by The Beatles. The purpose of the Hollywood session was to record a follow-up to *Satisfaction*, and it is remarkable that this was achieved in such convincing style. The track adopts a rock and roll approach (sometimes referred to as the 'Twist and Shout' chord method) and was a contrast to the rock/soul sound of *Satisfaction*. The lyrics exactly purveyed the pill-popping age of the 'sixties with the 'hey's and 'you's resonating in distinctive tones. More people were letting their inhibitions go, and the 'stoned' age, be it by drugs or alcohol, was beginning to run away from the establishment. Appearances on the by-now institutionalized BBC 'Top Of The Pops' TV show proved that the Stones had made their mark – *Get Off My Cloud* created a safe pedestal for a degree of experimentation on future single releases.

133. THE SINGER NOT THE SONG (Jagger, Richard)
6/7 September 1965: RCA, Hollywood. Producer: Andrew Oldham.
Engineer: Dave Hassinger.
UK B-side Get off My Cloud: 22 October 1965
USA LP DECEMBER'S CHILDREN: November 1965: No **4** *– 22 weeks*

An unremarkable track featuring acoustic guitars which duet in an amateurish fashion. The vocals lack the plush harmonies of their chart-topping counterparts, The Beatles, and the track sounds particularly off-key. This type of sound produced embarrassing smiles and was a temporary let-down to Andrew Oldham's creativeness. It should have remained a studio out-take and it is unfortunate such lightweight material should be used as a single flip-side, however, this was the tendency of the record company. The British were lucky they did not have to contend with the American DECEMBER'S CHILDREN album, which was a compiler's nightmare.

134. AS TEARS GO BY (Jagger, Richard, Oldham)
6/7 September 1965: RCA, Hollywood. Producer: Andrew Oldham.
Engineer: Dave Hassinger.
USA Single: December 1965: No **6** *– 6 weeks*
USA LP DECEMBER'S CHILDREN: November 1965: No **4** *– 22 weeks*
UK B-side 19th Nervous Breakdown: 4 February 1966
USA Compilation LP BIG HITS (HIGH TIDE AND GREEN GRASS):
March 1966: No **3** *– 35 weeks*
UK Compilation LP BIG HITS (HIGH TIDE AND GREEN GRASS):
November 1966: No **4** *– 43 weeks*
UK Compilation LP STONE AGE: 23 April 1971: No **4** *– 7 weeks*

This is the first Jagger, Richard composition which also credited Andrew Oldham as a songwriter. It tends to confirm that the track written in 1964 was intended as little more than a money-maker for Marianne Faithfull. In August, 1964, it achieved this with a Number 9 UK hit for Miss Faithfull. Possibly it surprised not only Andrew Oldham but also Jagger, Richard by its success (not to mention Lionel Bart, Miss Faithfull's previous musical mentor). Originally recorded in July 1964 as a demo, it was re-recorded in America at this session for the States where the soft ballad was in mode. The Stones were also concerned that the release of such a commercial ballad would have British critics saying it was yet another Beatle imitation (particularly of the song *Yesterday*). Mick Jagger played almost a solo role in the song. He was backed only by Keith on guitar and Andrew's string arrangements. The lyrics, inspired by girlfriend Marianne Faithfull, hence her unique involvement, were sentimental and soporific. The song was, however, a unique reminder of the softer Stones approach and musically was a milestone in their then short song-writing career. The comparison with *Yesterday* is unfair since the song was plainly written a year before the release of The Beatles' song. However, it can be argued that the final version did have slight Beatle leanings. An unusual Italian single release of this track exists with a different backing track, slightly more orchestrated, and features Mick Jagger singing in Italian *Con Le Mie Lacrime.*

135. SHE SAID YEAH (Roderick, Jackson, Christy)
11 November 1965: Hullabaloo TV Show, New York.
Bootleg only.

136. GET OFF MY CLOUD (Jagger, Richard)
11 November 1965: Hullabaloo TV Show, New York.
Bootleg only.

The band's 1965 schedule was intense and after the brief early September recordings they commenced yet another British tour featuring 24 dates. This finished mid-October and after a short rest they returned to the American continent for their fourth Stateside tour, which lasted almost two months. These recordings, which are available on bootleg, capture the enthusiasm of the audience and the adeptness of the performing band who manage to retain the spontaneity of the original record. The band had also recently acquired a road manager, Michael Gruber, who ensured the band had good fun on the road. His personality was such that the band, particularly Brian, Mick and Keith, came closer together for a period.

137. MOTHER'S LITTLE HELPER (Jagger, Richard)
3/8 December 1965: RCA, Hollywood. Producer: Andrew Oldham, assisted by Jack Nitzsche. Engineer: Dave Hassinger.
UK LP AFTERMATH: April 1966: No 1 – 28 weeks
USA Single: June 1966: No 8 – 8 weeks
USA Compilation LP FLOWERS: June 1967: No 3 – 18 weeks
UK Compilation LP THROUGH THE PAST DARKLY (BIG HITS VOL 2): 12 September 1969: No 2 – 37 weeks
USA Compilation LP THROUGH THE PAST DARKLY (BIG HITS VOL 2): September 1969: No 2 – 16 weeks

'What a drag it is getting old.' Brian Jones was determined to refute this by exploring different musical sounds and this track featured his current favourite instrument, the Indian sitar. An experimental song, it prepares the way for future leanings of this kind. Mick Jagger's lyrical enunciation of housewives' boredom which leads to popping yellow pills was perhaps condescending. Feminists took a stronger line, calling it male chauvinism. The human tones of sympathy and understanding were missed! The track was released in the States six months later as a single; it reached Number 8 and was a worthy single follow up to *Paint It, Black.* The musical similarity must have also been a contributory factor.

138. DONCHA BOTHER ME (a.k.a. DON'T YA FOLLOW ME) (Jagger, Richard)
3/8 December 1965: RCA, Hollywood. Producer: Andrew Oldham, assisted by Jack Nitzsche. Engineer: Dave Hassinger.
UK LP AFTERMATH: April 1966: No 1 – 28 weeks
USA LP AFTERMATH: June 1966: No 2 – 26 weeks

Back to the British recording roots of R 'n' B, *Doncha Bother Me* is played at a jaunty pace and includes bottleneck guitar. Harmonica is also incorporated after a few verses. The result is a strange dichotomy of blues, tinged with country leanings. There was no such unnecessary complication on the next track.

139. GOIN' HOME (Jagger, Richard)
3/8 December 1965: RCA, Hollywood. Producer: Andrew Oldham, assisted by Jack Nitzsche. Engineer: Dave Hassinger.
UK LP AFTERMATH: April 1966: No 1 – 28 weeks
USA LP AFTERMATH: June 1966: No 2 – 26 weeks

The first track to reach rock marathon status – it lasted 11 minutes and 45 seconds. *Goin' Home* is a blues jam which builds up incessantly. Mick Jagger leads the song's structure, thrusting the band forward and simmering them down as he feels appropriate. The whole band respond to the rock jargon he utters. Just before the climax, Mick Jagger sits back for a few seconds and hums evocatively along to the melody and then he strikes hard until the song has to relinquish. Brian Jones' contribution to this track was claimed to be minimal, the guitar pieces being played entirely by Keith Richards. The result swept aside the standard album cut format and was quite innovatory. The fact that the band had managed to maintain interest was significant and also characteristic of their live performance.

140. LOOKING TIRED (Jagger, Richard)
3/8 December 1965: RCA, Hollywood. Producer: Andrew Oldham, assisted by Jack Nitzsche. Engineer: Dave Hassinger.
Bootleg only.

Looking Tired was originally set for inclusion on an album titled COULD YOU WALK ON THE WATER? Press releases of the time indicated the album would also include *19th Nervous Breakdown, Sad Day, Take it Or Leave It, Think, Mother's Little Helper, Goin' Home, Sittin' On A Fence, Doncha Bother Me,* and *Ride On Baby.* A ten-page booklet of photos was prepared, the artwork for the album sleeve cover was also ready and was said to feature the group about to walk on water. Release was planned for March 1966 but when the product was presented to Decca they predictably panicked at the risqué album title and the cover sleeve. The Stones became bored and left 'the aftermath' to the record company. The album was, therefore, never released. The booklet of photos, however, did appear in November 1966 on the first official compilation album HIGH TIDE AND GREEN GRASS (BIG HITS) which featured their singles to date. *Looking Tired,* a mid-tempo rock song, featuring nimble acoustic guitar and a casually played piano, avoided official release. It is much sought after, but for its rarity appeal, rather than the musical quality.

141. TRY A LITTLE HARDER (Jagger, Richard)
December 1965: RCA, Hollywood.
USA B-side I Don't Know Why. 23 May 1975
UK B-side I Don't Know Why: 23 May 1975
*UK Compilation LP METAMORPHIS: 6 June 1975: No **45** – 1 week*
*USA Compilation LP METAMORPHIS: 6 June 1975: No **8** – 8 weeks*

Another track, presumably an out-take, which is difficult to date. The track has a ring of the American Dave Hassinger soul production sound. The opening bass sounds are powerful and set a strident pace. The Motown feel is accentuated by back-up vocals and inclusion of horns.

142. TAKE IT OR LEAVE IT (Jagger, Richard)
3/8 December 1965: RCA, Hollywood. Producer: Andrew Oldham, assisted by Jack Nitzsche. Engineer: Dave Hassinger.

*UK LP AFTERMATH: April 1966: No **1** – 28 weeks*
*USA Compilation LP FLOWERS: June 1967: No **3** – 18 weeks*

A schmaltzy, embarrassing song, written with little imagination, it epitomized the current direction Andrew Oldham was keen to follow. He seemed determined to emphasize the production and also condone the terrible harmony vocal arrangements. The track was later released in America on the compilation album FLOWERS in June, 1967.

143. **THINK** (Jagger, Richard)
3/8 December 1965: RCA, Hollywood. Producer: Andrew Oldham, assisted by Jack Nitzsche. Engineer: Dave Hassinger.
*UK LP AFTERMATH: April 1966: No **1** – 28 weeks*
*USA LP AFTERMATH: June 1966: No **2** – 26 weeks*

Keith Richards leads the attack on this mediocre rocker. Stun guitar effects are used but the song lacks the punch of other tracks with this technique, notably some of the single releases. Chris Farlowe, a British R 'n' B performer, thought the song was sufficiently good to allow Jagger, Richards and Oldham to produce a version for him. It was released as a single and was a moderate UK hit for a newcomer when it charted at Number 37.

144. **RIDE ON BABY** (Jagger, Richard)
3/8 December 1965: RCA, Hollywood. Producer: Andrew Oldham, assisted by Jack Nitzsche. Engineer: Dave Hassinger.
*USA Compilation LP FLOWERS: June 1967: No **3** – 18 weeks*

Another 'out-take' type of track which managed to find its way onto the FLOWERS compilation album. Brian Jones experimented with a new instrument, the mellotron, which gave the song a soft texture disguising the somewhat brash lyrics. Bongo drums are tapped in the background, emphasizing the newly acquired 'sixties nuance. A studio run-through of *Ride On Baby* is available on bootleg. *Ride On Baby* was also released as a single by Chris Farlowe, completing for him three successive Jagger, Richard covers. Mick Jagger was credited with the production.

145. **SITTIN' ON A FENCE** (Jagger, Richard)
3/8 December 1965: RCA, Hollywood. Producer: Andrew Oldham, assisted by Jack Nitzsche. Engineer: Dave Hassinger.
*USA Compilation LP FLOWERS: June 1967: No **3** – 18 weeks*
*UK Compilation LP THROUGH THE PAST DARKLY (BIG HITS VOL 2): 12 September 1969: No **2** – 37 weeks*

This track is also only available on the American compilation album FLOWERS. The prominent instruments are a classical sounding guitar and the background sound of Brian Jones' mellotron. A British duo, Twice As Much, copied the same classical style and popularized the song in the British charts by reaching Number 25. Andrew Oldham was the producer.

146. SAD DAY (a.k.a. SAD OL' DAY) (Jagger, Richard)
3/8 December 1965: RCA, Hollywood. Producer: Andrew Oldham,
assisted by Jack Nitzsche. Engineer: Dave Hassinger.
USA B-side 19th Nervous Breakdown: February 1966.
UK Single: 29 April 1973.

Sad Day was recorded and released and became the flip-side for the
next American single. It was overlooked by Decca, despite being lined
up for inclusion on the COULD YOU WALK ON THE WATER? album.
Seven years later it was eventually released on a quick Decca, cash-in-
hand, UK single. The song itself is a rocked-up ballad. Mick Jagger
seemed more at home with *Sad Day* than some of the more arranged
sounds of *Ride On Baby* and *Sittin' On A Fence*. He was able to shout and
cajole the lyrics, and the band seemed happy to return to the more
simple and familiar rock approach.

147. 19TH NERVOUS BREAKDOWN (Jagger, Richard)
3/8 December 1965: RCA, Hollywood. Producer: Andrew Oldham,
assisted by Jack Nitzsche. Engineer: Dave Hassinger.
*UK Single: 4 February 1966: No **2** – 8 weeks*
*USA Single: February 1966: No **2** – 9 weeks*
USA Compilation LP BIG HITS (HIGH TIDE AND GREEN GRASS):
*March 1966: No **3** – 35 weeks*
UK Compilation LP BIG HITS (HIGH TIDE AND GREEN GRASS):
*November 1966: No **4** – 43 weeks*

The lengthy Autumn '65 American tour was often described by Mick
Jagger in jest as his '19th nervous breakdown'. This phrase was immediately appropriated by the band and put forward as a possible song title,
the music being almost incidental. Despite this, it had the gusto of
previous singles. The heavy rock sound continued, the pace was fast and
also slightly erratic. *19th Nervous Breakdown* was certainly not as instantaneous or appealing as *Satisfaction* or *Get Off My Cloud*. It focused so
much on the band's thematic pills/mental breakdown saga, that Chrissie
Shrimpton paranoically believed it was written about her. References to
drugs are surreptitiously included, continuing the theme of the album cut
Mother's Little Helper. The vocals were, as usual, placed very much in
the background by Andrew Oldham's arrangement. The public and the
record company might, therefore, have missed the sole reference to 'a
teenager's first trip'. Glyn Johns was given the chance to re-mix the track
and to bring forward the vocals, but the band decided not to release that
version. The song is famous for Bill Wyman's 'dive bomb' bass lines at the
end which he put together rather haphazardly on his semi-acoustic
Framus bass. He describes it dismissively as a 'Bo Diddley thing'. In
Britain, the single only managed a Number 2 position to break their run of
five successive Number Ones. The Beatles were at that time on their
ninth consecutive British Number 1 and so the battle for chart record
supremacy was lost for ever. To this date, the achievement of five
consecutive number ones in Britain has only been surpassed by the
Beatles.

148. (I CAN'T GET NO) SATISFACTION (Jagger, Richard)
12 February 1966: Ed Sullivan TV Show, USA.
Bootleg only.

149. AS TEARS GO BY (Jagger, Richard, Oldham)
12 February 1966: Ed Sullivan TV Show, USA.
Bootleg only.

150. 19TH NERVOUS BREAKDOWN (Jagger, Richard)
12 February 1966: Ed Sullivan TV Show, USA.
Bootleg only.

1966 began with 'The New Year Starts Here', a 'Ready Steady Go' TV special featuring the Stones and other bands playing out 1965 and playing in 1966. January was a month of comparative rest, purchasing of expensive homes and general shopping sprees. The British musical newspaper *New Musical Express* on 14 January 1966 hailed the announcement of an EP featuring *As Tears Go By* and also the release of the next album COULD YOU WALK ON THE WATER? (both were subsequently aborted). The band then flew to the States quickly to promote the new single *19th Nervous Breakdown* plus their current Top Ten American single, *As Tears Go By* – for good measure *Satisfaction* was also included. The source of promotion was once again the Ed Sullivan TV Show. The Stones' performances on American TV were generating furore throughout America. The ecstatic scenes outside the television studios were unique. The actual recordings are, as usual, drowned by screams, the American vulnerability was epitomized by the 'beep' on *Satisfaction* when Mick Jagger tries to 'make some girl'. They then simmer down into *As Tears Go By*, which uses the single's orchestral back track, the pace quickens as they launch into *19th Nervous Breakdown*, a foretaste for the American public of the band's new single. After this sojourn in New York they flew to Australia and commenced an Australia/New Zealand nine-date tour.

151. OUT OF TIME (Jagger, Richard)
3/8 March 1966: RCA, Hollywood. Producer: Andrew Oldham.
Engineer: Dave Hassinger.
UK LP AFTERMATH: April 1966: No 1 – 28 weeks.
USA Compilation LP FLOWERS: June 1967: No 3 – 18 weeks

Mick Jagger later agreed that he thought that this was one of the better tracks available on the UK edition of the AFTERMATH album. Brian Jones was featured on yet another newly acquired instrument, the marimba. His experimentation and virtuosity on such instruments continued the rock allegiance with RUBBER SOUL period Beatles, and presumably contributed to some of the sounds on their forthcoming REVOLVER album. The Beatles were fully aware of this similarity and in one publicity photo John Lennon and George Harrison held high the covers of the AFTERMATH album and *19th Nervous Breakdown* single, proclaiming that they were attempting to come up with a couple of really original ideas! Subtle rhythm changes are the key to the song and also pleasant acoustic-sounding guitars. The track is over the standard length and as such is quite creditable.

152. OUT OF TIME (Jagger, Richard)
3/8 March 1966: RCA, Hollywood. 'Producer: Andrew Oldham.
UK Compilation LP METAMORPHIS: 6 June 1975: No **45** *– 1 week*
USA Compilation LP METAMORPHIS: 6 June 1975: No **8** *– 8 weeks*
UK Single: 5 September 1975: No **45** *– 2 weeks*
USA Single: 5 September 1975

This version was either recorded at the RCA Studios in Hollywood or possibly in England prior to the American visit as a demo for British singer Chris Farlowe. The track is orchestrated and features female backing vocal. Art Greenslade arranged the backing track which was also used for the Chris Farlowe single. Mick Jagger produced the single and thereby prompted a British Number 1 for Chris Farlowe in June, 1966. The contemptuous lyrics fired yet another swipe at the demeanour of women. Decca released the track as a single in 1975 from the dubious METAMORPHIS compilation. At the same time Chris Farlowe's version was rereleased and Dan McCafferty, ex-Nazareth Scottish rock singer, completed a bit of history with the unusual appearance of three versions of *Out Of Time* in the lower reaches of the British charts in September 1975.

153. LADY JANE (Jagger, Richard)
3/8 March 1966: RCA, Hollywood. Producer: Andrew Oldham.
Engineer: Dave Hassinger.
UK LP AFTERMATH: April 1966: No **1** *– 28 weeks*
USA LP AFTERMATH: June 1966: No **2** *– 26 weeks*
USA B-side Mother's Little Helper: June 1966
UK Compilation LP BIG HITS (HIGH TIDE AND GREEN GRASS):
November 1966: No **4** *– 43 weeks*
USA Compilation LP FLOWERS: June 1967: No **3** *– 18 weeks*

A tender, typically English ballad, which compromised Mick Jagger's stance on women. The publicity statements played on the Elizabethan feel to the record and claimed it was based on a letter written by Henry VIII to Jane Seymour, proclaiming his love for her and forecasting the end of his present wife by decapitation. Other much more plausible reasons for the song are Mick Jagger's flirtatious dealings with such British socialites as Jane Ormsby-Gore. The contribution by Brian Jones was again significant. American folk singer Richard Farina had introduced the dulcimer to him and Brian Jones plucks the instrument like a harpsichord. His contribution was innovative and confirmed Andrew Oldham's belief that the band's mid-'sixties musical success was due to Brian Jones' instrumental elaboration. Peter Whitehead directed and produced a live performance of *Lady Jane* incorporating wild crowd scenes with slow motion film techniques. The outcome was included in his film 'Tonight,

Let's All Make Love In London', a documentary of the times, which included Stones' interviews and footage.

154. IT'S NOT EASY (Jagger, Richard)
3/8 March 1966: RCA, Hollywood. Producer: Andrew Oldham.
Engineer: Dave Hassinger.
*UK LP AFTERMATH: April 1966: No **1** – 28 weeks*
*USA LP AFTERMATH: June 1966: No **2** – 26 weeks*

One of the less inspired inclusions on the AFTERMATH album. A chug-along R 'n' B rhythm ploughs the song forward on lacklustre lyrics. The album was let down by these mediocre tracks and emphasized the necessity for song-writing consistency for album inclusion.

155. STUPID GIRL (Jagger, Richard)
3/8 March 1966: RCA, Hollywood. Producer: Andrew Oldham.
Engineer: Dave Hassinger.
*UK LP AFTERMATH: April 1966: No **1** – 28 weeks*
USA B-side Paint It, Black: April 1966
*USA LP AFTERMATH: June 1966: No **2** – 26 weeks*
USA Compilation LP THE ROLLING STONES – PROMOTIONAL
ALBUM: October 1969

A better musical performance, but the lyrics again fall back on the female 'put-down' notion. The band's association with this theme is much debated. It may have been derived from insecurity or simply the boredom of impersonal hotel groupies. It created critical conflict and was politically derisory, but none the less fuelled the publicity machine.

156. PAINT IT, BLACK (Jagger, Richard)
3/8 March 1966: RCA, Hollywood. Producer: Andrew Oldham.
Engineer: Dave Hassinger.
*USA Single: April 1966: No **1** – 10 weeks*
*UK Single: 13 May 1966: No **1** – 10 weeks*
*USA LP AFTERMATH: June 1966: No **2** – 26 weeks*
UK Compilation LP BIG HITS (HIGH TIDE AND GREEN GRASS):
*November 1966: No **4** – 43 weeks*
USA Compilation LP THROUGH THE PAST DARKLY (BIG HITS VOL
*2): September 1969: No **2** – 16 weeks*
*UK Compilation LP STONE AGE: 23 April 1971: No **4** – 7 weeks*
Rolling Stones with Jack Nitzsche.

Keith Richards supplied the music to this, their next single, and Mick Jagger wrote the lyrics. Keith was not satisfied with the final take. He amusingly reckoned it would sound good as a funky eighteenth century sonata (!). Mick and Keith tried to sort out the problem. Bill Wyman became bored with the delay, started the tapes rolling and reproduced the melody by pedalling the organ as an 'impression' of their previous manager, Eric Easton, who in his youth had played the organ in English cinemas during the intermission. Charlie Watts took up the beat and

Brian Jones joined in on the sitar. Jack Nitzsche filled the sound in by playing what he claimed was a 'gypsy-style piano'. The song's transition was random and instantaneous. Brian Jones' virtuoso performance on the sitar was inspirational if not sardonically reminiscent of *Norwegian Wood*, The Beatles number. However, his attack on this instrument was unique. George Harrison reverently stroked the instrument, as opposed to Brian, who irremissibly rocked it up – so much so that he deeply cut the tops of his fingers. The vocals are sung in a sombre manner for the first few verses and are then followed by a coarser rock approach. It is said the track is about a funeral, or simply about a broken relationship; others, inspired by Decca's comma in the title, reckoned it was a racial attack. The over-all musical transition was notable, particularly for the single-only purchasers; the current public interest was intense and 300,000 advance orders produced a Number 1 single – both in Britain and the States.

157. LONG LONG WHILE (Jagger, Richard)
3/8 March 1966: RCA, Hollywood. Producer: Andrew Oldham. Engineer: Dave Hassinger.
UK B-side Paint It, Black: 13 May 1966

Keith Richards was again critical of the final sound created on *Paint It, Black*. Somehow, it typified the band's current success, which was due to four factors: the musical integrity led by Keith Richards, a unique musician in Brian Jones, the publicity connivance of Mick Jagger and Andrew Oldham and lastly the rhythm backbone of the band, Charlie Watts and Bill Wyman. This backbone provided the enthusiasm for this soul take. A boogie-woogie piano starts *Long Long While* off in Presleyesque style. The track uses the Righteous Brothers feel of a song which builds up unreservedly. It deserved to be more than just a banal flip-side but it can certainly not be classed as innovative.

158. UNDER MY THUMB (Jagger, Richard)
3/8 March 1966: RCA, Hollywood. Producer: Andrew Oldham. Engineer: Dave Hassinger.
UK LP AFTERMATH: April 1966: No 1 – 28 weeks
USA LP AFTERMATH: June 1966: No 2 – 26 weeks
USA Compilation LP THE ROLLING STONES – PROMOTIONAL ALBUM: October 1969

A lyrically revelistic and chauvinistic song, inspired by late-night groupie encounters. The song has a strong rhythmic base, with almost African connotations. This primeval feel is enhanced by the marimba, which is again played by Brian Jones. Bill Wyman prominently provides a fuzz-bass sound whilst Keith Richards plucks the guitar on the rhythm breaks. *Under My Thumb* is musically one of the more inspiring tracks released on the AFTERMATH album.

159. HIGH AND DRY (Jagger, Richard)
3/8 March 1966: RCA, Hollywood. Producer: Andrew Oldham.

Engineer: Dave Hassinger.
UK LP AFTERMATH: April 1966: No 1 – 28 weeks
USA LP AFTERMATH: June 1966: No 2 – 26 weeks

Ever since the band's first visit to the States, Keith Richards' fondness and interest for Country and Western music had been developing. *High And Dry* is one of the first songs recorded that he had written in this style – they were to be featured more strongly in the future. A hillbilly harmonica accompanies the country hick drawl of Mick Jagger's vocals. Mick was quick to mimic any dialect dictated by a song's style, and this was no exception. (He was to perfect and accentuate it on *Sweet Virginia* and *Far Away Eyes* in the 'seventies.) The lyrical content of *High And Dry* was insignificant and the song as a whole paled embarrassingly in comparison to the likes of Bob Dylan's conscience songs.

160. FLIGHT 505 (Jagger, Richard)
3/8 March 1966: RCA, Hollywood. Producer: Andrew Oldham.
Engineer: Dave Hassinger.
UK LP AFTERMATH: April 1966: No 1 – 28 weeks
USA LP AFTERMATH: June 1966: No 2 – 26 weeks

Ian Stewart plays the opening chords filling one channel on the stereo with a distant bar-room piano. The band then join in using both channels on this medium-paced Chuck Berry sound-a-like rocker. The song depicts the story of 'Flight Number 505' which crashes into oblivion. Their hectic touring schedule obviously produced its own nightmares. The track, despite fine piano playing, lacks the vivacious character of their more refined rockers.

161. I AM WAITING (Jagger, Richard)
3/8 March 1966: RCA, Hollywood. Producer: Andrew Oldham.
Engineer: Dave Hassinger.
UK LP AFTERMATH: April 1966: No 1 – 28 weeks
USA LP AFTERMATH: June 1966: No 2 – 26 weeks

The soft tones of the dulcimer, played by Brian Jones, provide a unique pitch for Mick Jagger to articulate somewhat malevolent lyrics – don't fear the reaper. The song is a quiet one which lurches forth on chorus lines – again not a particularly strong track, but one which encapsulated the newly found direction of 'art for art's sake'.

162. WHAT TO DO (Jagger, Richard)
3/8 March 1966: RCA, Hollywood. Producer: Andrew Oldham.
Engineer: Dave Hassinger.
UK LP AFTERMATH: April 1966: No 1 – 28 weeks

The final track on the British album, but not included on the American version due to the inclusion there of the hit single *Paint It, Black*. This was the last track of a week-long session which included the talents and merits of Jack Nitzsche, who was then the arranger/entrepreneur at Phil Spector's RCA Studios. The long session produced the AFTERMATH album, but was weighted in its attempts to progress musically. The successful ones, however, produced a monumental transgression and can be credited to one man, Brian Jones – take another look at *Paint It, Black, Mother's Little Helper* and *Lady Jane*. *What To Do* tried to eulogize the ordinary man who struggles for recognition.

163. PAINT IT, BLACK (Jagger, Richard)
May 1966: BBC TV, London.
Bootleg only.

Following the AFTERMATH sessions, the hectic touring schedule continued. The rest of March and part of April saw them on a brief European tour. May was a month of comparative rest in England. It was also a time for the band's mounting frustrations to come to the surface. Although Brian Jones' instrumental virtuosity on AFTERMATH was faultless, his remoteness at recording sessions was causing them concern, as was his seeming lack of interest in the electric guitar. Brian's problems revolved around Jagger and Richards' domination of the band, particularly the song-writing aspect. In the early days it was Brian who had formed the band and now he felt he had been pushed to one side. This insecurity was to manifest and lead to further problems. The preview of the newly written *Paint It, Black* was recorded live for BBC Television and was featured at the *New Musical Express* May Day concert for poll winners. Touring recommenced in America in June and July. It brought dramatic scenes of riot, even tear gas, and general press antagonism, as the band threaded their way through the States. The tension was not helped by the exclusion on a few dates of Brian Jones who was publicly suffering from pneumonia, and privately from tour excess. A double A-side single was released in the States to complement the tour and featured *Mother's Little Helper* with *Lady Jane*.

164. HAVE YOU SEEN YOUR MOTHER, BABY, STANDING IN THE SHADOW? (Jagger, Richard)
7 August 1966: RCA, Hollywood. Producer: Andrew Oldham.
Engineer: Dave Hassinger.
UK Single: 23 September 1966: No 5 – 8 weeks
USA Single: 23 September 1966: No 9 – 6 weeks
UK Compilation LP BIG HITS (HIGH TIDE AND GREEN GRASS):
November 1966: No 4 – 43 weeks
USA Compilation LP FLOWERS: June 1967: No 3 – 18 weeks
USA Compilation LP THROUGH THE PAST DARKLY (BIG HITS VOL 2): September 1969: No 2 – 16 weeks

The pattern of mid-'sixties singles releases culminated in *Have You Seen Your Mother?* It was described by Mick Jagger as the 'ultimate freakout'. He also said he was not interested in the band's chart positions, which was just as well since the single was not a success in Rolling Stones' terms – it just scraped a Top 10 position both sides of the Atlantic. The recording was a move away from single commercialism. It features guitar feedback at the beginning and end, and also brass which generates the song's attack. Bill Wyman's bass line and a raving piano glide the song as it dips and climbs around Mick Jagger's surging vocals. Keith Richards was critical of the final product. He felt it had been rushed to such an extent that the wrong mix was released. As a result the rhythm section was lost. Andrew Oldham, the producer, could obviously be criticized if there was such a slip-up; however, he could not be faulted for his publicity coups to accompany the single. The band decided to produce a promotional film to support the release, a revolutionary idea at the time. They used a young London Soho film maker, Peter Whitehead, who produced unique footage of the band. It starts with an apocalyptic stage entrance and continues showing clippage of Mick Jagger voyeuring Paris street art and the band being made up for a drag photo session in New York. The resultant photos by Jerry Schatzberg became the sleeve for the American release and the group in drag caused concern and outrage, particularly for Bill Wyman who was distastefully sat in a wheel-chair. It was all good mother-mocking fun, even if Keith Richards did appear slightly embarrassed by it all. The video finishes with the group adopting the same poses, this time out of landlady drag, Brian Jones yawns then smirks cheekily. The footage, suffice to say, did not appear on the British television music programme 'Top Of The Pops'.

165. WHO'S DRIVING YOUR PLANE? (Jagger, Richard)
7 August 1966: RCA, Hollywood. Producer: Andrew Oldham. Engineer: Dave Hassinger.
UK B-side Have You Seen Your Mother, Baby, Standing In The Shadow?: 23 September 1966
USA B-side Have You Seen Your Mother, Baby, Standing In The Shadow?: 23 September 1966

Who's Driving Your Plane? displays a heavier boogie approach to the blues. The lyrics concern themselves with the problems of a girl who because of dominant parents has no mind of her own. The vocals are sung with delayed echo, which gives a sophisticated edge to the song. This style was to pave the way for similar-sounding recordings made in the late 'sixties.

166. CAN'T BELIEVE (a.k.a. I CAN SEE IT and I'LL FEEL A WHOLE LOT BETTER) (Jagger, Richard)
3/12 August 1966: RCA, Hollywood. Producer: Andrew Oldham. Engineer: Dave Hassinger.
Bootleg only.

Recorded in between the AFTERMATH and BETWEEN THE BUTTONS sessions, *Can't Believe* is a lively rock and roll jaunt that missed its vocation and has since become a sought-after recording.

167. PAINT IT, BLACK (Jagger, Richard)
11 September 1966: Ed Sullivan TV Show, USA.
Bootleg only.

168. LADY JANE (Jagger, Richard)
11 September 1966: Ed Sullivan TV Show, USA.
Bootleg only.

169. HAVE YOU SEEN YOUR MOTHER, BABY, STANDING IN THE SHADOW? (Jagger,Richard)
11 September 1966: Ed Sullivan TV Show, USA.
Bootleg only.

Another Ed Sullivan TV appearance in September 1966 featured their last double-sided, American single and the forthcoming single, *Have You Seen Your Mother, Baby, Standing In The Shadow?* The performance was made with Brian Jones suffering from a broken hand. Reportedly, this had happened as a result of a climbing accident while holidaying in Morocco. Another version of the incident is that he had attempted to strike Anita Pallenberg at a Tangiers hotel, missed, and had hit a concrete post. The audience's reaction to the performance was ecstatic, as usual drowning the melodic strains of *Lady Jane* and making it hard for the Stones to out-sing the backing track of *Have You Seen Your Mother, Baby?*

170. UNDER MY THUMB (Jagger, Richard)
23 September 1966: Royal Albert Hall, London. Producer: Andrew Oldham. Engineer: Glyn Johns.
USA LP GOT LIVE IF YOU WANT IT!: November 1966: No **6** *– 11 weeks*

171. GET OFF MY CLOUD (Jagger, Richard)
23 September 1966: Royal Albert Hall, London. Producer: Andrew Oldham. Engineer: Glyn Johns.
USA LP GOT LIVE IF YOU WANT IT!: November 1966: No **6** *– 11 weeks*

172. LADY JANE (Jagger, Richard)
23 September 1966: Royal Albert Hall, London. Producer: Andrew Oldham. Engineer: Glyn Johns.
USA LP GOT LIVE IF YOU WANT IT!: November 1966: No **6** *– 11 weeks*

173. NOT FADE AWAY (Petty, Hardin)
23 September 1966: Royal Albert Hall, London. Producer: Andrew Oldham. Engineer: Glyn Johns.
USA LP GOT LIVE IF YOU WANT IT!: November 1966: No **6** *– 11 weeks*

174. I'VE BEEN LOVING YOU TOO LONG (Redding, Butler)
23 September 1966: Royal Albert Hall, London. Producer: Andrew Oldham. Engineer: Glyn Johns.
USA LP GOT LIVE IF YOU WANT IT!: November 1966: No **6** *– 11 weeks*

175. FORTUNE TELLER (Neville)
23 September 1966: Royal Albert Hall, London. Producer: Andrew Oldham. Engineer: Glyn Johns.
USA LP GOT LIVE IF YOU WANT IT!: November 1966: No **6** – 11 *weeks*

176. THE LAST TIME (Jagger, Richard)
23 September 1966: Royal Albert Hall, London. Producer: Andrew Oldham. Engineer: Glyn Johns.
USA LP GOT LIVE IF YOU WANT IT!: November 1966: No **6** – 11 *weeks*

177. 19TH NERVOUS BREAKDOWN (Jagger, Richard)
23 September 1966: Royal Albert Hall, London. Producer: Andrew Oldham. Engineer: Glyn Johns.
USA LP GOT LIVE IF YOU WANT IT!: November 1966: No **6** – 11 *weeks*

178. TIME IS ON MY SIDE (Meade, Norman)
23 September 1966: Royal Albert Hall, London. Producer: Andrew Oldham. Engineer: Glyn Johns.
USA LP GOT LIVE IF YOU WANT IT!: November 1966: No **6** – 11 *weeks*

179. I'M ALRIGHT (Nanker, Phelge)
23 September 1966: Royal Albert Hall, London. Producer: Andrew Oldham. Engineer: Glyn Johns.
USA LP GOT LIVE IF YOU WANT IT!: November 1966: No **6** – 11 *weeks*

180. HAVE YOU SEEN YOUR MOTHER, BABY, STANDING IN THE SHADOW? (Jagger,Richard)
23 September 1966: Royal Albert Hall, London. Producer: Andrew Oldham. Engineer: Glyn Johns.
USA LP GOT LIVE IF YOU WANT IT!: November 1966: No **6** – 11 *weeks*

181. (I CAN'T GET NO) SATISFACTION (Jagger, Richard)
23 September 1966: Royal Albert Hall, London. Producer: Andrew Oldham. Engineer: Glyn Johns.
USA LP GOT LIVE IF YOU WANT IT!: November 1966: No **6** – 11 *weeks*

The British tour kicked off on 23 September 1966 and the reel-to-reels engineered by Glyn Johns recorded the concert. The end result was produced (!) by Andrew Oldham and released on the GOT LIVE IF YOU WANT IT! album. The recording is horribly contrived; there are many bootlegs of better quality. It is basically a three-track recording: vocals, crowd screams and the band. The sound is layered and mixed in that order, the end product is terrible, and it pales into insignificance compared with the raunchy British EP of the same name. Two tracks are even studio out-takes. *I've Been Loving You Too Long* was initially recorded at the RCA Studios in Hollywood by Dave Hassinger on the 12/13 May 1965; the screams are over-dubbed. *Fortune Teller* is also over-dubbed and is an out-take of a track which was recorded in November 1963 at the Kingsway Studios. It was released, minus screams, on a compilation album, SATURDAY CLUB, in January 1964. The resulting album is a commercial 'cop out', the cover sleeve being more imaginative with evocative live photos taken by Gered Mankowitz. The sound-track lacks atmosphere and certainly does not convey the near-riot that nearly aborted the shows. The Stones had the sense not to release the end product in Britain. It has, however, appeared via import shops and also a few select tracks are available on an August 1972 compilation album GIMMIE SHELTER, distributed by Decca.

4

DANDELION AND THE FLOWER POWER GAME

NOVEMBER 1966 – SEPTEMBER 1967

182. RUBY TUESDAY (Jagger, Richard)
November 1966: Olympic, London. Producer: Andrew Oldham.
Engineer: Glyn Johns.
USA Single: 13 January 1967: No 1 – 9 weeks
UK B-side Let's Spend The Night Together: 13 January 1967
USA LP BETWEEN THE BUTTONS: 20 January 1967: No 2 – 19 weeks
USA Compilation LP FLOWERS: June 1967: No 3 – 18 weeks
UK Compilation LP THROUGH THE PAST DARKLY (BIG HITS VOL 2):
12 September 1969: No 2 – 37 weeks
USA Compilation LP THROUGH THE PAST DARKLY (BIG HITS VOL
2): September 1969: No 2 – 16 weeks

The Rolling Stones followed their stint in American studios by returning for a three-year period to the tranquillity of their native recording studios. *Ruby Tuesday* launched a significant change in direction and fortified the band's recent innovative moves made on AFTERMATH. The sound is romantic in nature, aided by Brian Jones playing the flute beautifully; the piano accompaniment is also superb. It was a well-deserved American

Number 1. The American public had tended to be served by the Stones with the more tepid (in beat) sounds. The rock had been reserved for the British public, hence the swap in A-sides in Britain. The song was written almost exclusively by Keith Richards and Brian Jones and is said to be about a well-known groupie. The Richard/Jones combination was a promising move to rekindle the band. An out-take of *Ruby Tuesday* exists without the vocals. In it, the structure of the song can be witnessed at first hand. Before the final take the viola was removed into the background.

183. DANDELION (Jagger, Richard)
November 1966: Olympic, London. Producer: Andrew Oldham.
Engineer: Glyn Johns.
UK B-side We Love You: 18 August 1967
USA Single: 18 August 1967: No 14 – 6 weeks
UK Compilation LP THROUGH THE PAST DARKLY (BIG HITS VOL 2):
12 September 1969: No 2 – 37 weeks
USA Compilation LP THROUGH THE PAST DARKLY (BIG HITS VOL
2): September 1969: No 2 – 16 weeks

The structure formulated on *Ruby Tuesday* was continued with *Dandelion*. The lyrics are loosely based on several nursery-rhyme themes. This enhanced the music, giving it a progressive, trippy feel. Perhaps this was the reason why it was not released until the next summer when it was to feature as the flip side of *We Love You*. The harmony vocals do seem a little stretched, but the over-all achievement was significant, Brian Jones being featured heavily on the orchestral sounds. Once the song fades out, the track winds into a segment of *We Love You*, which finishes as quickly as it starts.

184. LET'S SPEND THE NIGHT TOGETHER (Jagger, Richard)
November 1966: Olympic, London. Producer: Andrew Oldham.
Engineer: Glyn Johns.
UK Single: 13 January 1967: No 3 – 10 weeks
USA B-side Ruby Tuesday: 13 January 1967
USA LP BETWEEN THE BUTTONS: 20 January 1967: No 2 – 19 weeks
USA Compilation LP FLOWERS: June 1967: No 3 – 18 weeks
UK Compilation LP THROUGH THE PAST DARKLY (BIG HITS VOL 2):
12 September 1969: No 2 – 37 weeks
USA Compilation LP THROUGH THE PAST DARKLY (BIG HITS VOL
2): September 1969: No 2 – 16 weeks

The mood of the session changes and returns to a rock theme. The production, however, moved away from the familiar guitar thrash to a song led by the piano, supported by an incessant throbbing drum beat. The critics picked up the unashamed lyrics and developed them into a moralistic story, particularly in America. Either radio stations bleeped out the 'night' on the single, or settled for *Ruby Tuesday* on the other side. The fans were quick to point out that *Let's Spend The Night Together* was an honest love song depicting modern times. Andrew Oldham recalls the actual recording when two policemen decided to investigate the unusual noises emanating from the studio. Oldham, anxious to avoid any possible drugs scandal, rushed up to them, grabbed their truncheons and banged them together as though they were a long-lost tribal instrument and asked them to accompany the Stones on the next take.

185. MY OBSESSION (Jagger, Richard)
November/December 1966: Olympic, London. Producer: Andrew Oldham. Engineer: Glyn Johns.
UK LP BETWEEN THE BUTTONS: 20 January 1967: No **3** *– 22 weeks·*
USA LP BETWEEN THE BUTTONS: 20 January 1967: No **2** *– 19 weeks*

The recording of the next album, BETWEEN THE BUTTONS, commenced in the summer of '66 and finished in the last months of the year. Most sessions were recorded at the Olympic Studios in London, but it is likely that certain tracks were recorded in two stages at the RCA Studios in Hollywood, being engineered by Dave Hassinger, and also Olympic in London. The unique drum sound production on *My Obsession* provides a background for Keith Richards, who deploys a ricochet of stun guitar effects, and also for Ian Stewart, who subtly taps R 'n' B rhythms on the keyboard. As a solo performance for Charlie Watts the song is impressive. He unwittingly inspired the album title, the cover photo displaying a fashion-conscious Charlie.

186. ALL SOLD OUT (Jagger, Richard)
November/December 1966: Olympic, London. Producer: Andrew Oldham. Engineer: Glyn Johns.
UK LP BETWEEN THE BUTTONS: 20 January 1967: No **3** *– 22 weeks*
USA LP BETWEEN THE BUTTONS: 20 January 1967: No **2** *– 19 weeks*

Essentially the music on BETWEEN THE BUTTONS reflects the Carnaby Street revolution and musically contemporary British bands such as Cream, The Kinks and The Yardbirds. In short, it is certainly derivative as opposed to innovative. *All Sold Out* has a progressive,˙heavy feel – there is an undercurrent of electric guitar solos which somehow lead you to expect more, but exasperate by fading out before improvization starts. The shortness of the track at 2 minutes 15 seconds heightens this. The cymbal work and production of Charlie Watts percussion sound is the high spot again.

187. SHE SMILED SWEETLY (Jagger, Richard)
November/December 1966: Olympic, London. Producer: Andrew Oldham. Engineer: Glyn Johns.
UK LP BETWEEN THE BUTTONS: 20 January 1967: No **3** *– 22 weeks*
USA LP BETWEEN THE BUTTONS: 20 January 1967: No **2** *– 19 weeks*

She Smiled Sweetly is a ballad which features Keith Richards on his first venture on the church organ; it sounds as though he was determined not to miss a note, hence the methodical playing. Mick Jagger utters the sweet lyrics until the song attempts to climax. *She Smiled Sweetly* should have been saved for an out-take compilation such as FLOWERS.

188. **YESTERDAY'S PAPERS** (Jagger, Richard)
November/December 1966: Olympic, London. Producer: Andrew Oldham. Engineer: Glyn Johns.
UK LP BETWEEN THE BUTTONS: 20 January 1967: No **3** *– 22 weeks*
USA LP BETWEEN THE BUTTONS: 20 January 1967: No **2** *– 19 weeks*

Although the lyrics return to the chauvinistic theme of discarding women as waste paper, instrumentally *Yesterday's Papers* is a cut above the rest on the album. The harmonies also sound as though they have been worked upon; Keith Richards takes a prominent spot when playing a great guitar break with plenty of reverb and echo and the marimba is again used to astonishing effect by Brian Jones. This suggests the initial track may have been put to tape earlier in the year by Dave Hassinger in Hollywood. It was evident that Brian Jones' contribution later in the year was limited due to ill health.

189. **PLEASE GO HOME** (Jagger, Richard)
November/December 1966: Olympic, London. Producer: Andrew Oldham. Engineer: Glyn Johns.
UK LP BETWEEN THE BUTTONS: 20 January 1967: No **3** *– 22 weeks*
USA Compilation LP FLOWERS: June 1967: No **3** *– 18 weeks*

A roughneck, deranged *Not Fade Away* beat, inspired by the Diddley Daddy himself, accompanies this interpretation of mod music. Echoes on the vocals and Pete Townshend-type feed-back intermittently break into the song; it is a poor imitation of the aforementioned heroes. *Please Go Home* was not released on the American version of BETWEEN THE BUTTONS, but was included on FLOWERS, a compilation American LP released by London Records in June 1967.

190. **MISS AMANDA JONES** (Jagger, Richard)
November/December 1966: Olympic, London. Producer: Andrew Oldham. Engineer: Glyn Johns.
UK LP BETWEEN THE BUTTONS: 20 January 1967: No **3** *– 22 weeks*
USA LP BETWEEN THE BUTTONS: 20 January 1967: No **2** *– 19 weeks*

Miss Amanda Jones is refreshing. It is humorous, mischievous fun, if a little sexist – keep showing the suspenders. Miss Jones is a good-time girl who is the 'darling of the discotheque crowd'. The sound production enhances the humour. There are lead guitar parts cleverly thrown into the scenario; indeed, Keith Richards' guitar sounds strong and abrasive as he plays a raunchy twelve bar beat.

191. **BACK STREET GIRL** (Jagger, Richard)
November/December 1966: Olympic, London. Producer: Andrew Oldham. Engineer: Glyn Johns.

UK LP BETWEEN THE BUTTONS: 20 January 1967: No **3** – *22 weeks*
USA Compilation LP FLOWERS: June 1967: No **3** – 18 *weeks*

Mick Jagger rated *Back Street Girl* his favourite track of the BETWEEN THE BUTTONS sessions. It is a melodic sound, described by critics as a *valse musette*, or more understandably as a waltzy time song *à la fran- çaise*. The French accordion played by Brian Jones aids the Gallic atmosphere, but does nothing to hide the contemptuous, vitriolic lyrics of prostitution and forbidden sex which are concealed from the particip- ant's nice conventional home life. *Back Street Girl* was not to feature on the American release of the album, but again appeared on the FLOWERS album.

192. **IF YOU LET ME** (Jagger, Richard)
November/December 1966: Olympic, London. Producer: Andrew Oldham. Engineer: Glyn Johns.
UK Compilation LP METAMORPHIS: 6 June 1975: No **45** – 1 *week*
USA Compilation LP METAMORPHIS: 6 June 1975: No **8** – 8 *weeks*

Bill Wyman vetted this song in 1974/75 for inclusion on the Stones' version of a compilation album of out-takes provisionally titled 'Black Box'. The album was never released but *If You Let Me* was included on Allen Klein's METAMORPHIS compilation. The 'Black Box' product featured too many non-Jagger, Richard compositions and therefore the royalties to ABKCO Music (an Allen Klein subsidiary) would have been insignificant; this is the carousel of music politics. The song's appeal is its laid back approach to a summer's stroll in the country. The exact date of the recording cannot be specified, but its origin must lie in the '66 Olympic Studio!

193. **COOL, CALM AND COLLECTED** (Jagger, Richard)
November/December 1966: Olympic, London. Producer: Andrew Oldham. Engineer: Glyn Johns.
UK LP BETWEEN THE BUTTONS: 20 January 1967: No **3** – 22 *weeks*
USA LP BETWEEN THE BUTTONS: 20 January 1967: No **2** – 19 *weeks*

This composition is an audacious attempt at music-hall variety. The unlikely combination of instruments such as the kazoo and the banjo with a tinkering piano featured on a rock album are too much to comprehend. It loses any humour it was attempting to achieve and as a new rock form can be forgotten. Ray Davies and the Kinks had successfully carried it off to much better effect on *Dedicated Follower of Fashion* and *Sunny Afternoon*.

194. **SOMETHING HAPPENED TO ME YESTERDAY** (Jagger, Richard)
November/December 1966: Olympic, London. Producer: Andrew Oldham. Engineer: Glyn Johns.
UK LP BETWEEN THE BUTTONS: 20 January 1967: No **3** – 22 *weeks*
USA LP BETWEEN THE BUTTONS: 20 January 1967: No **2** – 19 *weeks*

Vaudevillism continues on *Something Happened To Me Yesterday.* Brian Jones leads the hysterics on trombone and other brass instruments. This five-minute concept of mockery on BETWEEN THE BUTTONS illustrated the need to take stock of the situation, as the pressure of touring and incessant studio work began to take its toll artistically. The Stones were recording products that they thought the public would like and not concentrating on extending their artistic repertoire. Keith Richards helps Mick Jagger out on the vocals as they take turns at discussing yesterday's trip; they are not sure what it was or if it is against the law. The song ends as Mick Jagger offers road safety advice – wear white, evening all! – Dixon of Dock Green style (a cosy British TV police series).

195. WHO'S BEEN SLEEPING HERE? (Jagger, Richard)
November/December 1966: Olympic, London. Producer: Andrew Oldham. Engineer: Glyn Johns.
UK LP BETWEEN THE BUTTONS: 20 January 1967: No **3** *– 22 weeks*
USA LP BETWEEN THE BUTTONS: 20 January 1967: No **2** *– 19 weeks*

The influences of Bob Dylan were displayed on this track. The summer of 1966 had brought the release of Dylan's classic album, BLONDE ON BLONDE, and comparisons were detectable. The Stones were by no means the only group affected by his folk charms, but the influences may have been stronger due to Brian Jones' friendship with Dylan. The excellent Dylan single *Like A Rolling Stone* was written for Brian Jones and Brian felt *Ballad Of A Thin Man* was also about him. Brian Jones' usual harmonica techniques were discarded on *Who's Been Sleeping Here?* as he plays in true Dylanesque style.

196. COMPLICATED (Jagger, Richard)
November/December 1966: Olympic, London. Producer: Andrew Oldham. Engineer: Glyn Johns.
UK LP BETWEEN THE BUTTONS: 20 January 1967: No **3** *– 22 weeks*
USA LP BETWEEN THE BUTTONS: 20 January 1967: No **2** *– 19 weeks*

The guitar and drum sound produced by Andrew Oldham on *My Obsession* was recreated again for the song *Complicated.* Keith Richards was obviously fond of this stun effect and a pleasing melody is played on the organ by Brian Jones.

197. CONNECTION (Jagger, Richard)
November/December 1966: Olympic, London. Producer: Andrew Oldham. Engineer: Glyn Johns.
UK LP BETWEEN THE BUTTONS: 20 January 1967: No **3** *– 22 weeks*
USA LP BETWEEN THE BUTTONS: 20 January 1967: No **2** *– 19 weeks*

The vocals are taken by Keith Richards on his first solo effort, although Mick Jagger stays close at hand and helps out in the background. The pace of the song seems to be a little fast. It was covered by American hard rock band Montrose to much better effect in 1974. The lyrical content evidently refers to drug taking, the morality of which would be severely tested within the next few months.

198. RUBY TUESDAY (Jagger, Richard)
January 1967: Ed Sullivan TV Show, USA.
Bootleg only.

199. LET'S SPEND THE NIGHT TOGETHER (Jagger, Richard)
January 1967: Ed Sullivan TV Show, USA.
Bootleg only.

Early in January the Stones flew to America to promote the release of the double A-sided single *Ruby Tuesday/Let's Spend The Night Together.* Ed Sullivan, eager not to corrupt his young audience, demanded that the lyrics were altered on *Let's Spend The Night Together.* A furious argument developed and a compromise of sorts was reached. The lyrics were altered to 'Let's Spend Some Time Together'. Mick Jagger later claimed he did not use this alternative version but the recording plainly confirms he did. This was not their only brush with television officialdom that January. They also upset British viewers on 22 January 1967 when they appeared on 'Sunday Night At The London Palladium'. They played the single but refused, at Mick Jagger's instigation, to stand with the rest of the artistes at the finale and wave to the audience. The British public, whipped up by the press, were insulted by this brash gesture. It was a two-finger salute that backfired on them, even with the fans.

200. WE LOVE YOU (Jagger, Richard)
July/August 1967: Olympic, London. Producer: Andrew Oldham.
Engineer: Glyn Johns.
*UK Single: 18 August 1967: No **8** – 8 weeks*
USA B-side Dandelion: 18 August 1967
UK Compilation LP THROUGH THE PAST DARKLY (BIG HITS VOL 2):
*12 September 1969: No **2** – 37 weeks*
Rolling Stones with John Lennon, Paul McCartney.

The atmosphere around the Stones throughout 1967 was heavily charged. On 12 February at Redlands, Keith Richards' country home, Mick Jagger and Keith Richards were busted; Mick for possession of amphetamines (alias Italian travel sickness pills) and Keith for allowing the use of cannabis in his home. It was a 'frame-up', supposedly instigated by the *News Of The World* Sunday newspaper. Awaiting court proceedings, March and April were spent touring Europe where riots and the arrest of youths were features of their concerts. The drugs trial commenced on 27 June, and sentences were passed on 29 June. The result was a preposterous three-month jail sentence for Mick Jagger and a year for Keith Richards. Robert Fraser, an art gallery friend, was sentenced to six months. Eventually, British justice awakened and on 30 June, having spent three nights in jail, Mick and Keith were released on bail awaiting appeal. The editor of *The Times* ran a famous leader on 1 July, 'Who Breaks A Butterfly On A Wheel?', attacking the rough justice and questioning the reasoning of the sentencer, Judge Block. To thank the fans and *The Times* for their support, not to mention such groups as The Beatles and The Who, *We Love You* was recorded. The lyrics were written by Mick Jagger on Her Majesty's notepaper during his prescribed stay at Lewes and Brixton jails. The Beatles had spent a period at Olympic Studios in June recording their next single *All You Need Is Love*. Mick Jagger and Keith Richards had contributed backing vocals. Brian Jones, on the flip side *Baby You're A Rich Man*, had played the oboe. The friendship and deed was reciprocated as John Lennon and Paul McCartney accompanied the Stones singing on *We Love You*. The result was a trippy, psychedelic song opened by heavy footsteps and clanging cell doors. The mellotron played by Brian Jones launches in and the band turn the other cheek declaring in typical hippy style 'We Love You'. As the song progresses the sounds become more weird, Brian Jones obviously enjoying the off-beat, Arabic brass arrangements. Peter Whitehead, following his film work on *Have You Seen Your Mother?*, was contacted again and asked to produce a promotional film for *We Love You*. It was a pastiche based on 'The Trials of Oscar Wilde' and due to its anti-establishment, provocative nature, was banned by the BBC. They were also lucky to avoid Wilde's fate of incarceration. Meanwhile, Robert Fraser continued his sentence devoid of a pardon or his freedom.

201. SHE'S A RAINBOW (a.k.a. **SHE COMES IN COLOURS**) (Jagger, Richard)
June/September 1967: Olympic Studio and Bell Sound, London.
Producer: Rolling Stones. Engineer: Glyn Johns.
USA LP THEIR SATANIC MAJESTIES REQUEST: November 1967: No **2** – *13 weeks*
UK LP THEIR SATANIC MAJESTIES REQUEST: December 1967: No **3** – *13 weeks*
USA Single: November 1967: No **25** – *4 weeks*
UK Compilation LP THROUGH THE PAST DARKLY (BIG HITS VOL 2): 12 September 1969: No **2** – *37 weeks*
USA Compilation LP THROUGH THE PAST DARKLY (BIG HITS VOL 2): September 1969: No **2** – *16 weeks*
Rolling Stones with John Paul Jones.

The SATANIC MAJESTIES sessions were spread through the summer of 1967, and were interrupted periodically by drug busts and various court appearances. Andrew Oldham became thoroughly disillusioned by the situation. The Stones deliberately antagonized him by entering the studio for days on end, playing bum sounds and generally freaking out. Andrew Oldham, frustrated at the growing arguments, gave up and walked out, leaving the Stones to Allen Klein and on this occasion also to produce themselves. *She's A Rainbow* was one of the first songs recorded at the sessions – demos originated from January 1967 – it continued the pretty Elizabethan sound started in *Ruby Tuesday* and *Dandelion*. The song's prominent instruments are the piano and the orchestral strings which were supplied by John Paul Jones who later found considerable fame with British supergroup Led Zeppelin. It was a suitable flower-power-type song, but was not released as a single in Britain.

202. SING THIS ALL ALTOGETHER (Jagger, Richard)
June/September 1967: Olympic Studio and Bell Sound, London.
Producer: Rolling Stones. Engineer: Glyn Johns.
USA LP THEIR SATANIC MAJESTIES REQUEST: November 1967: No
2 – 13 *weeks*
UK LP THEIR SATANIC MAJESTIES REQUEST: December 1967: No **3**
– 13 *weeks*

203. SING THIS ALL TOGETHER (SEE WHAT HAPPENS) (Jagger, Richard)
June/September 1967: Olympic Studio and Bell Sound, London.
Producer: Rolling Stones. Engineer: Glyn Johns.
USA LP THEIR SATANIC MAJESTIES REQUEST: November 1967: No
2 – 13 *weeks*
UK LP THEIR SATANIC MAJESTIES REQUEST: December 1967: No **3**
– 13 *weeks*

THEIR SATANIC MAJESTIES REQUEST was originally intended by Mick Jagger to be a concept album, inspired by the statement on British Passports 'Her Britannic Majesty's Principal Secretary of State for Foreign and Commonwealth Affairs Requests and Requires in the Name of Her Majesty...' For the sake of satirical brevity this was altered to 'Her Satanic Majesty Requests and Requires'. Decca were none too happy at this suggestion, hence the eventual title. At one stage, in readiness for Christmas release, the album was entitled 'Cosmic Christmas', but this title was also spurned. *Sing This All Together*, separated by other album tracks, opens and closes Side One. It was rumoured during the recordings that the album was to feature a twelve-minute track, and if the two halves had been coupled together this would have happened. At the time it was hip and psychedelic to introduce recurring themes, as in a dream – possibly the reason for the split in the track. The Beatles' album had included a reprise of the opening track *Sgt Pepper's Lonely Hearts Club Band.* Musically *Sing This All Together* spins around the lacklustre sing-along of 'Why don't we sing this song all together'. The discordant rhythms and instruments that accompany this give the song a psychedelic appeal. *Sing This All Together* contains the sing-along vocals, whereas *See What Happens* is essentially the dream-like sequence featuring a jam on electric guitar and experimentation of various exotic instruments. A recording is available of *Sing This All Together* on a bootleg.

204. 2000 LIGHT YEARS FROM HOME (Jagger, Richard)
June/September 1967: Olympic Studio and Bell Sound, London.
Producer: Rolling Stones. Engineer: Glyn Johns.
USA LP THEIR SATANIC MAJESTIES REQUEST: November 1967: No
2 – 13 *weeks*

USA B-side She's A Rainbow: November 1967
UK LP THEIR SATANIC MAJESTIES REQUEST: December 1967: No **3**
– 13 weeks
UK Compilation LP THROUGH THE PAST DARKLY (BIG HITS VOL 2):
12 September 1969: No **2** *– 37 weeks*
USA Compilation LP THROUGH THE PAST DARKLY (BIG HITS VOL
2): September 1969: No **2** *–* 16 *weeks*

The inspiration of psychedelia was genuinely captured on this track with echoes of the true hippy pilgrims, The Pink Floyd. The lyrics were supposedly written by Mick Jagger during his stay in jail. *2000 Light Years* is opened by Brian Jones gently feeling his way on the mellotron. Glyn Johns stated that Brian's weird spooky playing on the mellotron and strings generally saved the track from anonymity. Keith Richards' abrasive contribution on electric guitar added to the eerie atmosphere and the song became a firm favourite, although Mick Jagger felt it lost a lot on its stereo mix; an out-take of *2000 Light Years* is available on an alternative SATANIC MAJESTIES bootleg. A colour promotional film shows the band performing the track, Mick Jagger resplendent in druid head gear.

205. IN ANOTHER LAND (Wyman)

June/September 1967: Olympic Studio and Bell Sound, London.
Producer: Rolling Stones. Engineer: Glyn Johns.
USA LP THEIR SATANIC MAJESTIES REQUEST: November 1967: No
2 *– 13 weeks*
UK LP THEIR SATANIC MAJESTIES REQUEST: December 1967: No **3**
– 13 weeks
USA Single: December 1967
Rolling Stones with Nicky Hopkins, Steve Marriott.

Bill Wyman managed to break the dominant song-writing partnership during the 'Satanic' sessions. Glyn Johns had cancelled an evening's recording when Mick Jagger and Keith Richards were unavailable. He was unable to contact Bill Wyman or Charlie Watts and so they turned up dutifully on time, as usual. The piano foundations of the track were put down by Bill. Steve Marriott, who was recording in the next studio with The Small Faces, came in and placed down some lead guitar and Nicky Hopkins filled the tracks out by contributing some fine piano work. Bill Wyman's vocals were suitably disguised with some Glyn Johns robotic trickery. The final mix was decided upon after a number of takes, two of which are on the bootleg. The next evening it was played back to the group; they had to admit that it was OK and in keeping with the 'Satanic' mood. Backing vocals were overdubbed by Mick Jagger and Keith Richards, therefore maintaining the band's collectiveness. It proved that the song-writing duo would consider other material, but the circumstances of the recording were coincidental to say the least. The Stones recognized the recording by releasing it as a single in America, but it flopped without even entering the Top 40. Was the snoring at the end of the album cut an indication of Brian Jones' mounting boredom?!

206. CITADEL (Jagger, Richard)
June/September 1967: Olympic Studio and Bell Sound, London.
Producer: Rolling Stones. Engineer: Glyn Johns.
USA LP THEIR SATANIC MAJESTIES REQUEST: November 1967: No
2 – *13 weeks*
UK LP THEIR SATANIC MAJESTIES REQUEST: December 1967: No **3**
– 13 weeks

Citadel centres around a heavy guitar riff which was copied by Bryan Ferry in 1973 on his hit single *Street Life*. The song is said to be inspired by the early 1920s film *Metropolis*. Weird flute and brass arrangements are also added to what was originally quite a simple rock song.

207. 2000 MAN (Jagger, Richard)
June/September 1967: Olympic Studio and Bell Sound, London.
Producer: Rolling Stones. Engineer: Glyn Johns.
USA LP THEIR SATANIC MAJESTIES REQUEST: November 1967: No
2 – *13 weeks*
UK LP THEIR SATANIC MAJESTIES REQUEST: December 1967: No **3**
– 13 weeks
USA Compilation LP THE ROLLING STONES – PROMOTIONAL ALBUM: October 1969.

2000 Man begins with an acoustic guitar work-out and finishes as an electric thrash on organ and guitar. Mick Taylor, who played with John Mayall's Bluesbreakers; witnessed some of the 'Satanic' sessions and became aware of the friendly rivalry between the Stones and The Beatles which contributed to Mick Jagger's determination to produce at least an equal to the newly released SGT PEPPER'S LONELY HEARTS CLUB BAND. Musically the Stones failed; SGT PEPPER is melodic whereas SATANIC MAJESTIES is discordant and generally seems to lack direction.

208. GOMPER (a.k.a. THE LADY, THE LILLIES AND THE LAKE)
(Jagger, Richard)
June/September 1967: Olympic Studio and Bell Sound, London.
Producer: Rolling Stones. Engineer: Glyn Johns.
USA LP THEIR SATANIC MAJESTIES REQUEST: November 1967: No
2 – *13 weeks*
UK LP THEIR SATANIC MAJESTIES REQUEST: December 1967: No **3**
– 13 weeks

The weirdness and freakiness of the sessions were highlighted on *Gomper*. The flavour is eastern; Brian Jones plays the sitar and flute and bongo drums are gently tapped in the background. Once the vocals finish, the track develops into a musical freak-out lasting three or four minutes. Brian Jones had reached a difficult phase. Having escalated the Stones to the current pitch by his contribution on various instruments and also unintentionally furthering the far-out public image by his acid trips with Jimi Hendrix and company, he now felt enough was enough. He did not like the move away from the blues and thought it was time to divert his wiped-out talents elsewhere. This was unfortunately not helped by his current mental and physical state, which prompted various hospital visits and ultimately his drug bust in May 1967. His prison sentence was fortunately repealed in December 1967 following reports by his physician, Dr Green, which stated that imprisonment would throw Brian into the chasm of total despair.

209. THE LANTERN (Jagger, Richard)
June/September 1967: Olympic Studio and Bell Sound, London.
Producer: Rolling Stones. Engineer: Glyn Johns.
USA LP THEIR SATANIC MAJESTIES REQUEST: November 1967: No
2 – 13 *weeks*
UK LP THEIR SATANIC MAJESTIES REQUEST: December 1967: No **3**
– 13 *weeks*
USA B-side In Another Land: December 1967

The recordings at the Olympic Studio continued with or without the presence of Brian Jones (due to his unstable health). *The Lantern* commences with a gothic funeral song and continues at a slow pace. Acoustic and lead guitar supplied by Keith Richards do not help the weary 'sea of light' philosophy.

210. ON WITH THE SHOW (Jagger, Richard)
June/September 1967: Olympic Studio and Bell Sound, London.
Producer: Rolling Stones. Engineer: Glyn Johns.
USA LP THEIR SATANIC MAJESTIES REQUEST: November 1967: No
2 – 13 *weeks*
UK LP THEIR SATANIC MAJESTIES REQUEST: December 1967: No **3**
– 13 *weeks*

On With The Show is possibly a forerunner of 'The Rock 'n' Roll Circus' idea. It concludes the album with images of *Yellow Submarine* and is a cacophony of unrehearsed mayhem. The 'Satanic' project failed in terms of sales and was also critically a disaster. The album cover attempted to out-dress SGT PEPPER. The late Michael Cooper, a photographer, designed and photographed the gatefold sleeve. A 3D camera was used and the first album covers were sold with the animated band staring from their personalized Taj Mahal. Decca thankfully forbade a nude picture of Mick Jagger at the centre of the maze on the inner cover. Pictures of The Beatles were timidly hidden on the cover, as The Beatles themselves had done to the Stones on the SGT PEPPER cover (respect reciprocated). The three dimensional design proved too expensive to mass produce and so it reverted to the normal one-dimensional image. To this day, the Stones rate the album as one of their worst moments. Bill Wyman indicates that the band certainly came close to splitting up during the long recording marathon that led to the album.

211. SHADES OF ORANGE (Wyman, Gosling)
June/September 1967: Olympic, London. Producer: Bill Wyman.
Engineer: Glyn Johns.
Bootleg only.

For such a long period of recording from June to September, 1967, there are remarkably few out-takes of session material. Bill Wyman was working in the studio on various projects and he had co-written *Shades of Orange* with a group called The End, who had accompanied the Stones on a mid-'sixties British tour. It is difficult to tell if this particular version is an authentic Stones track; the vocals are not Jagger's but Charlie Watts is credited with playing the tabla. *Shades Of Orange* is similar to Bill Wyman's solo track *In Another Land*. It is played with a psychedelic feel and was re-recorded and released by The End in 1968. Bill Wyman also co-wrote *Loving Sacred Loving*, the flip-side of the *Shades Of Orange* single.

5

HONKY TONK COWBELL SUMMONS HYDE PARK HERD

MARCH 1968 – JULY 1969

212. JUMPIN' JACK FLASH (Jagger, Richard)
March/May 1968: Olympic, London. Producer: Jimmy Miller. Engineer: Glyn Johns.
*UK Single: 24 May 1968: No **1** – 11 weeks*
*USA Single: 24 May 1968: No **3** – 11 weeks*
*UK Compilation LP THROUGH THE PAST DARKLY (BIG HITS VOL 2): 12 September 1969: No **2** – 37 weeks*
*USA Compilation LP THROUGH THE PAST DARKLY (BIG HITS VOL 2): September 1969: No **2** – 16 weeks*

As a complete contrast to the heady recording period of 1967, the sound created on *Jumpin' Jack Flash* just six months later was a monumental transformation from the music realized during the SATANIC MAJESTIES sessions. The band's decision was to return to R 'n' B and this they did with the precision of Jimmy Miller at the controls. He was an aspiring blues musician whose production credits in 1966/67 included The Spencer Davis Group. He got on well with the Stones – so much so that he was to produce them for the next six years. It was a relationship which would severely test him and endanger him to the control-room scrap heap. The *Jumpin' Jack Flash* foundations were laid by Bill Wyman as he 'mucked around' with a chord sequence on the piano. Brian Jones and Charlie Watts improvised on it until Keith Richards and Mick Jagger entered the studio. The duo knew instantaneously that the sound had great possibilities. Mick had some nearly completed lyrics and so they set about recording. The heavy guitar chords which run throughout the track immediately assault the senses. Jagger shouts 'one two' and the band join in supplying the incessant riff around the uplifting vocals. Brian Jones shuffles his demonic maracas as Keith's wonderfully distorted lead guitar provides the Stones with their most powerful rock sound to date. An out-take of *Jumpin' Jack Flash* illustrates the undeniable enthusiasm for the track as the band shout 'yeah, yeah' and 'woah' between the choruses, a style to be copied in future live performances. Brian Jones was so happy with the end result that as soon as the session finished he contacted a friend of his, Ronny Money – wife of musician Zoot Money – and told her the Stones had returned to rock and roll with this thing called *Jumpin' Jack Flash*, it's a gas!' It gave the Stones a British Number 1 single and a world-wide hit. Originally, it was intended for release on BEGGARS BANQUET, the next album, but the overwhelming enthusiasm created by the track brought an early single release. Mick Jagger believes that the promotional film which accompanied the single's release ensured its success, but this was underestimating the Stones' now renewed rock popularity. The promotional film was shot by ITV's producer of 'Ready Steady Go', Michael Lindsay-Hogg. It was the start of an affiliation which was to last many years. The video simply portrays the band performing the song live in front of a camera. It was an awesome sight. The band, with the exception of Keith Richards, were heavily made up including symbolic forehead tattoos. Jagger, decked in warpaint, leered menacingly at the camera. Brian Jones atmospherically wore dark, green-rimmed sunglasses and his orange lipstick complimented his dyed auburn hair. The band's overall appearance was unnerving but vividly exciting. On 12 May 1968 they had an opportunity to preview the song to an audience at the NME Annual Pollwinners Concert. They were not included in the original bill, and so their surprise performance of three numbers, including *Jumpin' Jack Flash* and *Satisfaction* naturally created an amazing crowd reaction and renewed the band's vigour for going on the road.

213. CHILD OF THE MOON (Jagger, Richard)
March/May 1968: Olympic, London. Producer: Jimmy Miller. Engineer: Glyn Johns.
UK B-side Jumpin' Jack Flash: 24 May 1968
USA B-side Jumpin' Jack Flash: 24 May 1968

The rock resurgence created on *Jumpin' Jack Flash* continued with *Child Of The Moon*. The mood was of wizardry and sorcery, an interest ironically that would have been better suited to the SATANIC MAJESTIES album. The sound texture created on *Child Of The Moon* was akin to their mod heroes The Who, particularly the Daltrey type shouts and the Townshend guitar reverb at the start of the track. An incredibly lazy but effective electric guitar continues throughout, a style that Keith Richards had recently been improvising on. He was experimenting with open tuning, a technique that he felt blues musicians used effectively. The final chord sequence incidentally has to be the ultimate guitar chord finale to a rock song!

214. EVERYBODY PAYS THEIR DUES (Jagger, Richard)
March/June 1968: Olympic, London. Producer: Jimmy Miller. Engineer: Glyn Johns.
Bootleg only.

Keith Richards' house in the country, Redlands, was used as a base for rehearsing songs and laying ideas onto cassette. The tapes were then played to Jimmy Miller for suggestions and eventually they would set about cutting the track properly in the studio. This was the method for recording many of the tracks that ended up on BEGGARS BANQUET. *Everybody Pays Their Dues* is *Street Fighting Man* in disguise. It has a different set of lyrics which sound quite stilted and cumbersome compared with the well-known official release. The basis of the music is the same apart from a blistering guitar solo which attempts to run the duration of the track.

215. STREET FIGHTING MAN (Jagger, Richard)
March/June 1968: Olympic, London. Producer: Jimmy Miller. Engineer: Glyn Johns.
USA Single: August 1968
USA LP BEGGARS BANQUET: November 1968: No 5 – 13 weeks
UK LP BEGGARS BANQUET: 5 December 1968: No 3 – 12 weeks
UK Compilation LP THROUGH THE PAST DARKLY (BIG HITS VOL 2): 12 September 1969: No 2 – 37 weeks
USA Compilation LP THROUGH THE PAST DARKLY (BIG HITS VOL 2): September 1969: No 2 – 16 weeks
UK Single: 20 July 1970: No 21 – 8 weeks
UK Maxi-Single: 30 June 1972

Street Fighting Man is 'subversive', as Decca described it. It was inspired by the 1968 Spring student riots in Europe and more closely the riot at London's Grosvenor Square. Mick Jagger wanted to contribute something to the desperate situation and, therefore, produced an urban guerrilla rock anthem. He was politically disappointed at governments' 'compromise solution', but as he sings in the lyrics he was aware realistically that his vocation was to sing in a rock and roll band. He understood that revolution could not be started by a record alone. His contribution was of commentated voyeurism instead of practical participation, although he did voice meek discontent at protest marches. The song owes a lot to Keith Richards' acoustic guitar and the acoustic overdubs by Jimmy Miller, but the agitated atmosphere is created by the delivery of the lyrics by Mick. He lingers on notes for emphasis, which serve to build the song's aggression. The menacing quality of the song was made even more pointed by the fact that electric guitar was laid aside for Keith's subtle attack on the acoustic. Brian Jones' contribution was minimal. He performs almost unnoticed on sitar and percussively on the tamboura. The track was released in the States as a single in August due to the album's delay and was promptly banned in Chicago for fear of encouraging riot. Many other cities followed suit. The States were particularly unstable at that time after the Martin Luther King and Robert Kennedy assassinations. The authorities did not want to risk further fighting in the street which the song's message conveyed. The original picture sleeve on the single showed demonstrators being beaten by police in Los Angeles. This was quickly banned by the worried distributors. Decca Records in Britain did not risk conflict and the song was not released as a single until 1970. It was rereleased on a maxi single in 1972 when it eventually charted at Number 21.

216. NO EXPECTATIONS (Jagger, Richard)
March/June 1968: Olympic, London. Producer: Jimmy Miller. Engineer: Glyn Johns.
USA B-side Street Fighting Man: August 1968
USA LP BEGGARS BANQUET: November 1968: No 5 – 13 weeks
UK LP BEGGARS BANQUET: 5 December 1968: No 3 – 12 weeks
Rolling Stones with Nicky Hopkins.

Many guest artists were to feature on the BEGGARS BANQUET sessions. Various guitar players, including possibly Dave Mason, lent a hand due to Brian Jones' general unreliability. It is open to debate as to who the blues bottleneck guitar player is. Original cassette demos certainly featured Keith Richards, but it was ideal for Brian Jones, who was thrilled at the return to Robert Johnson country blues. But it is not clear whether his take was on the final version, the other contender being ace guitarist Ry Cooder, a friend of Jack Nitzsche's. Jimmy Miller and Glyn Johns were later to hint that Brian Jones contributed certain guitar passages on BEGGARS BANQUET and it is certain that this is one. *No Expectations* is a tranquil, pensive song; Nicky Hopkins lays down a soft melody on the piano and a skilful, effortless bottleneck guitar accompanies it. It was released in the States as the flipside to *Street Fighting Man* and was certainly an excellent foretaste of the album release.

217. THE DEVIL IS MY NAME (a.k.a. SYMPATHY FOR THE DEVIL)
(Jagger, Richard)
May 1968: Olympic, London. Producer: Jimmy Miller. Engineer: Glyn Johns.
Bootleg only.
Rolling Stones with Nicky Hopkins.

The Devil Is My Name was the working title for *Sympathy For The Devil*. All of it is captured during the filming of the Stones' cinematic debut. Jean-Luc Godard was a politically aware film producer whose anti-establishment reputation fitted in well with the Stones' image. The film cameras took the Olympic Studios over for two days and documented the rehearsals for *Sympathy For The Devil*. The film was provisionally titled 'One Plus One' but was changed for box office appeal to 'Sympathy For The Devil'. Uniquely, it captures the Stones' recording method, which is purposeful and spontaneous. The track builds up from what was once a country song, to an insane samba rhythm. Mick Jagger is shown playing acoustic guitar and indicates how he feels the song should build up; during difficult percussive pieces he would encourage Charlie Watts, 'Try to make it a bit more lively – it sounds a bit dead.' The film emphasized the rift between the Stones and Brian Jones, who was very much the outsider; at times he sat in the corner and was offered only a small acoustic guitar part. Keith Richards was industriously playing bass lines and lead guitar while Nicky Hopkins, who was now into the Stones' recording groove, plays competently on piano. One very interesting take of *Sympathy For The Devil* includes echo on Jagger's vocals; the film as a documentary of life in the studio is an essential Stones recording artefact.

218. SYMPATHY FOR THE DEVIL (a.k.a. THE DEVIL IS MY NAME)
(Jagger, Richard)
March/June 1968: Olympic, London. Producer: Jimmy Miller. Engineer: Glyn Johns.
*USA LP BEGGARS BANQUET: November 1968: No **5** – 13 weeks*
*UK LP BEGGARS BANQUET: 5 December 1968: No **3** – 12 weeks*
USA Compilation LP THE ROLLING STONES – PROMOTIONAL ALBUM: October 1969.
Rolling Stones with Nicky Hopkins.

The subject matter for *Sympathy For The Devil* is Satan and his madcap escapades into human life. Mick Jagger was influenced by Mikhail Bulgakov's novel The Master and Margarita, in which Satan looks at the effects of the Russian Revolution. Mick Jagger twists the tale further, evoking and inciting nightmare images. *Sympathy For The Devil* lyrically is a rock and roll masterpiece and confirms the dark images which were started in *Jumpin' Jack Flash*. The track starts gently enough as Mick Jagger and Charlie Watts play percussion to a samba beat. Nicky Hopkins enters on the piano and Mick Jagger invokes his irreligious taunts. Once the pace is right, Keith Richards bursts in with an electrifying solo guitar performance. The infamous background 'oo-oos' are supplied by the band and were inspired by Anita Pallenberg who, during one take, had started the chant. The guitar wanes for a few verses before entering again to a climactic crescendo.

219. DEAR DOCTOR (Jagger, Richard)
March/June 1968: Olympic, London. Producer: Jimmy Miller. Engineer: Glyn Johns.
*USA LP BEGGARS BANQUET: November 1968: No **5** – 13 weeks*
*UK LP BEGGARS BANQUET: 5 December 1968: No **3** – 12 weeks*

A certain maturity is displayed in this musical interpretation of a 'down in Virginia' country music song. Mick Jagger practises his newly acquired affected drawl and illustrates an amusing scene of despair and happiness. A wedding is set for a poor unfortunate to a bow-legged, sow of a woman. Bourbon cannot drown the feelings of the wedding day and as he searches in his wedding-suit pocket for the ring he finds a note which says the sow has run off with his cousin. There follow tears of relief – the doctor can put away his stethoscope; the blood pressure is now under control. The story was typically fashioned around the irony of the blues, a depressing but most uplifting music form, a strange dichotomy derived from ethnic roots. The musical quality on the original album version and an out-take are superb.

220. DOWNTOWN SUZIE (Wyman)
March/June 1968: Olympic, London. Producer: Jimmy Miller. Engineer: Glyn Johns.
*UK Compilation LP METAMORPHIS: 6 June 1975: No **45** – 1 week*
*USA Compilation LP METAMORPHIS: 6 June 1975: No **8** – 8 weeks*

The good fortune of having his composition included on the SATANIC MAJESTIES album made Bill Wyman determined to write further songs. He knew the musical quality had to be maintained and he admitted that *Downtown Suzie* did not warrant inclusion on BEGGARS BANQUET. Brian Jones did not respond quite so objectively to the Jagger/Richard dominance. Keith Richards indicates that Brian never actually produced a finished product and, therefore, this part of his insecurity was mostly self-inflicted. The music on *Suzie* is good-time boogie with a portion of acoustic blues. An out-take is available on bootleg; the original eventually appeared on the mid-'seventies Decca compilation, METAMORPHIS, making it only the second Wyman composition to feature on a Rolling Stones' album.

221. PRODIGAL SON (Wilkins)
March/June 1968: Olympic, London. Producer: Jimmy Miller. Engineer: Glyn Johns.
*USA LP BEGGARS BANQUET: November 1968: No **5** – 13 weeks*
*UK LP BEGGARS BANQUET: 5 December 1968: No **3** – 12 weeks*
USA Compilation LP THE ROLLING STONES – PROMOTIONAL ALBUM: October 1969
Rolling Stones with Ry Cooder.

The Reverend Robert Wilkins' gospel song of biblical parallels was convincingly attempted by the band. Duelling acoustic guitars and wailing harmonica provide the background for Jagger to sing another Chicago blues track. The result is impressively impromptu. Ry Cooder helped to create the blues flavour, as he plucked the strings with Keith Richards. Brian Jones was conspicuously absent; ironic since he favoured the return to the blues. On 21 May 1968 Brian was arrested and charged with possession of cannabis. He was bailed out but the pressure brought by the establishment (the plain-clothes detectives who constantly followed and harassed Mick, Keith and Brian) was taking its toll. In short, the prodigal son was cracking under the imposed strain. His musical talents floundered, interest waned and he failed to turn up for many session dates. The band did little to halt this decline.

222. I'M A COUNTRY BOY (Jagger, Richard)
March/June 1968: Olympic, London. Producer: Jimmy Miller. Engineer: Glyn Johns.
Bootleg only.

An instrumental track but not as you would expect played in the country vein. Several versions exist, one including a vocal mix.

223. GIVE ME A HAMBURGER (a.k.a. **HAMBURGER TO GO** and **STUCK OUT ALL ALONE**) (Jagger, Richard)
March/June 1968: Olympic, London. Producer: Jimmy Miller. Engineer: Glyn Johns.
Bootleg only.

224. SILVER BLANKET (Jagger, Richard)
March/June 1968: Olympic, London. Producer: Jimmy Miller. Engineer: Glyn Johns.
Bootleg only.

225. LADY (Jagger, Richard)
March/June 1968: Olympic, London. Producer: Jimmy Miller. Engineer: Glyn Johns.
Bootleg only.

The BEGGARS BANQUET sessions in the Spring of '68 produced a number of unreleased tracks including *I'm a Country Boy, Silver Blanket, Lady* and *Give Me A Hamburger. Silver Blanket* is an up-tempo number. *Lady* was a serious contender for inclusion on the BEGGARS BANQUET album, but was dropped at the last minute. *Hamburger* like *Lady* is a soft ballad, possibly using one of the 'many friends' who were supposed to be present at some of the sessions. One of these may have been Eric Clapton...the press rumoured he was about to sign as replacement guitarist for Brian Jones, whose health problems were now jeopardizing the future of the band.

226. JIGSAW PUZZLE (Jagger, Richard)
March/June 1968: Olympic, London. Producer: Jimmy Miller. Engineer: Glyn Johns.
*USA LP BEGGARS BANQUET: November 1968: No **5** – 13 weeks*
*UK LP BEGGARS BANQUET: 5 December 1968: No **3** – 12 weeks*
Rolling Stones with Nicky Hopkins.

Nicky Hopkins, since his introduction during the 'Satanic' sessions, was beginning to contribute a more prominent role in the band's over-all sound and they used him to good effect on this track. The blues feel is still retained with some fine slide guitar by Keith Richards, but the song's rhythm is controlled by Nicky Hopkins incessantly pounding on the ivory keys. The song written by Mick Jagger caused anxiety among critics – the imagery is bizarre and unrelated, the jigsaw puzzle was left uncompleted.

227. PARACHUTE WOMAN (Jagger, Richard)
March/June 1968: Olympic, London. Producer: Jimmy Miller. Engineer: Glyn Johns.
USA LP BEGGARS BANQUET: November 1968: No 5 – 13 weeks
UK LP BEGGARS BANQUET: 5 December 1968: No 3 – 12 weeks

The foundations are very simple on this prototypical R 'n' B showcase. The mood is purposeful and the formula of harmonica, steel guitar is successful. Electric guitar dubbed on at the end satisfactorily completes this uptempo number, which Keith Richards recalls was initially put down in a rough form on a cassette. The lyrics are lewdly plain, particularly the last verse.

228. FAMILY (Jagger, Richard)
March/June 1968: Olympic, London. Producer: Jimmy Miller. Engineer: Glyn Johns.
UK Compilation LP METAMORPHIS: 6 June 1975: No 45 – 1 week
USA Compilation LP METAMORPHIS: 6 June 1975: No 8 – 8 weeks

The creation of *Family* may be traced by means of collecting two out-takes on bootleg. They are obviously abbreviated versions prior to the recording of the final take; the lyrics were certainly not completed. The end result lacks the necessary Stones finish and it is easy to see why it was excluded from BEGGARS BANQUET. It does not have the recurrent R 'n' B theme which was so prevalent on BEGGARS BANQUET.

229. SALT OF THE EARTH (Jagger, Richard)
March/June 1968: Olympic, London. Producer: Jimmy Miller. Engineer: Glyn Johns.
USA LP BEGGARS BANQUET: November 1968: No 5 – 13 weeks
UK LP BEGGARS BANQUET: 5 December 1968: No 3 – 12 weeks
Rolling Stones with Nicky Hopkins.

Acoustic guitar kicks off a rousing anthem to the working class. Keith Richards is in charge of the vocals on the first verse, his first recorded solo. Another first is the inclusion of female singers who provide the vocal sustenance to the backbone of the world during the track's finale. One has to acknowledge that *Salt Of The Earth* is the Stones' sing-along equal to The Beatles' *All You Need Is Love*. The poignant message contained is open to being misconstrued; since when did the Stones have any pretensions of being working class?

230. STRAY CAT BLUES (Jagger, Richard)
March/June 1968: Olympic, London. Producer: Jimmy Miller. Engineer: Glyn Johns.
USA LP BEGGARS BANQUET: November 1968: No 5 – 13 weeks
UK LP BEGGARS BANQUET: 5 December 1968: No 3 – 12 weeks

The semi-pornographic overtones captured in the lyrics of *Stray Cat Blues* overshadow the excellent musical quality of the blues. The song concerns itself with sleazy under-age groupie sex. The musical accompaniment is atmospherically excellent, enhancing the sordid message. The Stones failed to play live during 1968, but on the 1969 tours the song became a firm stage favourite. Mick Jagger claimed later that the 'Velvet Underground sound' (a.k.a. *Heroin*) was the inspiration and basis for some of the BANQUET sound, but in particular *Stray Cat*.

231. FACTORY GIRL (Jagger, Richard)
March/June 1968: Olympic, London. Producer: Jimmy Miller. Engineer: Glyn Johns.
*USA LP BEGGARS BANQUET: November 1968: No **5** – 13 weeks*
*UK LP BEGGARS BANQUET: 5 December 1968: No **3** – 12 weeks*

The working class sentiments tackled on *Salt Of The Earth* are repeated on *Factory Girl*, although in a much more dismissive manner. The track is a short acoustic song with slight country/hillbilly leanings. The fiddle was Nicky Hopkins' idea and was encouraged by Jimmy Miller. Although adequate, *Factory Girl* would certainly not win the track of the album award. With the album now complete, the task of sleeve design came next. A cartoon design was considered, but dismissed in favour of a photograph taken by Barry Feinstein showing a toilet decked in graffiti. The Stones liked the idea, and did a quick redecorating job by producing their own graffiti with track listings and acknowledgements for the back cover. When Decca Records were shown the design, they immediately rejected it on grounds of bad taste. The ensuing argument held up the release of the album for four months. Mick Jagger suggested a compromise of packaging the sleeve in a plain paper bag and labelling it 'Unfit for Children'. Decca, however, insisted, as they did with the March 1966 cover for COULD YOU WALK ON THE WATER?, that the sleeve had to be changed. If the recorded product was ever to be made available the Stones had to agree. A simple plain white gatefold sleeve was chosen, which led to immediate parallels with the just released Beatles' WHITE ALBUM – could they never win?

232. MIDNIGHT RAMBLER (Jagger, Richard)
March/June 1968: Olympic, London. Producer: Jimmy Miller. Engineer: Glyn Johns.
*USA LP LET IT BLEED: November 1969: No **3** – 19 weeks*
*UK LP LET IT BLEED: December 1969: No **1** – 29 weeks*

Early renditions of three tracks later to appear on the LET IT BLEED album were recorded during the BEGGARS BANQUET sessions. The most controversial was certainly *Midnight Rambler*. It is a gutsy reminder of the Boston Strangler – the lyrics even include part of Albert de Salvo's confession. Keith Richards is the prime instrumentalist overdubbing guitar parts and creating subtle tempo changes that intensify Jagger's homicidal dialogue. *Midnight Rambler* builds up menacingly until it reaches the 'Don't do that' passage, Keith Richards controlling the direction as Mick Jagger blows away on the harmonica. The song's theatrical leanings allow anger to be vented in drama and not in insane violence. Live performances of the track allowed the song to be extended; Keith Richards and Mick Jagger both enjoyed the malevolent atmosphere it created – it was a challenge to perform on stage.

233. YOU GOT THE SILVER (Jagger, Richard)
March/June 1968: Olympic, London. Producer: Jimmy Miller. Engineer: Glyn Johns.
USA LP LET IT BLEED: November 1969: No 3 – 19 weeks
UK LP LET IT BLEED: December 1969: No 1 – 29 weeks
Rolling Stones with Nicky Hopkins.

This country song was written by Keith Richards, who also performed the vocals not for one verse as on *Salt Of The Earth* but for the complete song – his first solo project. The finished track was chosen by Michelangelo Antonioni for inclusion on the sound-track of his film *Zabriskie Point*. An out-take of *You Got The Silver* features Mick Jagger on vocals allowing Keith to get on with the business of playing the steel acoustic guitar and also the lead blues lick on electric.

234. YOU CAN'T ALWAYS GET WHAT YOU WANT (Jagger, Richard)
March/June 1968: Olympic, London. Producer: Jimmy Miller. Engineer: Glyn Johns. Vocal arranger: Jack Nitzsche.
USA LP LET IT BLEED: November 1969: No 3 – 19 weeks
UK LP LET IT BLEED: December 1969: No 1 – 29 weeks
UK B-side Honky Tonk Women: 11 July 1969
USA B-side Honky Tonk Women: 11 July 1969
UK B-side Sad Day: 29 April 1973
Rolling Stones with Al Kooper, London Bach Choir, Madelaine Bell, Doris Troy, Nanette Newman, Rocky Dijon, Jimmy Miller.

'Slightly over the top' is an understatement. The song includes Al Kooper on organ and French horn, producer Jimmy Miller aids Charlie Watts on drums, and Rocky Dijon plays percussion, not to mention three female vocalists and a choir who help Mick Jagger out on vocals. The end result is a production by the Stones unparalleled to this day. It is an adventurous attempt at a rock opera, running in at over seven minutes. The track was shortened for it to be featured as the flip side of *Honky Tonk Women*. The London Bach Choir, although content with their contribution, were not over-impressed with the rest of the album's content (e.g. *Midnight Rambler*) and wished to renounce their rôle in it. However, it was too late. An abbreviated version without the orchestral theatrics is obtainable on bootleg and is a rough antidote to the released version. *You Can't Always Get What You Want* has been a tour favourite ever since.

235. SISTER MORPHINE (Jagger, Richard) (Some credit Marianne Faithfull)
March/October 1968: Olympic, London. Producer: Jimmy Miller. Engineer: Glyn Johns.

UK LP STICKY FINGERS: 23 April 1971: No 1 – 25 weeks
USA LP STICKY FINGERS: June 1971: No 1 – 26 weeks
Rolling Stones with Ry Cooder, Jack Nitzsche.

Sister Morphine was written in 1968 and early recordings probably come from the Olympic sessions. It was cut on tape late in '68 and again in June, 1969. Jack Nitzsche tinkered on the piano keys and Ry Cooder excelled himself on the bottleneck guitar. Once the song was released Marianne Faithfull put in a claim that she was co-writer of the song. Jagger and Richards signed an acknowledgement of this and she recorded it for single release in February 1969. The producer was Mick Jagger and the arranger Jack Nitzsche. *Sister Morphine* is a harrowing tale of drug addiction and the ultimate overdose. The version which appears on STICKY FINGERS, two or three years after its original recording, depicts this nightmare – so much so that the Spanish version of the album substituted another track to avoid any youth subversion. In fact, it is musically quite beautiful, the solo guitar is purposeful and the acoustic back-drop resplendent.

236. STILL A FOOL (a.k.a. TWO TRAINS) (Jagger, Richard)
July 1968: Mobile at Redlands and Olympic. Producer: Jimmy Miller.
Engineer: Glyn Johns.
Bootleg only.

The Summer of '68 produced a variety of songs this way from the Redlands base, a number of which have been bootlegged. *Still A Fool* is a return to the *Little Red Rooster* style blues. Slide guitar, wailing harmonica, piano and Jagger moaning in true southern delta fashion create a track lasting over nine minutes, which should be sought by blues critics and Stones' official collectors alike. It returns to the past but also is predictive of the future. Rated as essential collecting material.

237. HIGHWAY CHILD (a.k.a. THE VULTURE) (Jagger, Richard)
July 1968: Mobile at Redlands and Olympic. Producer: Jimmy Miller.
Engineer: Glyn Johns.
Bootleg only.

238. HOLD ON I'M COMING (Hayes, Porter)
July 1968: Mobile at Redlands. Producer: Jimmy Miller. Engineer: Glyn Johns.
Bootleg only.

239. ROCK ME BABY (King, Josea, James, Taub)
July 1968: Mobile at Redlands. Producer: Jimmy Miller. Engineer: Glyn Johns.
Bootleg only.

Blues was the name of the game at Redlands. Various favourites were recorded, including B. B. King's *Rock Me Baby*. *Highway Child* seemed a possibility for release, since the tape was later mastered by Jimmy Miller at the Olympic Studio. It is played in the hard rock vogue and has quite a memorable riff. *Hold On I'm Coming* is a lengthy blues track, which lacks the raw edge of *Still A Fool* but despite this is still very collectable.

240. MEMO FROM TURNER (Jagger, Richard)
October 1968: Olympic, London. Producer: Jack Nitzsche. Conductor: Randy Newman.
UK LP PERFORMANCE (A motion picture sound-track): 19 September 1970
USA LP PERFORMANCE (A motion picture sound-track): 19 September 1970
UK Single: November 1970. (Credited as Mick Jagger only)

241. MEMO FROM TURNER (Jagger, Richard)
May-October 1968: Olympic, London. Producer: Jack Nitzsche.
*UK Compilation LP METAMORPHIS: 6 June 1975: No **45** – 1 week*
*USA Compilation LP METAMORPHIS: 6 June 1975: No **8** – 8 weeks*
Rolling Stones with Steve Winwood, Jim Capaldi.

While Mick Jagger was playing his first film rôle as Turner in *Performance* Keith Richards felt creatively remote. His girlfriend Anita Pallenberg was playing opposite Mick Jagger, and this involved bed scenes, some of which were cut from the final film. The insecurity mounted and the Jagger, Richard composition intended by writer and co-producer Donald Connell to be the major score of the film was still missing. Keith attempted to retaliate by delaying the sessions as long as possible. Mick Jagger countered by inviting Steve Winwood and Jim Capaldi to play on a rough composition which can be witnessed on the 1975 Compilation album METAMORPHIS. The result is a freaky work-out so different to the film score release. The content is interesting, but a shadow of the R 'n' B version with Keith Richards.

242. YER BLUES (Lennon, McCartney)
10,11 December 1968: BBC, London. Producer: Allen Klein. Engineer: Glyn Johns.
Bootleg only.
Keith Richard, John Lennon, Eric Clapton, Mitch Mitchell, Yoko Ono.

243. ROUTE 66 (Troup)
10, 11 December 1968: BBC, London. Producer: Allen Klein. Engineer: Glyn Johns.
Bootleg only.
Rolling Stones with Rocky Dijon.

244. CONFESSIN' THE BLUES (Brown, McShann)
10, 11 December 1968: BBC, London. Producer: Allen Klein. Engineer: Glyn Johns.
Bootleg only.
Rolling Stones with Rocky Dijon.

245. JUMPIN' JACK FLASH (Jagger, Richard)
10, 11 December 1968: BBC, London. Producer: Allen Klein. Engineer: Glyn Johns.
Bootleg only.

246. PARACHUTE WOMAN (Jagger, Richard)
10, 11 December 1968: BBC, London. Producer: Allen Klein. Engineer: Glyn Johns.
Bootleg only.

247. YOU CAN'T ALWAYS GET WHAT YOU WANT (Jagger, Richard)
10, 11 December 1968: BBC, London. Producer: Allen Klein. Engineer: Glyn Johns.
Bootleg only.

248. YONDERS WALL (Clark)
10, 11 December 1968: BBC, London. Producer: Allen Klein. Engineer: Glyn Johns.
Bootleg only.

249. NO EXPECTATIONS (Jagger, Richard)
10, 11 December 1968: BBC, London. Producer: Allen Klein. Engineer: Glyn Johns.
Bootleg only.

250. SYMPATHY FOR THE DEVIL (Jagger, Richard)
10, 11 December 1968: BBC, London. Producer: Allen Klein. Engineer: Glyn Johns.
Bootleg only.

251. SALT OF THE EARTH (Jagger, Richard)
10, 11 December 1968: BBC, London. Producer: Allen Klein. Engineer: Glyn Johns.
Bootleg only.
Rolling Stones with The Who, John Lennon, Yoko Ono, Eric Clapton.

The Rolling Stones' 'Rock And Roll Circus' was an extravaganza recorded in early December and intended for a BBC TV Christmas special to promote the BEGGARS BANQUET album. The filming was directed by Michael Lindsay-Hogg. The star-studded array of performers disguised in clown outfits with Mick Jagger typically dressed as a ring-master was incongruous and unreal. The Stones were dissatisfied with the outcome – it was even considered that they were upstaged by The Who. 'The Circus' was never released; the film was carefully kept in Mick Jagger's vaults. The notable tracks bootlegged from the sound-track are *Parachute Woman*, an acoustic version, the new track, *Yonders Wall* and the climax *Salt Of The Earth*, which used the same musical track recorded at Olympic, but with the vocal inclusion of the 'Rock And Roll Circus' cast. There were half-a-dozen takes of *Jumpin' Jack Flash*. The invited crowd soon became fed up with the considerable delays and only a devoted few were there for the climax of *Salt Of The Earth* at six o'clock in the morning. 'Rock And Roll Circus' is sadly the last Stones' performing work with Brian Jones. It was the end of an era.

252. **HONKY TONK WOMEN** (Jagger, Richard)
May 1969: Olympic, London. Producer: Jimmy Miller. Engineer: Glyn Johns.
UK Single: 11 July 1969: No **1** *– 17 weeks*
USA Single: 11 July 1969: No **1** *– 14 weeks*
UK Compilation LP THROUGH THE PAST DARKLY (BIG HITS VOL 2): 12 September 1969: No **2** *– 37 weeks*
USA Compilation LP THROUGH THE PAST DARKLY (BIG HITS VOL 2): September 1969: No **2** *– 16 weeks*
Rolling Stones with Mick Taylor.

A short session in May 1969 enabled Mick Taylor to establish himself as suitable for an honorary guitar position with the Stones. He possibly performed on two unreleased tracks, *Toss The Coin* and *Old Glory*, but certainly contributed to the prestigious *Honky Tonk Women*. Charlie Watts taps out the first few beats on the cowbell. He then hits the snare and kicks into the bass drum. Keith Richards follows shortly with the guitar riff. *Honky Tonk* is a unique piece of rhythm artistry and as a single has not been equalled by the Stones to this day. The released take features brass instruments in the background. The song was written by Jagger, Richard during a visit to South America. Earlier recordings of the track feature Brian Jones on guitar, but it was later re-recorded with the aspiring young guest musician Mick Taylor. Ry Cooder was also present at the sessions. Once *Honky Tonk Women* was released, he argued that he had written the opening chords, a dispute which inevitably caused a rift between himself and Keith Richards, the credited writer. Keith cannot, however, deny that the open guitar tuning used on the single had been inspired and copied from Ry Cooder's book of guitar riffs. On the other hand, the drum sound created by Charlie and the production team of Jimmy Miller and Glyn Johns is recognized as one of the most original and best drum sounds released on disc. It was a perfect foundation for the rest of the band to rock along to, creating an immensely successful dance record. The public echoed those sentiments ensuring a world-wide Number 1 hit.

253. **LET IT BLEED** (Jagger, Richard)
June/July 1969: Olympic, London. Producer: Jimmy Miller. Engineer: Glyn Johns. Assistant Engineers: Bruce Botnick, Jerry Hansen, George Chkiantz.
USA LP LET IT BLEED: November 1969: No **3** *– 19 weeks*
UK LP LET IT BLEED: December 1969: No **1** *– 29 weeks*

On 9 June 1969 the original line-up of The Rolling Stones was finally broken. It was publicly stated that Brian Jones was quitting the band due to the age-old 'musical differences'. Mick Jagger, Keith Richards and

Charlie Watts had just visited Brian at his East Grinstead ten-acre home, formerly Winnie The Pooh's (i.e. A. A. Milne's) idyllic Cotchford Farm. The Stones had not toured for two years and were eager to finalize details for an American tour to promote the forthcoming album LET IT BLEED. They asked Brian to go with them, but he thoughtfully declined and it was then that they hinted that Mick Taylor was ready and willing to join the band. It was agreed that the split should be formally announced. Brian Jones did not play any further part in recording sessions. *It should be noted that for sessionography purposes Mick Taylor is now Rolling Stones 'personnel'.* In Hyde Park, London on 13 June 1969 the Stones held a press conference to confirm this and also that arrangements were under way for a free concert to be held at Hyde Park on 5 July 1969. On the album track of *Let It Bleed* Ian Stewart replaces Nicky Hopkins momentarily on the 'joanna' for an R 'n' B fashioned song that became the title track of the new album. Jimmy Miller recalls that Keith Richards was always at pains to arrive at a precise sound. He over-dubbed various guitar parts to create the perfect sound, being in danger at times of overdoing it. As Dave Hassinger found in Los Angeles, his sheer musical professionalism was one of the mainstays of the band. The lyrics have some obvious sex and drugs connotations which Marianne Faithfull believed referred to her hazy existence.

254. LOVE IN VAIN (Payne)
June/July 1969: Olympic, London. Producer: Jimmy Miller. Engineer: Glyn Johns. Assistant Engineers: Bruce Botnick, Jerry Hansen, George Chkiantz.
USA LP LET IT BLEED: November 1969: No 3 – 19 weeks
UK LP LET IT BLEED: December 1969: No 1 – 29 weeks
USA Compilation LP THE ROLLING STONES – PROMOTIONAL ALBUM: October 1969
Rolling Stones with Ry Cooder, Nicky Hopkins.

Marianne Faithfull convinced Mick Jagger to record a song formerly played by one of his blues idols, Robert Johnson. Mick chose *Love In Vain.* Ry Cooder was brought in to play a mandolin passage and the song evolved around the distinctive blues format. A purely acoustic version was recorded which ended up on a much-sought-after promotional album, simply titled THE ROLLING STONES. It features tracks from the early days, *Walking The Dog,* and leads up to the late 'sixties' culminating in the rare version of *Love In Vain.* Intended for radio promotional purposes only, copies were released to radio stations in the States and only 200 for the press in the UK. Decca have since released a version of the album in Australia which has a different track listing. Import copies are obtainable.

255. I'M GOING DOWN (Jagger, Richard, Taylor)
June/July 1969: Olympic, London. Producer: Jimmy Miller. Engineer: Glyn Johns.
UK Compilation LP METAMORPHIS: 6 June 1975: No 45 – 1 week
USA Compilation LP METAMORPHIS: 6 June 1975: No 8 – 8 weeks

The current level of productiveness and the purposeful quality of the material had encouraged the Stones to think of a two-album release in 1969. They said in June that an album titled STICKY FINGERS would be released in September and another was set for a Christmas release. The promise was broken and certain material never made an official release, including *I'm Going Down* which had to wait for the METAMORPHIS Decca compilation in 1975. *I'm Going Down* is a mid-tempo rock song featuring brass sounds. It missed the boat – a certain amount of confusion remains over the credited songwriter. The disc's inner circle credits Mick Taylor in addition to Jagger and Richard whilst the sleeve prints only Jagger, Richard. An out-take on bootleg is the same track, without fade-outs, that emerges on METAMORPHIS.

256. I DON'T KNOW WHY (Wonder, Riser, Hunter, Hardaway)
July 1969: Olympic, London. Producer: Jimmy Miller. Engineer: Glyn Johns.
UK Single: 23 May 1975
USA Single: 23 May 1975
UK Compilation LP METAMORPHIS: 6 June 1975: No 45 – 1 week
USA Compilation LP METAMORPHIS: 6 June 1975: No 8 – 8 weeks

The date was 3 July 1969 and the band were busy recording a version of Stevie Wonder's *I Don't Know Why*. Late into the night a 'phone call from the wife of Brian Jones' chauffeur interrupted the session. She described to Mick the tragic events whereby Brian had accidentally drowned in his own swimming pool. The band's sentiments and the reasons for Brian's death have been publicly aired and trawled for years. The national press still run stories regarding the circumstances of his death. Let's simply remember Brian's epitaph, 'Please Don't Judge Me Too Harshly' and continue with the music he loved. Earlier in March 1969 Stevie Wonder had had a small hit with *I Don't Know Why* (Number 14 UK, Number 39 USA). The Stones cover is played very much in Stevie Wonder's mould and incorporates the now familiar brass sounds which were mixed in at the October '69 Elektra sessions. Out-takes of *I Don't Know Why* include lengthy 7–8 minute versions. Release on the intended '69 Christmas album did not materialize and so it was picked up again by Decca in 1975 and released as a UK single. The first 1,000 copies were erroneously credited to Jagger, Richard. The American marketeers went one better declaring Jagger, Richard and Taylor as the songwriters!

257. MONKEY MAN (Jagger, Richard)
June/July 1969: Olympic, London. Producer: Jimmy Miller. Engineer: Glyn Johns. Assistant Engineers: Bruce Botnick, Jerry Hansen, George Chkiantz.
USA LP LET IT BLEED: November 1969: No 3 – 19 weeks
UK LP LET IT BLEED: December 1969: No 1 – 29 weeks
Rolling Stones with Nicky Hopkins, Jimmy Miller.

Monkey Man originated from some song-writing trips to Naples in Italy during the BEGGARS BANQUET period. Powered by a heavy guitar and

Nicky Hopkins' piano, the song pushes out a tongue-in-cheek stance of satanic messianicism to entrap the fans.

258. JIVING SISTER FANNY (Jagger, Richard)
June/July 1969: Olympic, London. Producer: Jimmy Miller. Engineer: Glyn Johns.
*UK Compilation LP METAMORPHIS: 6 June 1975: No **45** – 1 week*
*USA Compilation LP METAMORPHIS: 6 June 1975: No **8** – 8 weeks*
UK B-side Out Of Time: 5 September 1975
USA B-side Out Of Time: 5 September 1975
Rolling Stones with Nicky Hopkins.

A twelve-bar blues tune which was strangely placed as the flip side of a 1975 single *Out Of Time*. It is played in true chug along rock 'n' roll style and was so noticeably an anachronism that it was not included on an album of its own period. Mick Taylor features heavily on lead guitar – its non-release surely could not have anything to do with his prominent 'jiving' role! Again, brass instruments are used, a favourite song-enhancement of the period. A bootlegged out-take is in existence.

259. I'M YOURS, AND I'M HERS (Winter)
5 July 1969: Hyde Park, London.
Bootleg only.

260. JUMPIN' JACK FLASH (Jagger, Richard)
5 July 1969: Hyde Park, London.
Bootleg only.

261. MERCY MERCY (Covay, Miller)
5 July 1969: Hyde Park, London.
Bootleg only.

262. STRAY CAT BLUES (Jagger, Richard)
5 July 1969: Hyde Park, London.
Bootleg only.

263. NO EXPECTATIONS (Jagger, Richard)
5 July 1969: Hyde Park, London.
Bootleg only.

264. I'M FREE (Jagger, Richard)
5 July 1969: Hyde Park, London.
Bootleg only.

265. DOWN HOME GIRL (Leiber, Butler)
5 July 1969: Hyde Park, London.
Bootleg only.

266. HONKY TONK WOMEN (Jagger, Richard)
5 July 1969: Hyde Park, London.
Bootleg only.

267. LOVE IN VAIN (Payne)
5 July 1969: Hyde Park, London.
Bootleg only.

268. GIVE ME A DRINK (a.k.a. **LOVING CUP**) (Jagger, Richard)
5 July 1969: Hyde Park, London.
Bootleg only.

269. MIDNIGHT RAMBLER (Jagger, Richard)
5 July 1969: Hyde Park, London.
Bootleg only.

270. STREET FIGHTING MAN (Jagger, Richard)
5 July 1969: Hyde Park, London.
Bootleg only.

271. (I CAN'T GET NO) SATISFACTION (Jagger, Richard)
5 July 1969: Hyde Park, London.
Bootleg only.

272. SYMPATHY FOR THE DEVIL (Jagger, Richard)
5 July 1969: Hyde Park, London.
Bootleg only.

At 6 o'clock in the evening on 5 July 1969 the Stones prepared to take the stage in front of a quarter of a million sun-drenched music revellers. They came to London's Hyde Park for a day of pop music, previously unparalleled in England. The crowd (more than twice the size of the annual Wembley FA Cup Final) had been entertained by Screw, Battered Ornaments, Third Ear Band, Alexis Korner's New Church, King Crimson and Family. A documentary filmed by Granada TV captures the historic day. It contrasts the celebration of the 'new' Rolling Stones line-up and the mourning of a lost friend, Brian Jones. The band, mid-afternoon, were ensconced in a Park Lane hotel, looking over the massed crowd made up of mods, rockers, angels (the security) and spaced-out hippies. They were unusually nervous as they entered the arena in an armoured truck just fifteen minutes before showdown. The angels cleared a path to the back-stage caravan where Mick Taylor and Keith Richards tuned up practising blues riffs. Charlie Watts handed apples and other provisions out of the window to some waiting fans. At last they were introduced to the crowd, and Mick Jagger, resplendent in Greek dress, was given the unenviable task of quietening them down in order to say a few words about Brian. He spoke a few stanzas of a Shelley poem, and then waiting helpers released thousands of white butterflies. The band promptly started the first sound *I'm Yours, And I'm Hers*, an unreleased number written by Johnny Winter and often misquoted as 'Lemon Squeezer'. *Jumpin' Jack Flash* followed as they moulded themselves into a format of loose rock. The sound was slightly untogether, but gradually their confidence grew. The tracks played were mostly new and taken from the recent blues-tinged BEGGARS BANQUET and LET IT BLEED sessions. *Midnight Rambler*, *Stray Cat Blues* and *Love In Vain* were improvised and extended from the album versions. *Loving Cup*, to be included on the EXILE ON MAIN ST double album, was tried out on the appreciative audience. Finally, the band launched into what Mick Jagger described as 'a samba', tribal bongo drummers tapped the rhythm out while the escalating guitars of Mick Taylor and Keith Richards come beautifully to a hypnotic climax. The show was a renowned success and has become a legend amongst concert goers. For the Stones, it was a distinct turning-point in their career. As a footnote, those who helped to clean the park up on the Sunday after the performance were given freebies of the newly released single *Honky Tonk Women*.

6

GIMMIE SHELTER FROM ALTAMONT

OCTOBER 1969 – MARCH 1971

273. GIMMIE SHELTER (Jagger, Richard)
October/November 1969: Elektra, Hollywood. Producer: Jimmy Miller. Engineer: Glyn Johns.
USA LP LET IT BLEED: November 1969: No 3 – 19 weeks
UK LP LET IT BLEED: December 1969: No 1 – 29 weeks
Rolling Stones with Nicky Hopkins, Jimmy Miller, Merry Clayton.

Four months passed after the Hyde Park Concert before a tour was arranged in the States. Meanwhile, Mick Jagger was filming in Australia for the starring rôle in *Ned Kelly*. Just before the USA tour started on 7 November in Colorado, the Stones went briefly into the studio to finish two uncompleted songs and to record a different version of *Honky Tonk Women*. These recordings would then complete the LET IT BLEED album. *Gimmie Shelter* is a hard rock track. It features the strong vocals of Merry Clayton and centres around the heavy lead guitar of Keith Richards. Jimmy Miller enhances the percussion techniques, a knack which he was keen to develop on future Stones mixes. *Gimmie Shelter* is a very strong contemporary sound which stands the test of time and is ideal for the opening cut on the album.

274. LIVE WITH ME (Jagger, Richard)
October/November 1969: Elektra, Hollywood. Producer: Jimmy Miller. Engineer: Glyn Johns.
USA LP LET IT BLEED: November 1969: No 3 – 19 weeks
UK LP LET IT BLEED: December 1969: No 1 – 29 weeks
Rolling Stones with Nicky Hopkins, Leon Russell, Bobby Keys.

Live With Me is the forerunner of the sound so successfully captured the following month on *Brown Sugar*. It was one of the first tracks Mick Taylor performed. Originally conceived at the Olympic sessions in June, it was completed in Hollywood in November. The rhythm section of Bill Wyman and Charlie Watts provide a powerful back beat on what is a simple rock song. The lyrics are also bawdily simplistic, which caused some concern with the London Bach Choir included on the LET IT BLEED album. Leon Russell provides the inspiration for the saxophone arrangements and assists on piano. *Live With Me* features for the first time the talents of saxophonist Bobby Keys. He had been introduced to the Stones by Jimmy Miller and his rock pedigree was undisputed: he was still in his mid-teens when he played with Buddy Holly. Coincidentally, he shares the same birthday as Keith Richards and was playing with Bobby Vee as support to the Stones on their USA '64 visit to San Antoni. He has consistently played with the Stones off and on ever since and has contributed significantly to their development.

275. ALL DOWN THE LINE (Jagger, Richard)
October/November 1969: Elektra, Hollywood. Producer: Jimmy Miller. Engineer: Glyn Johns.
Bootleg only.

All Down The Line was rerecorded in 1971 for the EXILE ON MAIN ST album. This version recorded in October 1969 was principally instrumental, Mick Jagger only sang a brief vocal line indicating the lyrics were unfinished. Testimony to this, the earlier recording date can be confirmed by reference to the copyright credits which were the same as other 'sixties material (Essex Music International Ltd, 19/20 Poland Street, London W1).

276. COUNTRY HONK (Jagger, Richard)
October/November 1969: Elektra, Hollywood. Producer: Jimmy Miller. Engineer: Glyn Johns.
USA LP LET IT BLEED: November 1969: No 3 – 19 weeks
UK LP LET IT BLEED: December 1969: No 1 – 29 weeks
Rolling Stones with Byron Berline, Nanette Newman.

Originally it was intended that *Honky Tonk Women* was to be expressed as a typical 'thirties country song, but this was dramatically changed when Mick Taylor experimented with the riff on guitar. Determined to attempt a country version, and pushed along by country rock artist Gram Parsons, they hired Byron Berline to play the fiddle. It is rumoured that in order to get an authentic sound on the fiddle he recorded his part on the boulevard's sidewalk (pavement), hence the car honk mixed in at the beginning and end of the track. An out-take lacks this subtle addition. *Country Honk* with the lyrics slightly changed in the first verse is a country version of *Honky Tonk Women* and is a refreshing change. The album was now complete, a wealth of material being included which literally spanned a decade. Once released, it leapt to Number 1 in Britain and remained in the UK charts well into the Summer of 1970. On reflection, many will find that LET IT BLEED contains many of the elements of a classic rock album.

277. I DON'T KNOW THE REASON WHY (Jagger, Richard)
October/November 1969: Elektra, Hollywood. Producer: Jimmy Miller. Engineer: Glyn Johns.
Bootleg only.
Rolling Stones with Bobby Keys.

I Don't Know The Reason Why is a seven-minute excursion into the blues. Mick Taylor is evident on electric guitar playing in the traditional English 'blues breakers' mould of Eric Clapton and John Mayall. The saxophone work of Bobby Keys can also be heard. The stereo recording elevates *I Don't Know The Reason Why* into a worthy collector's piece.

278. HONKY TONK WOMEN (Jagger, Richard)
November 1969: David Frost TV Show, USA
Bootleg only.

279. YOU CAN'T ALWAYS GET WHAT YOU WANT (Jagger, Richard)
November 1969: David Frost TV Show, USA.
Bootleg only.

280. GIMMIE SHELTER (Jagger, Richard)
18/19 November 1969: Ed Sullivan TV Show, USA.
Bootleg only.

281. LOVE IN VAIN (Payne)
18/19 November 1969: Ed Sullivan TV Show, USA.
Bootleg only.

282. HONKY TONK WOMEN (Jagger, Richard)
18/19 November 1969: Ed Sullivan TV Show, USA.
Bootleg only.

Another American tour led to reappearances on the Ed Sullivan Show and also on this occasion the David Frost Programme. The opportunity was used to promote material from the forthcoming BEGGARS BANQUET album and the by now chart fading single *Honky Tonk Women*.

283. JUMPIN' JACK FLASH (Jagger, Richard)
27/28 November 1969: Madison Square Gardens, New York. Producer: Rolling Stones, Glyn Johns. Engineer: Glyn Johns.
*UK LP GET YER YA-YA's OUT: 29 September 1970: No **1** – 15 weeks*
*USA LP GET YER YA-YA's OUT: 29 September 1970: No **6** – 10 weeks*

284. CAROL (Berry)
27/28 November 1969: Madison Square Gardens, New York. Producer: Rolling Stones, Glyn Johns. Engineer: Glyn Johns.
*UK LP GET YER YA-YA's OUT: 29 September 1970: No **1** – 15 weeks*
*USA LP GET YER YA-YA's OUT: 29 September 1970: No **6** – 10 weeks*

285. STRAY CAT BLUES (Jagger, Richard)
27/28 November 1969: Madison Square Gardens, New York. Producer: Rolling Stones, Glyn Johns. Engineer: Glyn Johns.
*UK LP GET YER YA-YA's OUT: 29 September 1970: No **1** – 15 weeks*
*USA LP GET YER YA-YA's OUT: 29 September 1970: No **6** – 10 weeks*

286. LOVE IN VAIN (Payne)
27/28 November 1969: Madison Square Gardens, New York. Producer: Rolling Stones, Glyn Johns. Engineer: Glyn Johns.
*UK LP GET YER YA-YA's OUT: 29 September 1970: No **1** – 15 weeks*
*USA LP GET YER YA-YA's OUT: 29 September 1970: No **6** – 10 weeks*

287. MIDNIGHT RAMBLER (Jagger, Richard)
27/28 November 1969: Madison Square Gardens, New York. Producer: Rolling Stones, Glyn Johns. Engineer: Glyn Johns.
*UK LP GET YER YA-YA's OUT: 29 September 1970: No **1** – 15 weeks*
*USA LP GET YER YA-YA's OUT: 29 September 1970: No **6** – 10 weeks*

288. SYMPATHY FOR THE DEVIL (Jagger, Richard)
27/28 November 1969: Madison Square Gardens, New York. Producer: Rolling Stones, Glyn Johns. Engineer: Glyn Johns.
*UK LP GET YER YA-YA's OUT: 29 September 1970: No **1** – 15 weeks*
*USA LP GET YER YA-YA's OUT: 29 September 1970: No **6** – 10 weeks*

289. LIVE WITH ME (Jagger, Richard)
27/28 November 1969: Madison Square Gardens, New York. Producer: Rolling Stones, Glyn Johns. Engineer: Glyn Johns.
*UK LP GET YER YA-YA's OUT: 29 September 1970: No **1** – 15 weeks*
*USA LP GET YER YA-YA's OUT: 29 September 1970: No **6** – 10 weeks*

290. LITTLE QUEENIE (Berry)
27/28 November 1969: Madison Square Gardens, New York. Producer: Rolling Stones, Glyn Johns. Engineer: Glyn Johns.
*UK LP GET YER YA-YA's OUT: 29 September 1970: No **1** – 15 weeks*
*USA LP GET YER YA-YA's OUT: 29 September 1970: No **6** – 10 weeks*

291. HONKY TONK WOMEN (Jagger, Richard)
27/28 November 1969: Madison Square Gardens, New York. Producer: Rolling Stones, Glyn Johns. Engineer: Glyn Johns.
UK LP GET YER YA-YA's OUT: 29 September 1970: No **1** *– 15 weeks*
USA LP GET YER YA-YA's OUT: 29 September 1970: No **6** *– 10 weeks*

292. STREET FIGHTING MAN (Jagger, Richard)
27/28 November 1969: Madison Square Gardens, New York. Producer: Rolling Stones, Glyn Johns. Engineer: Glyn Johns.
UK LP GET YER YA-YA's OUT: 29 September 1970: No **1** *– 15 weeks*
USA LP GET YER YA-YA's OUT: 29 September 1970: No **6** *– 10 weeks*

The seventeen-date tour of North America provided the Stones and their new member, Mick Taylor, a chance to fine-tune their act. By the time the show reached New York, they were ready and capable of delivering the proverbial goods. Touts increased ticket prices and celebrities such as Andy Warhol, Jimi Hendrix and Janis Joplin crowded back-stage areas. Mick Jagger entered the arena wearing a stars and stripes top-hat, determined to test the mettle of the American public. The stray fifteen year-old girls in *Stray Cat Blues* became thirteen-year-olds and the rendition that day of *Midnight Rambler* confirmed its theatrical soft-porn status. The concerts at New York were recorded by Glyn Johns using techniques considerably more advanced than those on the 1965 GOT LIVE IF YOU WANT IT!. The band were captured in electrifying form, Keith Richards and Mick Taylor pairing up well. *Sympathy For The Devil* enabled them to toss guitar solos back and forth. *Midnight Rambler* was extended to a work out lasting eight and a half minutes. It was full of subtle rhythm changes which built the crowd up to fever pitch. For collectors, the album contains a version of *Little Queenie*, a Chuck Berry rock and roll standard not previously recorded. The concert recording was made available by Decca to cash in on a live market currently furnished by a new era of professional bootleggers. Bob Dylan, The Beatles and the Stones were their chief targets. An unscrupulous roadie had allowed a recording to be made of the Stones third concert at Oakland – it was mixed on an eight-track and was of high stereo quality. It created the basis for the legendary bootleg album 'Liver Than You'll Ever Be' and sold astonishingly well. To counter this threat, Decca released GET YER YA-YA's OUT, the title originating from a voodoo chant. Mick Jagger wanted it to be a double album featuring also the tour's support acts, B. B. King and Ike and Tina Turner. Although a master was produced, Decca were not impressed. Financial logistics prevented the release and so only the single album was made available. Test pressings of the double album are extremely rare and valuable. The tracks were in a different order to the released version and lacked the obligatory guitar overdubs.

293. WILD HORSES (Jagger, Richard)
1 December 1969: Muscle Shoals, Alabama. Producer: Jimmy Miller. Engineer: Glyn Johns, Jimmy Johnson.
UK LP STICKY FINGERS: 23 April 1971: No **1** *– 25 weeks*

*USA LP STICKY FINGERS: June 1971: No **1** – 26 weeks*
*USA Single: June 1971: No **28** – 5 weeks*
*UK Compilation LP MADE IN THE SHADE: 6 June 1975: No **14** – 12 weeks*
*USA Compilation LP MADE IN THE SHADE: 6 June 1975: No **6** – 9 weeks*
Rolling Stones with Jimmy Dickinson.

Shortly after the conclusion of the US tour in Florida, the Stones decided to record two recently written compositions at the infamous home of southern soul music, the Muscle Shoals Studio in 'sweet home' Alabama. One of these recordings was *Wild Horses.* It is a soft country ballad lasting a lengthy six minutes. Mick Taylor plays a Nashville strung guitar, a technique used by established country and western artistes. Jimmy Dickinson, a Nashville session man who happened to be present at the studio, is featured on piano. Keith Richards had written the song, again collaborating with his friend Gram Parsons, who recorded it himself with The Flying Burrito Brothers. It was released on the Burritos' 1970 album BURRITO DELUXE. The lyrics apparently concern Keith's reluctance to go on the '69 tour because it left Anita alone to cope with their newly born son, Marlon. The sentiments captured can, however, purport to any strained relationship, and they were said also to relate to the demands placed on Mick Jagger by Marianne Faithful following her suicide attempt in Australia in July '69, an incident which finally led to the ending of the romance early in 1970. In fact, the exact subject matter is not important. The moving quality of Mick's vocals, which twist and turn, serve their purpose: 'Wild, wild horses couldn't drag me away'. The backing vocals of Pete Townshend and Ronnie Lane may have been on the final mix, but it is unlikely, as an out-take from the sessions does not testify to their presence. Various jams known loosely as 'Muscle Shoals Jam' have also been bootlegged. Gram Parsons would have featured on these out-takes, indeed one version of *Wild Horses* includes his guitar playing. *Wild Horses* was released as a single in the States but only attained a Number 28 position – the Stones most unsuccessful chart ranking to date.

294. YOU GOTTA MOVE (McDowell)
1 December 1969: Muscle Shoals, Alabama. Producer: Jimmy Miller.
Engineer: Glyn Johns, Jimmy Johnson.
*UK LP STICKY FINGERS: 23 April 1971: No **1** – 25 weeks*
*USA LP STICKY FINGERS: June 1971: No **1** – 26 weeks*

You Gotta Move is a short, simplistic tune written by an aged blues gospel artist Mississippi Fred McDowell. The song contains a languid steel slide guitar and the singular pounding of a bass drum. The gospel image is intensified as the whole band sing along camp-fire style. Despite the simplicity, it took the Stones numerous attempts before the final master was made. *You Gotta Move* and the two other tracks recorded at Muscle Shoals were given their first public airing at the much publicized free concert at Altamont. While they were recording in Alabama various messages originating from California indicated the organizers were trying to overcome insurmountable problems. Mick Jagger wanted to organize an event on the scale of Woodstock. At such short notice the Stones' staff were trying to achieve the impossible.

295. BROWN SUGAR (a.k.a. BLACK PUSSY) (Jagger, Richard)
1 December 1969: Muscle Shoals, Alabama. Producer: Jimmy Miller. Engineer: Glyn Johns, Jimmy Johnson.
*UK Single: 16 April 1971: No **2** – 13 weeks*
*UK LP STICKY FINGERS: 23 April 1971: No **1** – 25 weeks*
*USA Single: May 1971: No **1** – 12 weeks*
*USA LP STICKY FINGERS: June 1971: No **1** – 26 weeks*
*UK Compilation LP MADE IN THE SHADE: 6 June 1975: No **14** – 12 weeks*
*USA Compilation LP MADE IN THE SHADE: 6 June 1975: No **6** – 9 weeks*
*UK Re-released Single: June 1984: No **58** – 2 weeks*
Rolling Stones with Bobby Keys.

Brown Sugar is literally a rock and roll overdose – although critics who claim the song is about brown sugar *à la Mexicocaine* were becoming hooked themselves on too many drug references. The lyrical message written in the studio is, in fact, a lot more sordid. It concerns the slave trade and the *buannas* who buy girls for illicit purposes, and after their work is done in the cotton fields, 'hear the boss whip the women and taste them just around midnight'. The song's working title, derived from one of Mick's early lyrics, was soon dropped. Bobby Keys contributed enormously to the success of *Brown Sugar* – his driving sax is inspirational, but the rock riff merchant, Keith Richards, created the foundation for the huge hit single. Keith, also on the acoustic guitar, emphasizes the *Street Fighting* anthem similarity, while Jagger's 'Yeah, Yeah, Yeah, Woah' at the end prompts the ritual raised fist. The single was the first to be released on their own label (courtesy of Ahmet Ertegun and Atlantic Records) with a tongue logo designed by Andy Warhol. The Stones' relationship with Allen Klein had been strained for some time and the air was fraught with law suits and counter law suits. The Stones claimed Klein had duped them, their royalties having been deposited into Klein's company Nanker Phelge Music, Inc. instead of Nanker Phelge Music Ltd. A £29-million law suit was at issue and in July 1970 the Stones officially divorced themselves from Klein. Inevitably, there was a delay before any issue of new material and seventeen months elapsed before *Brown Sugar* hit the streets.

296. UNDER MY THUMB (Jagger, Richard)
6 December 1969: Altamont Speedway, Livermore, California.
Bootleg only.

Determined to put on a free show, and attempting to out-do Woodstock, the Stones' management searched California, where it would still be warm in December, for a suitable festival site. After much delay, Alta-mont was found, but this allowed little time to organize such an extrava-gant event. Support artists for a crowd of over 250,000 included Gram Parson's Flying Burrito Brothers, Crosby, Stills, Nash, and Young, Santana and the Jefferson Airplane. The Hell's Angels were the 'police' for the event. There had been some trouble during Jefferson Airplane's set, but things had simmered at dusk as the Stones were awaited on stage. Meanwhile, backstage, all was chaos. Fans and the Angels mixed freely with the Stones. The band scrambled their way to the stage and for a couple of numbers all was OK, despite the poor sound quality. It was during *Sympathy For The Devil* that outbursts of trouble started. Angels, armed with pool cues, fought with the crowd and mayhem generally ruled, stopping *Sympathy* before its opening rhythm had properly started. Keith Richards bravely uttered some strong words against the Angels, but Mick Jagger had lost his usual 'under my thumb' pull over the crowd. The Stones eventually restarted and jammed, playing the blues, for a few minutes. While *Under My Thumb* was sending out its strong bass rhythm the infamous killing occurred. Meredith Hunter, an eigh-teen-year-old youth with gun in hand, was seen pushing his way towards the stage. Instantly, the angels pounced on him; the ensuing struggle left Meredith Hunter dying from knife wounds. The Stones and the majority of the crowd were unaware until later of the awesome happening, the band still playing *Under My Thumb*. The show continued, the crowd, fed by the acid, lazily accepted the Stones, but the damage had been done and another nail had been placed in the coffin of the hippies' peace, love and understanding. The 1969 American tour had been filmed by the Maysles Brothers, and they witnessed on camera the macabre murder. It was Mick's idea to record the concert and release it as soon as possible, thus pre-empting the *Woodstock* film. It was released under the title *Gimmie Shelter*, and still does the cinematic rounds to this day.

297. COCKSUCKER BLUES (a.k.a. SCHOOLBOY BLUES) (Jagger, Richard)
June 1970: Olympic, London. Producer: Jimmy Miller. Engineer: Glyn Johns.
Bootleg only.

As the Stones terminated their contract with Decca an executive remind-ed them that they still had to deliver one further single. The Stones duly obliged, presenting them with the master tape of *Cocksucker Blues*. It was the Stones' last two-finger salute to the record company, who, through the years, continually voiced censorship against album covers and product alike. Decca were morally obliged not to release the 'X'-rated *Cocksucker Blues*. It is a slow blues song featuring just acoustic guitar and Mick Jagger's wailful tones. The lyrics freely describe homo-sexual practices. The track was later retitled *Schoolboy Blues* when it was included in the stage production of *The Trials of Oz* by Geoff Robertson. Original demos were recorded in a mobile recording unit in Newbury, Berkshire.

298. BITCH (Jagger, Richard)
*June 1970: Olympic, London. Producer: Jimmy Miller. Engineer: Glyn
Johns, Andy Jones, Chris Kimsey, Jimmy Johnson.
UK B-side Brown Sugar: 16 April 1971, June 1984
UK LP STICKY FINGERS: 23 April 1971: No 1 – 25 weeks
USA B-side Brown Sugar: May 1971
USA LP STICKY FINGERS: June 1971: No 1 – 26 weeks
UK Compilation LP MADE IN THE SHADE: 6 June 1975: No 14 – 12
weeks
USA Compilation LP MADE IN THE SHADE: 6 June 1975: No 6 – 9
weeks
UK Compilation LP TIME WAITS FOR NO ONE – ANTHOLOGY 1971
– 1977: May 1978
USA Compilation LP TIME WAITS FOR NO ONE – ANTHOLOGY
1971 – 1977: May 1978
Rolling Stones with Bobby Keys, Jimmy Miller, Jim Price.*

The Keith Richards/Bobby Keys partnership that started on *Live With
Me* and culminated on *Brown Sugar* proved fruitful on *Bitch*. The track
again centres on one of Keith's famous riffs, but on this occasion Jim Price
was used to enhance the brass sound. He was a friend of Bobby Keys and
played trumpet and piano on some of the STICKY FINGERS sessions.
Bitch was good enough to merit its own single status but due to some 'sex'
comments was banned from the air-waves.

299. MOONLIGHT MILE (a.k.a. **THE JAPANESE THING**) (Jagger, Richard)
*June 1970: Olympic, London. Producer: Jimmy Miller. Engineer: Glyn
Johns, Andy Jones, Chris Kimsey, Jimmy Johnson.
UK LP STICKY FINGERS: 23 April 1971: No 1 – 25 weeks
USA LP STICKY FINGERS: June 1971: No 1 – 26 weeks
Rolling Stones with Paul Buckmaster, Jim Price.*

Recording methods were changing considerably – the Stones had set up
a mobile unit in an air-conditioned truck and this was used by Keith
Richards early in 1970 to put some ideas (hence *The Japanese Thing*) on
to tape for the next album. *Moonlight Mile* was conceived in this way.
Mick Taylor took the beginnings and wrote the rest of the track – he felt it
deserved a co-writer credit, but Mick Jagger denied him. Paul Buckmaster, who was one of Elton John's cohort, arranged the strings to create
a track that was a significant change of direction for the band. Mick
Taylor plays a haunting acoustic guitar and the song gradually builds up
under Paul Buckmaster's direction, Jim Price being used to great effect
on piano. Keith Richards reckons part of his original guitar workings
were included near the end of the track.

300. I GOT THE BLUES (Jagger, Richard)
*June 1970: Olympic, London. Producer: Jimmy Miller. Engineer: Glyn
Johns, Andy Jones, Chris Kimsey, Jimmy Johnson.
UK LP STICKY FINGERS: 23 April 1971: No 1 – 25 weeks*

USA LP STICKY FINGERS: June 1971: No 1 – 26 weeks
Rolling Stones with Bobby Keys, Billy Preston, Jim Price.

Billy Preston, who had found brief pop fame with The Beatles in 1969 when he had played keyboards on *Get Back* and *Don't Let Me Down*, joined the Stones to play organ on this tease of the Stax sound. *I Got The Blues* is played in a slow blues mould and again includes the brass sounds of Bobby Keys and Jim Price. The outcome is not a classic – it could have sounded better if played at a faster tempo.

301. SWAY (Jagger, Richard)
June 1970: Olympic, London. Producer: Jimmy Miller. Engineer: Glyn Johns, Andy Johns, Chris Kimsey, Jimmy Johnson.
UK LP STICKY FINGERS: 23 April 1971: No 1 – 25 weeks
USA LP STICKY FINGERS: June 1971: No 1 – 26 weeks
USA B-side Wild Horses: June 1971
Rolling Stones with Nicky Hopkins, Paul Buckmaster.

Nicky Hopkins was rested on STICKY FINGERS following his hefty contribution to the BEGGARS BANQUET and LET IT BLEED albums. *Sway* is the only track he played on, playing with Buckmaster's orchestra and leaving Ian Stewart on the other cuts to cope with Jim Price, Billy Preston and Jimmy Dickinson. Mick Taylor displays some searing solo guitar work, a job with which Keith Richards felt uncomfortable. Keith was used to laying down riffs and providing the band with its unique rhythm. Mick Taylor was to add a heavier virtuoso dimension as demonstrated on *Sway*. Having left his guitar on the stand, with both Mick Taylor and Mick Jagger taking the guitar rôles, Keith helped out on vocals.

302. CAN'T YOU HEAR ME KNOCKING (Jagger, Richard)
June 1970: Olympic, London. Producer: Jimmy Miller. Engineer: Glyn Johns, Andy Johns, Chris Kimsey, Jimmy Johnson.
UK LP STICKY FINGERS: 23 April 1971: No 1 – 25 weeks
USA LP STICKY FINGERS: June 1971: No 1 – 26 weeks
Rolling Stones with Bobby Keys, Billy Preston, Jimmy Miller, Rocky Dijon.

Another guitar riff provides the basis for *Can't You Hear Me Knocking.* Keith Richards used it to test his new brother-in-arms, Mick Taylor, and sparred alike with Bobby Keys' sax, Billy Preston's organ and the percussion sounds of Jimmy Miller and Rocky Dijon. It was a 'jam' in the vein of *Goin' Home*. Keith moves aside half way through to allow Mick Taylor to practise his distant solos (sounds as though they were recorded in the corridor). The album, now almost complete, was left in the can until the band returned from their Autumn 1970 tour of Europe. In November various guitar overdubs were made, but a release awaited the outcome of the Klein publishing rights trials.

303. DEAD FLOWERS (Jagger, Richard)
June 1970: Olympic, London. Producer: Jimmy Miller. Engineer: Glyn Johns, Andy Johns, Chris Kimsey, Jimmy Johnson.

*UK LP STICKY FINGERS: 23 April 1971: No **1** – 25 weeks*
*USA LP STICKY FINGERS: June 1971: No **1** – 26 weeks*

Treading now on ever more familiar ground, *Dead Flowers* is another Nashville ringer. It features Ian Stewart on the piano and the country-sloven vocals of Mick Jagger on some humorously ironic lyrics. The love for country and western was not simply a popular fashion – the Stones seemed to have an in-built love for the music and country songs were included on most future albums. STICKY FINGERS featured a host of musicians and took seven months to record but, due to protracted record company deals and various law suits, was not released for a further ten to twelve months. Andy Warhol had designed the controversial cover – its sexual innuendo was not subtle, but the only country to object was Spain. The Spanish Group of Atlantic Records changed the cover and also substituted *Let It Rock* for the needle-inspired *Sister Morphine*. The album became their biggest selling release to date and topped the charts internationally. It heralded a new business acumen and launched the Stones into the 'seventies while their counterparts, The Beatles, remained entrenched in the 'sixties.

304. AIN'T GONNA LIE (a.k.a. **MEAN WOMAN BLUES**) (Jagger, Richard)
17/31 October 1970: Mobile, Newbury and Olympic Sound, London.
Producer: Jimmy Miller. Engineer: Glyn Johns.
Bootleg only.

Following the early summer recording session to complete tracks for the STICKY FINGERS album, September and the beginning of October was spent touring Europe (excluding Britain). These were the Stones' first European dates since 1967. The tour was a relatively quiet affair marred only by rioting and arrests in Milan, Italy on 1 October. Ironically, while Marianne Faithfull was being divorced by John Dunbar – Mick Jagger cited as the cause for the marriage failure – Bianca Perez Moreno de Macias accompanied Mick on the Stones' European travels. Separate hotel rooms indicated the situation was serious! *Ain't Gonna Lie* recorded in the serenity of the English countryside is a slow twelve-bar blues lightweight in content.

305. GOOD TIME WOMAN (a.k.a. **TUMBLING DICE**) (Jagger, Richard)
17/31 October 1970: Mobile, Newbury and Olympic Sound, London.
Producer: Jimmy Miller. Engineer: Glyn Johns.
Bootleg only.
Rolling Stones with Bobby Keys, Jim Price, Nicky Hopkins.

With a different set of lyrics, *Good Time Woman* was the embryo of *Tumbling Dice*. It is played at a faster pace, driven by the lead guitar of Mick Taylor and the integral boogie piano power of Ian Stewart. The marked difference between *Good Time Woman* and the eventual out-come *Tumbling Dice*, which is skilfully slovenly, is the rhythm artistry of Keith Richards. He performed the lead and rhythm guitar while Mick

Taylor played the bass. In so doing, he transformed the track from anonymity to chart success.

306. BROWN SUGAR (Jagger, Richard)
18 December 1970: Olympic, London. Producer: Jimmy Miller.
Engineer: Glyn Johns.
Bootleg only.
Rolling Stones with Eric Clapton, Bobby Keys, Al Kooper.

Jimmy Miller announced a joint birthday party at the Olympic Studio for Keith Richards and Bobby Keys. Axe hero Eric Clapton was invited and soon the party developed into a jam session. Glyn Johns managed to roll the tape on this cover of *Brown Sugar*. The result has always been classed as a unique piece of live studio work. The atmosphere is great: Al Kooper swings on his boogie piano, but the significant contribution was, of course, Eric Clapton's rasping slide guitar. Keith is heard prominently on the vocals for nobody had the heart to turn down his vocal level! Although obviously a bit rough, the spontaneity caused the Stones to wonder if it should be released officially, but technically it was not as good as the original recorded in Muscle Shoals and so version two remained on Olympic's dusty shelves.

307. LET IT ROCK (Anderson)
13 March 1971: Leeds University. Producer: Glyn Johns.
UK B-side Brown Sugar: 16 April 1971.

308. (I CAN'T GET NO) SATISFACTION (Jagger, Richard)
13 March 1971: Leeds University. Producer: Glyn Johns.
Bootleg only.

309. LITTLE QUEENIE (Berry)
13 March 1971: Leeds University. Producer: Glyn Johns.
Bootleg only.

Before the release of *Brown Sugar* and STICKY FINGERS the Stones embarked on a short nine-date tour of England and Scotland. They were the first concerts in Britain since the Hyde Park spectacle and the first tour since October 1966. It was billed in the press as a farewell tour because plans were advanced for the Stones to quit England for the tax haven of France. The English fans were rewarded with this tour and by way of a souvenir *Let It Rock* was coupled (only in Britain) with *Bitch*, on the flip-side of the new single *Brown Sugar*. The tour contained a foretaste of the new album but was predominantly based on the maxim good-time rock 'n' roll. *Let It Rock* is a good example. Keith Richards is in hot form on electric guitar playing Chuck Berry riffs while lead solos by Mick Taylor bombard the crawdaddy senses. *Let It Rock* was written by Chuck Berry under a pseudonym. Keith reckoned it to be one of his finest works. Chuck agreed, including it in a 'top ten list' of his own compositions. *Satisfaction* and *Little Queenie* capture the band in a hard-driving boogie frame of mind. Recordings from two concerts were bootlegged on the 1971 British tour, the aforementioned Leeds concert on 13 March courtesy of a live BBC broadcast, and a day later the gig at the Roundhouse in London. And so in the Spring, France beckoned, and on 12 May 1971, Mick Jagger formally hitched himself to Bianca Perez-Mora in St Tropez, on the French Riviera. Bianca, Nicaraguan by birth, an aspiring model/socialite, agreed to marry Mick just eight months after their first meeting in Paris.

7

EXILES ENJOY STAR STAR TREATMENT

MAY 1971 – APRIL 1974

310. SHAKE YOUR HIPS (a.k.a. **HIP SHAKE**) (Moore)
May–September 1971: Rolling Stones Mobile Unit, Nellcote, France.
Producer: Jimmy Miller. Engineer: Andy Johns, Glyn Johns, Joe
Zaganno, Jeremy Gee.
UK LP EXILE ON MAIN ST: 12 May 1972: No 1 – 16 weeks
USA LP EXILE ON MAIN ST: 12 May 1972: No 1 – 17 weeks
Rolling Stones with Bobby Keys, Jim Price.

This Slim Harpo (the late James Moore) composition is played in rockabilly fashion. Charlie Watts tick-tacks the rhythm throughout on the drum rim while the lead guitars interweave authentic 'fifties sounds. Mick Jagger warbles on the harmonica as the song fades out. The 1971 'Tropical Disease' sessions, as they became known, had started. They were recorded at a villa Keith Richards rented near Villefranche on the sunny French Côte D'Azur. The basement kitchen had been temporarily converted into a studio and electric wires led to the mobile recording unit stationed outside. This simple set-up created a unique laid-back atmosphere – the *vin ordinaire* and music flowed in voluminous quantities. Jimmy Miller reports that such was the quantity of material that two double albums could have been created from the available tapes.

311. VENTILATOR BLUES (Jagger, Richard, Taylor)
May–September 1971: Rolling Stones Mobile Unit, Nellcote, France.
Producer: Jimmy Miller. Engineer: Andy Johns, Glyn Johns, Joe
Zaganno, Jeremy Gee.
UK LP EXILE ON MAIN ST: 12 May 1972: No 1 – 16 weeks

USA LP EXILE ON MAIN ST: 12 May 1972: No **1** *– 17 weeks*
Rolling Stones with Bobby Keys, Jimmy Price, Nicky Hopkins.

As the title indicates, the song is a pondering blues track. The song-writing team includes for the second time the merits of Mick Taylor. The vocals are not sung in the usual blues mould and the horns contributed by the brass twins Bobby Keys and Jimmy Price do not exactly recreate the classic sound. However, Nicky Hopkins is suitably carried away on the piano.

312. **TORN AND FRAYED** (Jagger, Richard)
May–September 1971: Rolling Stones Mobile Unit, Nellcote, France.
Producer: Jimmy Miller. Engineer: Andy Johns, Glyn Johns, Joe
Zaganno, Jeremy Gee.
UK LP EXILE ON MAIN ST: 12 May 1972: No **1** *– 16 weeks*
USA LP EXILE ON MAIN ST: 12 May 1972: No **1** *– 17 weeks*
Rolling Stones with Al Perkins, Jim Price, Nicky Hopkins.

A country rock song which delves into the mythology of a touring band (a reckless, restless guitar player is hooked on codeine, his coat torn and frayed) gives this a certain self-mocking display. Mick Taylor and Jim Price put down their more familiar instruments to play bass and organ, respectively, while Al Perkins is featured on steel guitar, a one-off contribution which could have been made when the album was mixed at Sunset Sound, Hollywood, in the Fall of '71.

313. **LOVING CUP** (a.k.a. **GIVE ME A DRINK**) (Jagger, Richard)
May–September 1971: Rolling Stones Mobile Unit, Nellcote, France.
Producer: Jimmy Miller. Engineer: Andy Johns, Glyn Johns, Joe
Zaganno, Jeremy Gee.
UK LP EXILE ON MAIN ST: 12 May 1972: No **1** *– 16 weeks*
USA LP EXILE ON MAIN ST: 12 May 1972: No **1** *– 17 weeks*
Rolling Stones with Bobby Keys, Jim Price, Nicky Hopkins, Jimmy
Miller.

The original basis for this track was written prior to the 1969 Hyde Park concert and was performed there as *Give Me A Drink*. It was nearly recorded at the Muscle Shoals sessions in December 1969. The tone of the song is similar to *Torn And Frayed*. It does not follow the usual macho stance, but deals compassionately with a guy who is unable to spill the beans with his girl – one of Keith's foibles perhaps?! Engineer Jeremy (Bear) Gee was recruited by Ian Stewart to assist with the Mobile unit. Later in the year he took the unit to Montreux and played a successful rôle capturing the sound of heavy rock merchants Deep Purple on their Number 1 album, MACHINE HEAD.

314. **LET IT ROCK** (Anderson)
May–September 1971: Rolling Stones Mobile Unit, Nellcote, France.
Bootleg only.

A studio cover, as opposed to the live version that was initially released on the British B-side of *Brown Sugar*, has never been released and the exact recording origin is unknown. The instrumental breaks are taken by Mick Jagger on the harmonica, while Keith Richards is temporarily restrained on lead guitar.

315. TURD ON THE RUN (Jagger, Richard)

May–September 1971: Rolling Stones Mobile Unit, Nellcote, France.
Producer: Jimmy Miller. Engineer: Andy Johns, Glyn Johns, Joe Zaganno, Jeremy Gee.
UK LP EXILE ON MAIN ST: 12 May 1972: No 1 – 16 weeks
USA LP EXILE ON MAIN ST: 12 May 1972: No 1 – 17 weeks
Rolling Stones with Nicky Hopkins, Bill Plummer.

The problems of recording in a family situation at the villa were evident. Tempers became frayed, the band being particularly annoyed when Keith Richards would disappear for hours as he put his son, Marlon, to bed. He would reappear in the early hours ready to record until dawn. Other band members, bored at the delay, would venture into the night life of either Nice or Monte Carlo. The frustrations were accentuated by Mick Jagger who disappeared at regular intervals to visit his newly wedded, mid-term pregnant Bianca in Paris. It is surprising in these circumstances that such a cohesive album was created and Keith must take much of the credit. *Turd On The Run* is a short country-style rocker. The upright bass is played by Bill Plummer and the rebel yells at the end create 'fifties images. The subject matter is the thematic jungle disease.

316. ALL DOWN THE LINE (Jagger, Richard)

May–September 1971: Rolling Stones Mobile Unit, Nellcote, France.
Producer: Jimmy Miller. Engineer: Andy Johns, Glyn Johns, Joe Zaganno, Jeremy Gee.
UK LP EXILE ON MAIN ST: 12 May 1972: No 1 – 16 weeks
USA LP EXILE ON MAIN ST: 12 May 1972: No 1 – 17 weeks
USA B-side Happy: June 1972.
UK Compilation LP TIME WAITS FOR NO ONE – ANTHOLOGY 1971 – 1977: May 1978.
Rolling Stones with Bobby Keys, Jimmy Price, Nicky Hopkins, Jimmy Miller, Kathi McDonald, Bill Plummer.

One of the strong contenders on the album for a single release, it was considered at one time a stronger track than *Tumbling Dice* but it lost the battle and was displaced to the flip-side of *Happy*, a single which was only released in the States. *All Down The Line* has since featured as a favourite on most Stones' tours. It is easy to see why. It is an infectious up-beat rocker in the vein of some of their previously successful singles. The sax twins open up the throttle and create the familiar *Brown Sugar* clash with the axe men, Keith Richards and Mick Taylor. Bill Plummer helps out on bass, Jimmy Miller on percussion and a newcomer to the Stones' crew, Kathi McDonald, provides backing vocals. An alternative, acoustic run-through of the song was originally recorded in 1969. The pace is generally slower, Mick Jagger's vocals are more pronounced and less hurried.

317. TUMBLING DICE (a.k.a. **GOOD TIME WOMAN**) (Jagger, Richard)
May–September 1971: Rolling Stones Mobile Unit, Nellcote, France.
Producer: Jimmy Miller. Engineer: Andy Johns, Glyn Johns, Joe
Zaganno, Jeremy Gee.
UK Single: 14 April 1972: No **5** *– 8 weeks*
USA Single: 14 April 1972: No **7** *– 9 weeks*
UK LP EXILE ON MAIN ST: 12 May 1972: No **1** *– 16 weeks*
USA LP EXILE ON MAIN ST: 12 May 1972: No **1** *– 17 weeks*
UK Compilation LP MADE IN THE SHADE: 6 June 1975: No **14** *– 12 weeks*
USA Compilation LP MADE IN THE SHADE: 6 June 1975: No **6** *– 9 weeks*
Rolling Stones with Bobby Keys, Jim Price, Nicky Hopkins, Clydie King, Vanetta Fields.

Tumbling Dice obtained Top 10 positions on both sides of the Atlantic, but its spell in the charts was comparatively short-lived, compared with the Stones' previous single successes. Although not a strong single release, *Tumbling Dice* is a convincing album track. Mick Jagger contributes a guitar piece and Mick Taylor aids Bill Wyman on his bass lines. The song rocks along in a relaxed manner – Keith Richards plays some effortless guitar licks and on this occasion Mick is complemented by Clydie King and Vanetta Fields on backing vocals. The latter's vocals and some of Jimmy Miller's production finesse are missing on one bootlegged demo; another demo is governed by a slower pace, on which Keith Richards is heard more prominently on backing vocals. These versions may be the original 'Nellcote' material. The released version of *Tumbling Dice* is charmingly untogether, a knack which was being perfected by another skilfully slovenly British group The Faces who included Rod Stewart, a certain Ron Wood, and remnants of The Small Faces.

318. SWEET BLACK ANGEL (a.k.a. **BLACK ANGEL** (see album cover) and **BENT GREEN NEEDLES**) (Jagger, Richard)
May–September 1971: Rolling Stones Mobile Unit, Nellcote, France.
Producer: Jimmy Miller. Engineer: Andy Johns, Glyn Johns, Joe
Zaganno, Jeremy Gee.
UK B-side Tumbling Dice: 14 April 1972.
USA B-side Tumbling Dice: 14 April 1972.
UK LP EXILE ON MAIN ST: 12 May 1972: No **1** *– 16 weeks*
USA LP EXILE ON MAIN ST: 12 May 1972: No **1** *– 17 weeks*
Rolling Stones with Nicky Hopkins, 'Amyl Nitrate', Jimmy Miller.

Jimmy Miller provides a hypnotic percussive sound full of Caribbean flavour on this simple acoustic song. Mick Jagger saunters on the harmonica and a touch of the Brian Jones' sound is created by 'Amyl Nitrate' on the marimba. At a concert on the North American Tour on 4 June 1972

Sweet Black Angel was sympathetically dedicated to the exploits of a black militant, Angela Davis, who on that day was released from a framed 'conspiracy to murder' charge. *Sweet Black Angel* became a foretaste of the album as it was placed on the flip-side of *Tumbling Dice*. The song was captured on the slowest side of the double album. Mick Jagger arguing that EXILE was an album of four single sides and should not be played collectively but in twenty-minute bursts. An instrumental version of *Sweet Black Angel* has been bootlegged.

319. I JUST WANT TO SEE HIS FACE (a.k.a. JUST WANNA (see album cover)) (Jagger, Richard)
May–September 1971: Rolling Stones Mobile Unit, Nellcote, France.
Producer: Jimmy Miller. Engineer: Andy Johns, Glyn Johns, Joe Zaganno, Jeremy Gee.
UK LP EXILE ON MAIN ST: 12 May 1972: No 1 – 16 weeks
USA LP EXILE ON MAIN ST: 12 May 1972: No 1 – 17 weeks
Rolling Stones with Nicky Hopkins, Bill Plummer, Jimmy Miller, Clydie King, Vanetta Fields, Jerry Kirkland.

Just Wanna (see inset of album cover) fades in from the remnants of *Ventilator Blues*. It is a gospel-inspired song, complete with choralists – namely Clydie King, Vanetta Fields and Jerry Kirkland. These backing vocals were included at the mixing stage using the foundations of the initial track recorded at Nellcote. The unlikely Keith Richards delivers a haunting melody on piano and the normal rhythm section of Charlie Watts and Bill Wyman is enhanced by bass guitarists Bill Plummer and Mick Taylor. Jimmy Miller assists the percussion.

320. SWEET VIRGINIA (Jagger, Richard)
May–September 1971: Rolling Stones Mobile Unit, Nellcote, France.
Producer: Jimmy Miller. Engineer: Andy Johns, Glyn Johns, Joe Zaganno, Jeremy Gee.
UK LP EXILE ON MAIN ST: 12 May 1972: No 1 – 16 weeks
USA LP EXILE ON MAIN ST: 12 May 1972: No 1 – 17 weeks
Rolling Stones with Bobby Keys, Jim Price.

Keith Richards' fraternization with country and western music was evident at the 'Jungle Disease' sessions – while band members were arriving or eating he was usually seen playing 'cowboy' songs. Andy Johns, the engineer, hearing the outcome, was insistent that Keith should put out an album of his own songs. But Keith claimed he would request the services of the other Stones, thereby defeating the original purpose with a quasi-Stones product, a distorted logic which meant only the occasional release of a potential country classic. Ian Stewart managed to regain the piano seat momentarily from Nicky Hopkins on this pure country song, which stood apart from the other tracks on EXILE. It received full media attention via Wolfman Jack, the famous American disc-jockey. He played *Sweet Virginia* on his AM prime-network radio station KDAY. The song's reference to drugs of 'speed' and 'shit' ensured an air-wave hit with the youth, but it remained as an album cut only. Nashville survived to live another day!

321. **RIP THIS JOINT** (Jagger, Richard)

May–September 1971: Rolling Stones Mobile Unit, Nellcote, France.
Producer: Jimmy Miller. Engineer: Andy Johns, Glyn Johns, Joe Zaganno, Jeremy Gee.
*UK LP EXILE ON MAIN ST: 12 May 1972: No **1** – 16 weeks*
*USA LP EXILE ON MAIN ST: 12 May 1972: No **1** – 17 weeks*
*UK Compilation LP MADE IN THE SHADE: 6 June 1975: No **14** – 12 weeks*
*USA Compilation LP MADE IN THE SHADE: 6 June 1975: No **6** – 9 weeks*
Rolling Stones with Bill Plummer, Bobby Keys, Jim Price, Nicky Hopkins.

Kick ass and roll; the Stones shift their butts on this two-minute electric rock 'n' roller. Nicky Hopkins pounces on the black-and-white keys and the sax squeals in surprise while Bill 'winkle pickers Comet' Plummer plays the upright bass. The track's foundation, however, is the enraged guitar work of Keith Richards and the *Route 66* type lyrics of Mick Jagger which travel the States. Ah, let it rock, wham bam, round and round we go! Mention is made of the President, Richard Nixon, and the first lady, Pat Nixon.

322. **HAPPY** (Jagger, Richard)

May–September 1971: Rolling Stones Mobile Unit, Nellcote, France.
Producer: Jimmy Miller. Engineer: Andy Johns, Glyn Johns, Joe Zaganno, Jeremy Gee.
*UK LP EXILE ON MAIN ST: 12 May 1972: No **1** – 16 weeks*
*USA LP EXILE ON MAIN ST: 12 May 1972: No **1** – 17 weeks*
*USA Single: June 1972: No **22** – 4 weeks*
*UK Compilation LP MADE IN THE SHADE: 6 June 1975: No **14** – 12 weeks*
*USA Compilation LP MADE IN THE SHADE: 6 June 1975: No **6** – 9 weeks*
Rolling Stones with Bobby Keys, Jim Price, Nicky Hopkins, Jimmy Miller.

Happy is a simply brilliant rock song, full of optimistic euphoria. It revolves around one of Keith Richards' unique guitar riffs. He also supplies some bass guitar parts but most noticeably the lead vocal – the first occasion since *You Got The Silver*. Bobby Keys not only contributes some percussion work with Jimmy Miller, but again teams up with Jim Price to sway some brass sounds and mesh them with Keith Richards' guitar. It provided the Stones in July 1972 with a Top 30 American hit and was the second US single to be released from the double album. Britain was only granted the one single *Tumbling Dice*. *Happy* has since become a favourite on tours and during a long set it enabled Mick Jagger to rest and catch a quick malt liquor.

323. SOUL SURVIVOR (Jagger, Richard)
May–September 1971: Rolling Stones Mobile Unit, Nellcote, France.
Producer: Jimmy Miller. Engineer: Andy Johns, Glyn Johns, Joe
Zaganno, Jeremy Gee.
UK LP EXILE ON MAIN ST: 12 May 1972: No 1 – 16 weeks
USA LP EXILE ON MAIN ST: 12 May 1972: No 1 – 17 weeks
Rolling Stones with Nicky Hopkins.

The true lead guitar of Mick Taylor resumes on *Soul Survivor*. Keith
Richards provides a rhythm back drop and also lays down a bass line.
Nicky Hopkins is at the fore, taking a prime rôle on what is a very guitar-
and piano-orientated track. He was well used to the pressures of rec-
ording with the Stones. Mick Taylor, it is fair to say, did not settle so well.
The nomadic life was stretching his home situation and it was noticeable
on EXILE that he was not as inspiring as on the forthcoming GOATS
HEAD SOUP album.

324. STOP BREAKING DOWN (Johnson credited to 'trad arranged by Jagger, Richard' on album sleeve)
May–September 1971. Rolling Stones Mobile Unit, Nellcote, France.
Producer: Jimmy Miller. Engineer: Glyn Johns, Andy Johns, Joe
Zaganno, Jeremy Gee.
UK LP EXILE ON MAIN ST: 12 May 1972: No 1 – 16 weeks
USA LP EXILE ON MAIN ST: 12 May 1972: No 1 – 17 weeks
Rolling Stones with Nicky Hopkins.

A Robert Johnson classic, arranged by Jagger, Richard, Wyman, Taylor
and Watts into a semi-rhythm 'n' blues mould. Again, instrumentally the
lead is shared by Mick Taylor, who plays a rasping solo, and the piano is
styled on this occasion by Ian Stewart. Mick Jagger plays a guitar piece
and blows the life out of his harmonica.

325. ROCKS OFF (Jagger, Richard)
May–September 1971: Rolling Stones Mobile Unit, Nellcote, France.
Producer: Jimmy Miller. Engineer: Andy Johns, Glyn Johns, Joe
Zaganno, Jeremy Gee.
UK LP EXILE ON MAIN ST: 12 May 1972: No 1 – 16 weeks
USA LP EXILE ON MAIN ST: 12 May 1972: No 1 – 17 weeks
Rolling Stones with Bobby Keys, Jim Price, Nicky Hopkins.

Rocks Off is an arousing sleaze song of sexual incapability, the exploits
with a dancer friend being memorable. Bobby Keys and Jim Price drive
hard around the familiar playing of Keith 'Riff Hard'. It is the opening cut
on the first side of the double; a first side that leaves you breathless. The
Stones were aware that the release of a double album would inevitably
lead to claims that there were weak tracks but it was agreed that all
tracks were worth release. Commercially, it sold relatively well despite
costing more as a double. Many fans and critics alike argue that EXILE is
in fact the Stones' artistic peak, but as Mick says 'the sunshine bores the
daylights out of me'.

326. CASINO BOOGIE (Jagger, Richard)
May–September 1971: Rolling Stones Mobile Unit, Nellcote, France.
Producer: Jimmy Miller. Engineer: Andy Johns, Glyn Johns, Joe
Zaganno, Jeremy Gee.
UK LP EXILE ON MAIN ST: 12 May 1972: No 1 – 16 weeks
USA LP EXILE ON MAIN ST: 12 May 1972: No 1 – 17 weeks
Rolling Stones with Nicky Hopkins, Bobby Keys, Jim Price.

A boogie song in classic blues tradition. The music is more worthy than the clandestine, abstract lyrics – who plays suicidal Russian roulette these days? Mick Jagger accentuates the words, Keith Richards plays a hand of bass while Mick Taylor deals a mean lead. Nicky Hopkins is determined not to be forgotten and studies form in the corner. The Monte Carlo Casino had a lot to answer for.

327. LET IT LOOSE (Jagger, Richard)
May–September 1971: Rolling Stones Mobile Unit, Nellcote, France.
Producer: Jimmy Miller. Engineer: Andy Johns, Glyn Johns, Joe
Zaganno, Jeremy Gee.
UK LP EXILE ON MAIN ST: 12 May 1972: No 1 – 16 weeks
USA LP EXILE ON MAIN ST: 12 May 1972: No 1 – 17 weeks
Rolling Stones with Nicky Hopkins, Bobby Keys, Jim Price, Tammi
Lynn, Shirley Goodman, Mac Rebennack (Dr John), Vanetta Fields,
Clydie King, Joe Gree.

Let It Loose is an evocative 'holier than thou' song aided by an entourage of backing vocalists. Nicky Hopkins on keyboards shines for the first few verses until the Spanish-sounding horns of Jim Price take the struggle on half-way through. The Stones themselves were taking a side-saddle to the very capable session musicians. A rogue guitar line and an unpolished saxophone break can be heard on an out-take of the track. The backing vocal talents of Vanetta Fields and Clydie King have since been used on the Stones' solo projects such as Bill Wyman's STONE ALONE in 1976 and Ron Wood's 1234 in 1981.

328. SHINE A LIGHT (Jagger, Richard)
May–September 1971: Rolling Stones Mobile Unit, Nellcote, France.
Producer: Jimmy Miller. Engineer: Andy Johns, Glyn Johns, Joe
Zaganno, Jeremy Gee.
UK LP EXILE ON MAIN ST: 12 May 1972: No 1 – 16 weeks
USA LP EXILE ON MAIN ST: 12 May 1972: No 1 – 17 weeks
Rolling Stones with Nicky Hopkins, Bobby Keys, Jim Price, Billy
Preston, Clydie King, Joe Green, Vanetta Fields, Jerry Kirkland, Jimmy
Miller.

Featuring the expertise of Billy Preston on organ and piano, *Shine A Light* is essentially the anthem of the album. It incorporates gospel tones, torn images and sexual failings, all so prevalent on the album. It is played with a reggae beat and combines the talents of lead guitarist Mick Taylor, who contributes solo after solo, and the undoubted rising star of the company, Billy Preston.

329. EXILE ON MAIN STREET BLUES (Jagger, Richard)
*Week ending 29 April 1972: NME Flexi Disc: New Musical Express
music magazine.*

Following the release of the *Tumbling Dice* single the *New Musical
Express*, British weekly music paper, provided the fans with a sampler of
the album which was to be released in two weeks. Mick Jagger, plus a
piano accompaniment, is heard singing *Exile On Main Street Blues*
which incorporates various song titles from the album. Excerpts of tracks
featured are: *All Down The Line, Tumbling Dice, Shine A Light* and
Happy.

330. TUMBLING DICE (Jagger, Richard)
*April 1972: Rialto Theatre, Montreux, Switzerland.
Bootleg only.*

331. BLUEBERRY JAM (Nanker, Phelge)
*April 1972: Rialto Theatre, Montreux, Switzerland.
Bootleg only.*

332. SHAKE YOUR HIPS (Moore)
*April 1972: Rialto Theatre, Montreux, Switzerland.
Bootleg only.*

In April 1972 the EXILE ON MAIN ST double album was just about to be
released and the band found themselves in Switzerland rehearsing for
the American tour planned for June and July 1972. The reason for the
Swiss detour was that Anita Pallenberg had entered a private hospital to
deliver a daughter, Dandelion, and also to undergo treatment for drug
addiction. Keith naturally wished to remain in close proximity and the
band joined him. They rehearsed secretly in a disused cinema. *Blueberry Jam*, a traditional-style blues, is collectable material. Two versions
of *Tumbling Dice* are also performed and *Shake Your Hips* from EXILE
ON MAIN ST.

333. DON'T LIE TO ME (Berry)
*20/21 July 1972: Spectrum, Philadelphia, USA.
Bootleg only.
Rolling Stones with Bobby Keys.*

The Stones' Rock And Roll Circus hit America in the summer and performed to vast crowds. Riots were a by-product. *For sessionography
purposes it is not possible to document all live recordings on this and
future tours. The bootleggers' tenacity and prolific output make the task
impossible. Only previously unavailable material or tracks of musical
significance will therefore be mentioned.* To counter the unofficial
demand for live material, a double album of the tour, including support
artist Stevie Wonder, was planned. Artwork was prepared for a sleeve
design, but the product never made the shops due to Decca Records'
insistence that the new versions of Stones' old numbers could not be

released. One such number, *Don't Lie To Me*, a Chuck Berry rocker, was originally recorded at the Chess Studios in 1964. The Philadelphia live recording was the first time it had been heard because the 1964 studio version was not released on disc until 1975. The 1972 American tour was filmed by Robert Frank, the cuttings were edited and the film was provisionally titled 'Cocksucker Blues', but due to its X-rated content of mile high club activities was not released. Marshall Chess's film recording of the Stones', Fort Worth, Texas gig on the 24 June 1972 faired better – it was released in 1974 under the title 'Ladies and Gentlemen, The Rolling Stones'.

334. BLOOD RED WINE (Jagger, Richard)
November 1972: Elektra, Hollywood. Producer: Jimmy Miller.
Bootleg only.
Rolling Stones with Nicky Hopkins.

The EXILE ON MAIN ST sessions had been mixed and recorded at the Elektra studios and so the Stones returned nearly a year later to record EXILE out-takes and new songs. *Blood Red Wine* is a slow track with strumming acoustic guitars and a smooth piano providing the back-drop for Mick Jagger's mournful vocals.

335. TRAVELLIN' MAN (Jagger, Richard)
November 1972: Elektra, Hollywood. Producer: Jimmy Miller.
Bootleg only.
Rolling Stones with Nicky Hopkins.

An up-tempo number, used by Mick Taylor to whip his guitar into action. He plays a lengthy solo which ducks and dives for the duration of the track. All the Elektra tracks are available in stereo on bootleg and the sound quality is almost perfect. Some tracks originated from the EXILE sessions in France.

336. LEATHER JACKET (Jagger, Richard)
November 1972: Elektra, Hollywood. Producer: Jimmy Miller.
Bootleg only.
Rolling Stones with Nicky Hopkins.

Leather Jacket is an instrumental track; vocals may have been intended at a later date. The track consists solely of a repetitive melody supplied by Mick Taylor and is obviously unfinished.

337. DANCING IN THE LIGHT (Jagger, Richard)
November 1972: Elektra, Hollywood. Producer: Jimmy Miller.
Bootleg only.
Rolling Stones with Nicky Hopkins.

A Stones' instrumental featuring Nicky Hopkins on keyboard and the guitar work of Mick Taylor and Keith Richards.

338. POTTED SHRIMP (Jagger, Richard)
November 1972: Elektra, Hollywood. Producer: Jimmy Miller.
Bootleg only.
Rolling Stones with Nicky Hopkins.

Again an instrumental but featuring one of Keith Richards' riffs extracted from his extensive repertoire. This time it has an air of familiarity. It worried Keith that a riff he thought to be new may in fact have been a sound culled from his subconscious.

339. ALADDIN STORY (Jagger, Richard)
November 1972: Elektra, Hollywood. Producer: Jimmy Miller.
Bootleg only.
Rolling Stones with Jim Price, Nicky Hopkins.

This track certainly seemed to be a possibility for eventual release. The backing instrumentation includes horns and Nicky Hopkins on organ.

340. TRIDENT JAM (Unknown)
November 1972: Elektra, Hollywood. Producer: Jimmy Miller.
Bootleg only.

A guitarist work-out intended to warm up a session. The Stones would often play old standards to limber up prior to the principal recording of the evening. It was inevitable that some of these jam sessions ended up on an engineer's tape.

341. COMING DOWN AGAIN (Jagger, Richard)
25 November – December 1972: Dynamic Sounds, Kingston, Jamaica.
Producer: Jimmy Miller. Engineer: Andy Johns. Assistant Engineer:
Carlton Lee, Howard Kilgour, Doug Bennett.
UK LP GOATS HEAD SOUP: 31 August 1973: No 1 – 14 weeks
USA LP GOATS HEAD SOUP: 31 August 1973: No 1 – 19 weeks
Rolling Stones with Jimmy Miller, Pascal, Rebop, Nicky Hopkins,
Bobby Keys, Jim Horn, Chuck Finley.

Nicky Hopkins gently nestles his way into *Coming Down Again*, thereby starting the so-called 'Goats Head Patties' sessions in November 1972. They lasted four weeks and were consolidated by Jimmy Miller to produce the GOATS HEAD SOUP album. Keith Richards wrote this soft country-style song and he also featured in the singing role on various verses ('Where are all my friends?'). His wah-wah guitar effects helped to create a soft edge upon which Nicky Hopkins so instinctively thrived.

342. WINTER (Jagger, Richard)
25 November – December 1972: Dynamic Sounds, Kingston, Jamaica.
Producer: Jimmy Miller. Engineer: Andy Johns. Assistant Engineer:
Carlton Lee, Howard Kilgour, Doug Bennett. String arrangement:
Nicky Harrison.
UK LP GOATS HEAD SOUP: 31 August 1973: No 1 – 14 weeks

USA LP GOATS HEAD SOUP: 31 August 1973: No **1** *– 19 weeks*
Rolling Stones with Jimmy Miller, Pascal, Rebop, Nicky Hopkins.

Winter is an evocative reminder of North winds and Christmas-tree
lights. Nicky Harrison's strings escalate the song to an epic status. But
Mick Jagger contributed a guitar line or two to keep the track safely on
the ground! Jimmy Miller was not totally happy with the finished vocals.
He wanted something a little more powerful but Mick, having laid down
three or four takes, was called away from the studio by Bianca and the
'magic' take was never made. Mick Taylor's unnerving lead guitar helps
to make this one of the most powerful tracks originating from what were
dubbed the 'Jamaican Patties' sessions.

343. SEPARATELY (Jagger, Richard)
25 November – December 1972: Dynamic Sounds, Kingston, Jamaica.
Producer: Jimmy Miller.
Bootleg only.
Rolling Stones with Nicky Hopkins.

An instrumental which features Nicky Hopkins on keyboard and the
slightly echoed guitar of Mick Taylor. Keith Richards or Mick Jagger
accompany the unreleased track on acoustic guitar.

344. WHO AM I (SEE I LOVE YOU)? (Jagger, Richard)
25 November – December 1972: Dynamic Sounds, Kingston, Jamaica.
Producer: Jimmy Miller.
Bootleg only.

Rightly discarded as substandard. *Who Am I To Say I Love You?* is
played with a repetitive calypso beat.

345. CAN YOU HEAR THE MUSIC (Jagger, Richard)
25 November – December 1972: Dynamic Sounds, Kingston, Jamaica.
Producer: Jimmy Miller. Engineer: Andy Johns. Assistant Engineer:
Carlton Lee, Howard Kilgour, Doug Bennett.
UK LP GOATS HEAD SOUP: 31 August 1973: No **1** *– 14 weeks*
USA LP GOATS HEAD SOUP: 31 August 1973: No **1** *– 19 weeks*
Rolling Stones with Jimmy Miller, Pascal, Rebop, Nicky Hopkins, Jim
Horn.

The entire GOATS HEAD SOUP session credits the percussion works of
Pascal and Rebop, local session musicians. Rebop had also played with
Stevie Winwood. They are heard along with Charlie Watts and Jimmy
Miller on *Can You Hear The Music?*, a strange rhetorical, almost 'psy-
chedelia revisited' track which explores synthesized vocal playbacks
and the eerie flute playing of Jim Horn. The original guitar riff written by
Keith Richards is lost in the track's unintended complexity. Mick Taylor
contributes the main guitar lines.

346. DANCING WITH MR D (Jagger, Richard)

25 November – December 1972: Dynamic Sounds, Kingston, Jamaica.
Producer: Jimmy Miller. Engineer: Andy Johns. Assistant Engineer:
Carlton Lee, Howard Kilgour, Doug Bennett.
UK LP GOATS HEAD SOUP: 31 August 1973: No 1 – 14 weeks
USA LP GOATS HEAD SOUP: 31 August 1973: No 1 – 19 weeks
USA B-side Doo Doo Doo Doo (Heartbreaker): December 1973.
UK Compilation LP TIME WAITS FOR NO ONE – ANTHOLOGY 1971
– 1977: May 1978
Rolling Stones with Jimmy Miller, Pascal, Rebop, Nicky Hopkins.

Sympathy For The Devil Part Two, and the album's opening cut which delves into the more day-to-day exploits of 'Mister Fire and Brimstone'. The tantalizing dealings with Satan seemed to have a voodoo effect on the Stones' supporting cast. Andy Johns became ill and was unable to finish the sessions, while Jimmy Miller managed to hang on, but fell emaciated to the wayside and was not used again as a Stones' producer. The doomsday images were heightened by the photographic artwork of David Bailey on the album cover. This featured the band in funereal mask poses. *Dancing* is one of the LP's few up-beat numbers. It was one of the album cuts that stood the test of time, being used as a single flip-side in America and also as fodder for subsequent tours.

347. ANGIE (Jagger, Richard)

25 November – December 1972: Dynamic Sounds, Kingston, Jamaica.
Producer: Jimmy Miller. Engineer: Andy Johns. Assistant Engineer:
Carlton Lee, Howard Kilgour, Doug Bennett. String arrangement:
Nicky Harrison.
UK Single: 20 August 1973: No 5 – 10 weeks
USA Single: 20 August 1973: No 1 – 13 weeks
UK LP GOATS HEAD SOUP: 31 August 1973: No 1 – 14 weeks
USA LP GOATS HEAD SOUP: 31 August 1973: No 1 – 19 weeks
UK Compilation LP MADE IN THE SHADE: 6 June 1975: No 14 – 12 weeks
USA Compilation LP MADE IN THE SHADE: 6 June 1975: No 6 – 9 weeks
UK Compilation LP TIME WAITS FOR NO ONE – ANTHOLOGY 1971
– 1977: May 1978
Rolling Stones with Jimmy Miller, Pascal, Rebop, Nicky Hopkins.

The gently strumming acoustic guitars of Keith Richards and Mick Taylor, the soft piano touch of Nicky Hopkins and the strings incorporated by Nicky Harrison aided and abetted a world-wide hit single. *Angie* was the first ballad to be released as a single in Britain, and the public, although at first shocked by the incongruous nature of the song, launched it to Number 5 in the UK; in the States and other countries it became a mighty Number 1. It must be remembered that at this time the Stones were contending for chart positions in Britain with a record-buying public purchasing Donny Osmond, The Carpenters and Gary Glitter. In America, at least, they were still dealing with contemporary artists Cher (whom they knocked off the top position) and Eddie Kendricks, formerly of The Temptations. Rumours abounded that the song was about David Bowie's wife, Angela, who had been seen socially in Jagger's company. A Michael Lindsay-Hogg promotional film accompanied the release of *Angie*. The band are shown sitting on the stage edge resplendent in flared suits as they perform the song. Rose petals flutter down, creating a languid, inert atmosphere – Charlie and Bill seemingly nod off at the end.

348. SILVER TRAIN (Jagger, Richard)
25 November – December 1972: Dynamic Sounds, Kingston, Jamaica.
Producer: Jimmy Miller. Engineer: Andy Johns. Assistant Engineer:
Carlton Lee, Howard Kilgour, Doug Bennett.
UK B-side Angie: 20 August 1973
USA B-side Angie: 20 August 1973
UK LP GOATS HEAD SOUP: 31 August 1973: No 1 – 14 weeks
USA LP GOATS HEAD SOUP: 31 August 1973: No 1 – 19 weeks
Rolling Stones with Jimmy Miller, Pascal, Rebop.

Mick Jagger and Keith Richards wrote *Silver Train* for the talented white bluesman, Johnny Winter. He recorded it for single release in the Spring of 1973, pre-empting the Stones' version which was released as a flip-side antidote to the *Angie* single. Ian Stewart is heard rocking on piano while Mick Jagger honks an aggressive harp and plays a lick of electric guitar. The main guitars of Mick Taylor and Keith Richards slide furiously up and down the guitar fretboards on what is a well-heeled south-bound blues rocker. Two out-takes can be heard on bootleg recordings; one is very similar to the original, the other is a rarer acoustic version, which uses a completely different vocal track to the finished article. The latter was probably recorded in 1969/70 at the Olympic Studios.

349. 100 YEARS AGO (Jagger, Richard)
25 November – December 1972: Dynamic Sounds, Kingston, Jamaica.
Producer: Jimmy Miller. Engineer: Andy Johns. Assistant Engineer:
Carlton Lee, Howard Kilgour, Doug Bennett.
UK LP GOATS HEAD SOUP: 31 August 1973: No 1 – 14 weeks
USA LP GOATS HEAD SOUP: 31 August 1973: No 1 – 19 weeks
Rolling Stones, Jimmy Miller, Pascal, Rebop, Billy Preston.

Written in the late 'sixties/early 'seventies by Mick Jagger, *100 Years Ago* was eventually recorded and released for the GOATS HEAD SOUP album. Billy Preston was invited to perform at one of the 'Goat Patties' sessions and this time he plays the clavinet. The Stones were lucky to have a wealth of keyboardsmen to call upon. Mick Taylor unpretentiously delivers a winding and lengthy guitar solo using talents nurtured from his crusading days with the John Mayall's Bluesbreakers.

350. HIDE YOUR LOVE (Jagger, Richard)
25 November – December 1972: Dynamic Sounds, Kingston, Jamaica.
Producer: Jimmy Miller. Engineer: Andy Johns. Assistant Engineer:
Carlton Lee, Howard Kilgour, Doug Bennett.

UK LP GOATS HEAD SOUP: 31 August 1973: No 1 – 14 weeks
USA LP GOATS HEAD SOUP: 31 August 1973: No 1 – 19 weeks
Rolling Stones with Jimmy Miller, Pascal, Rebop.

Hide Your Love is one of the weakest tracks recorded at the sessions. It includes Mick Jagger tampering in out-take manner on piano and Mick Taylor who again attempts to revive a flagging song with a blistering lead solo. The track has a poor ending which served to underline an over-all lack of depth and power, a criticism of the GOATS HEAD sessions. The up-tempo numbers such as *Star Star* and *Heartbreaker* are the gems. *Winter* and *Angie* are the only memorable slower tracks. The band's recent album successes demanded a consistent standard of work, which was not forthcoming on GOATS HEAD SOUP.

351. SAVE ME (Jagger, Richard)
25 November – December 1972: Dynamic Sounds, Kingston, Jamaica.
Producer: Jimmy Miller.
Bootleg only.

The up-tempo sound of *Save Me* is a refreshing, humorous song. With completed lyrics it could have been considered suitable for release, although the band were conscious that too many rock numbers could have spoilt the album's balance. In hindsight, they may have reconsidered this decision.

352. DOO DOO DOO DOO (HEARTBREAKER) (Jagger, Richard)
25 November – December 1972: Dynamic Sounds, Kingston, Jamaica.
Producer: Jimmy Miller. Engineer: Andy Johns. Assistant Engineer: Carlton Lee, Howard Kilgour, Doug Bennett.
UK LP GOATS HEAD SOUP: 31 August 1973: No 1 – 14 weeks
USA LP GOATS HEAD SOUP: 31 August 1973: No 1 – 19 weeks
USA Single: December 1973: No 15 – 6 weeks
UK Compilation LP MADE IN THE SHADE: 6 June 1975: No 14 – 12 weeks
USA Compilation LP MADE IN THE SHADE: 6 June 1975: No 6 – 9 weeks
Rolling Stones with Jimmy Miller, Pascal, Rebop, Billy Preston, Bobby Keys, Jim Price, Jim Horn, Chuck Finley.

A Mick Taylor 'wah-wah' guitar purposefully opens the second American single to be taken from the album. Keith Richards takes time out to play bass and the song is swept along by the horn arrangement inspired by Jim Price. The lyrics are vengeful, describing two incidents in the alleyways of New York: a boy shot by police in a case of mistaken identity and the OD of a ten-year-old girl on a street corner. There was no prescribed solution, but one can be sure the New York Police did not help to make it a Number 15 hit!

353. STAR STAR (a.k.a. STARFUCKER) (Jagger, Richard)
25 November – December 1972: Dynamic Sounds, Kingston, Jamaica.

Producer: Jimmy Miller. Engineer: Andy Johns. Assistant Engineer: Carlton Lee, Howard Kilgour, Doug Bennett.
UK LP GOATS HEAD SOUP: 31 August 1973: No **1** *– 14 weeks*
USA LP GOATS HEAD SOUP: 31 August 1973: No **1** *– 19 weeks*
USA B-side Doo Doo Doo Doo (Heartbreaker): December 1973
UK Compilation LP TIME WAITS FOR NO ONE – ANTHOLOGY 1971 – 1977: May 1978
Rolling Stones with Jimmy Miller, Pascal, Rebop.

One of the final tracks recorded at the GOATS HEAD sessions, *Star Star* created a furore with Atlantic Record's President Ahmet Ertegun. 'Starfucker' hit too close to the belt for his liking and he insisted it was retitled on the album's sleeve work to *Star Star*. The lyrics are certainly racy: 'bet you keep your pussy clean' and 'giving head to Steve McQueen'. Mick defended that he only wrote about what he saw (he must have been friendly with Steve) and star fuckers are a way of life in the entertainment industry. Atlantic Records were keen to disrupt the release of the album due to the inclusion of this track and told the Stones that Steve McQueen would sue. The band quickly responded by sending him a tape of the song and requested his written permission to release it, which he simply did. It is fair to say, however, that Atlantic Records were conscious of anti-pornographic legislation being billed in Congress; and so the American version of *Star Star* was remixed to bludgeon out the reference to 'pussy' and lyric sheets were also suitably altered – the chorus became 'starbucker'! It was ironic that for promotion purposes, a sampler EP of GOATS HEAD SOUP featured four tracks, including the original mix of *Star Star* (side one, track one), was released with the full blessing of Atlantic. The BBC in Britain banned the song from all air-play. The music itself is basically the definitive rip-off of a Chuck Berry song that has never been written. Keith Richards' R 'n' B riff is lead guitar at its best and served to put the cream on top of an otherwise sagging album.

354. THROUGH THE LONELY NIGHTS (Jagger, Richard)
25 November – December 1972 or March 1973: Dynamic Sounds, Kingston, Jamaica. Producer: The Glimmer Twins. Engineer: Keith Harwood, Glyn Johns.
UK B-side It's Only Rock 'N' Roll: 26 July 1974
USA B-side It's Only Rock 'N' Roll: 26 July 1974
Rolling Stones with Jimmy Page.

With the declining health of Andy Johns and Jimmy Miller, the Stones were left officially to try their production techniques on some out-takes and also two tracks, *Through The Lonely Nights* and *Tops*, which received belated official releases. Keith Harwood, who had been working with Led Zeppelin, stepped in to engineer these tracks, and out-takes permanently locked up include *Jamaica*, *After Muddy And Charlie* and *Chris Cross. Through The Lonely Nights* appeared as the flip-side of the 1974 single, *It's Only Rock 'N' Roll* and as such is obviously a bonus issue; an indication that the Stones themselves wanted the track released. It is an acoustic ballad and is said to feature guitarist Jimmy Page, a rumour which could easily be a fact since Keith Harwood, a Led Zeppelin engineer, was involved in the sessions and Jimmy Page was known to the Stones having previously played on demo material, notably the tracks available on the Decca-compiled METAMORPHIS album.

355. TOPS (Jagger, Richards)
25 November – December 1972 or March 1973: Dynamic Sounds, Kingston, Jamaica. Producer: The Glimmer Twins.
UK LP TATTOO YOU: 24 August 1981: No 2 – 29 weeks
USA LP TATTOO YOU: 24 August 1981: No 1 – 30 weeks
Rolling Stones with Nicky Hopkins.

Tops resurfaced on the TATTOO YOU album eight to nine years later, much to Mick Taylor's annoyance since he had departed the Stones. He sued the Stones for royalties as there was no credit on the album cover to suggest he was playing and it was obvious the basis of the track was the one recorded back in Jamaica in 1972/73. Various over-dubs may have been overlaid on to the original take but both Bill Wyman and Keith Richards have since indicated that very little alteration was made to the initial recording. It can be noted that since *Tops* was released in 1981, Keith Richards is credited under his full name (i.e. with 's').

356. BYE BYE JOHNNY (Berry)
28 September 1973: Olympiahalle, Munich, West Germany. Bootleg only.
Rolling Stones with Bobby Keys, Billy Preston.

1973 was a busy year for the Stones Touring Party. Having pulled off the American leg of the world tour in the summer of 1972 they concentrated on the European leg in 1973. However, they did not forget the 'down under' stretch, visiting Hawaii, Hong Kong, New Zealand and Australia in January and February 1973. In September and October they played Europe, concentrating on the home countries, England and Scotland (a planned concert at Cardiff Castle, Wales was cancelled) and also Germany. *Bye Bye Johnny* illustrates the band's desire to rock it up. Bobby Keys is in excellent form on sax and Billy Preston aids the band on keyboards. The tour also illustrated the new-found camp, glitter image. Make-up was lavish and Mick Jagger wore an array of zipped jump-suits, particularly revealing at crutch level. In June Keith Richards found that British law was still ready to pounce on tour-stressed stars when he was arrested for possession of cannabis and an unauthorized handgun. For the rest of the year band members fulfilled their own projects and whims, which included the recording of Bill Wyman's first solo album MONKEY GRIP – he was the first member to complete a solo project.

357. AIN'T TOO PROUD TO BEG (Whitfield, Holland)
March–April 1974: Musicland, Munich, West Germany. Producer: The Glimmer Twins. Engineer: Andy Johns, Keith Harwood. Assistant Engineers: Tapani Tapanainen, Rod Thear, Howard Kilgour, Mac 'Munich', George Chkiantz.

*UK LP IT'S ONLY ROCK 'N' ROLL: 18 October 1974: No **2** – 9 weeks*
*USA LP IT'S ONLY ROCK 'N' ROLL: 18 October 1974: No **1** – 11 weeks*
*USA Single: October 1974: No **17**   7 weeks*
Rolling Stones with Billy Preston, Ed Leach, Ray Cooper.

The Stones entered the München Studios in 1974 and set about performing material for an album planned for a quick release later in the year.
This recording format was a return to the spontaneity captured in sessions such as BEGGARS BANQUET. However, the use of Jimmy Miller as
the band's producer was now at an amicable end so Mick Jagger and
Keith Richards naturally drifted into producing themselves; hence the
Glimmer Twins (a pseudonym for the duo originating from the band's
motto 'Give us a Glimmer') credited with production. Very occasionally,
Tamla Motown tracks provided the band with undoubted inspiration;
their copies of *Can I Get A Witness* and *Hitch Hike* are instantly recal-
lable. It is no surprise that they tackled this Temptations number giving it
the Stones treatment in their own unique manner, thereby allowing a new
generation to verse themselves in Motown history. Billy Preston leads the
band into the song on clavinet, promptly followed by Charlie Watts who
launches into the beat, kicking his foot pedals. The track also features
Elton John's percussion man, Ray Cooper, on bongos and Ed Leach
rapping the cowbell. Keith Richards is inspirational, playing a particularly raw electric guitar. *Ain't Too Proud To Beg* was released as a single in
the States just reaching the Billboard Top 20 – The Temptations version
had previously peaked at Number 13 in November 1966.

358. DRIFT AWAY (Gray)
March–April 1974: Musicland, Munich. Producer: The Glimmer Twins.
Bootleg only.
Rolling Stones with Nicky Hopkins.

So you want to get lost in rock and roll? This the Stones adequately do on
Dobie Gray's 1973 USA hit. Mick Jagger sings the lyrics with sparse
accompaniment, save the piano work of Nicky Hopkins. Recorded live in
the studio, it is a typical studio 'run-through'.

359. IF YOU CAN'T ROCK ME (Jagger, Richard)
March–April 1974: Musicland, Munich, West Germany. Producer: The
Glimmer Twins. Engineer: Andy Johns, Keith Harwood. Assistant
Engineers: Tapani Tapanainen, Rod Thear, Howard Kilgour, Mac
'Munich', George Chkiantz.
*UK LP IT'S ONLY ROCK 'N' ROLL: 18 October 1974: No **2** – 9 weeks*
*USA LP IT'S ONLY ROCK 'N' ROLL: 18 October 1974: No **1** – 11 weeks*
Rolling Stones with Billy Preston, Ray Cooper.

The Stones' tax exile status meant that they could not record in Britain and
temporarily bored with American shores, they landed in Munich. *If You
Can't Rock Me*, the opening cut, sets the tone for a non-revolutionary but
competent album. The band's on stage and it's one of those nights – 'let's
rock and roll'. Charlie Watts' drum sound is more upfront, resonating like

a machine gun, while Mick Taylor's guitar pierces the airwaves through Keith Richards' incessant riff machine.

360. FINGERPRINT FILE (Jagger, Richard)
March–April 1974: Musicland, Munich, West Germany. Producer: The Glimmer Twins. Engineer: Andy Johns, Keith Harwood, Glyn Johns. Assistant Engineers: Tapani Tapanainen, Rod Thear, Howard Kilgour, Mac 'Munich', George Chkiantz.
UK LP IT'S ONLY ROCK 'N' ROLL: 18 October 1974: No 2 – 9 weeks
USA LP IT'S ONLY ROCK 'N' ROLL: 18 October 1974: No 1 – 11 weeks
Rolling Stones with Billy Preston, Nicky Hopkins, Ray Cooper, Charlie Jolly.

Standing at six minutes and forty seconds, *Fingerprint File* is the longest track on IT'S ONLY ROCK 'N' ROLL. *Fingerprint* describes the paranoia of an American society with Mick Jagger playing the role of a guy being followed by the F.B.I. His vocals are the key to the theme of the song as he hustles the song's rhythm forward in rap manner. Mick Jagger also takes up a guitar joining the 'slaves of rhythm', while Bill Wyman and Mick Taylor experiment with synthesizers. The tabla player is an unknown quantity – Charlie Jolly. Glyn Johns is credited solely with mixing the resultant track, his one and only contribution to the album. *Fingerprint File* is the ultimate studio track, using all available techniques to create a unique atmosphere.

361. TILL THE NEXT GOODBYE (Jagger, Richard)
March–April 1974: Musicland, Munich, West Germany. Producer: The Glimmer Twins. Engineer: Andy Johns, Keith Harwood. Assistant Engineers: Tapani Tapanainen, Rod Thear, Howard Kilgour, Mac 'Munich', George Chkiantz.
UK LP IT'S ONLY ROCK 'N' ROLL: 18 October 1974: No 2 – 9 weeks
USA LP IT'S ONLY ROCK 'N' ROLL: 18 October 1974: No 1 – 11 weeks
Rolling Stones with Nicky Hopkins, Ray Cooper.

This is a country-sounding song featuring Jaggeresque lilted vocals and steel guitar work. It is reminiscent of earlier workings and may have originated from previous sessions, for instance the EXILE ON MAIN STREET period. Nicky Hopkins contributes a piano line which is over-familiar. In short, it is adequate, but is also on the verge of being a throw-away.

362. IT'S ONLY ROCK 'N' ROLL (BUT I LIKE IT) (Jagger, Richard)
March–April 1974: Musicland, Munich, West Germany. Producer: The Glimmer Twins. Engineer: Andy Johns, Keith Harwood. Assistant Engineers: Tapani Tapanainen, Rod Thear, Howard Kilgour, Mac 'Munich', George Chkiantz.
UK Single: 26 July 1974: No 10 – 7 weeks
USA Single: 26 July 1974: No 16 – 7 weeks
UK LP IT'S ONLY ROCK 'N' ROLL: 18 October 1974: No 2 – 9 weeks

USA LP IT'S ONLY ROCK 'N' ROLL: 18 October 1974: No **1** *– 11 weeks*
UK Compilation LP MADE IN THE SHADE: 6 June 1975: No **14** *– 12 weeks*
USA Compilation LP MADE IN THE SHADE: 6 June 1975: No **6** *– 9 weeks*
Rolling Stones with Ron Wood, Ray Cooper, Kenny Jones, Willy Weeks, David Bowie.

The reason for such a personnel gathering on this record is mainly due to the inimitable Ron Wood. He had played for many years with Rod Stewart and The Faces and in 1974 had started to record a solo project titled I'VE GOT MY OWN ALBUM TO DO. Keith Richards, Mick Taylor and Mick Jagger contributed quite extensively to this album. One evening, *It's Only Rock And Roll* started to evolve. Mick Jagger and Ron Wood were on guitars, Willie Weeks on bass guitar, Kenny Jones the drums and David Bowie took some backing vocals. Ron Wood handed the end product to Mick Jagger who took the tape back to Munich. Guitar overdubs were made by Keith Richards – rumour has it that Ron's lead part was wiped by Keith, the vocals were redone and Ian Stewart supplied a piano melody. Mick Taylor was in hospital for some of the Munich sessions, and had missed one of the two major get-togethers. Perhaps this is why he made some rather jaded remarks concerning the song's forced rock and roll nature. *It's Only Rock 'n' Roll* is not an out-and-out rocker – it is played mid-tempo with some acoustic parts. It seemed contrived at the time, particularly the 'suicide on stage' lyrics, combating with mid-'seventies glam rock stars. But it has stood the test of time, being featured on most Stones' tours since its release. To promote the single release, a Michael Lindsay-Hogg film was shot. The Stones, dressed in mock American Navy uniforms, entered a large blown up perspex tent and performed the single. All was normal until foam bubbles started to enter the tent at such a pace that they were soon shoulder high in them – not a problem until they realize that Charlie Watts is still sitting at his drum kit. He is seen exiting stage right, not amused!

363. **IF YOU REALLY WANT TO BE MY FRIEND** (Jagger, Richard)

March–April 1974: Musicland, Munich, West Germany. Producer: The Glimmer Twins. Engineer: Andy Johns, Keith Harwood. Assistant Engineers: Tapani Tapanainen, Rod Thear, Howard Kilgour, Mac 'Munich', George Chkiantz.
UK LP IT'S ONLY ROCK 'N' ROLL: 18 October 1974: No **2** *– 9 weeks*
USA LP IT'S ONLY ROCK 'N' ROLL: 18 October 1974: No **1** *– 11 weeks*
Rolling Stones with Nicky Hopkins, Ray Cooper, Blue Magic.

A slow, pleading love song, it has some charm. Backing vocals are provided by an acquaintance, Blue Magic, which give it some distinctive qualities; Mick Taylor accordingly responds with a nimble solo, but the track is again light-weight, not really tugging on the intended heart strings, but more forceful than *Till The Next Goodbye*.

364. TIME WAITS FOR NO ONE (Jagger, Richard)

March–April 1974: Musicland, Munich, West Germany. Producer: The Glimmer Twins. Engineer: Andy Johns, Keith Harwood. Assistant Engineers: Tapani Tapanainen, Rod Thear, Howard Kilgour, Mac 'Munich', George Chkiantz.
*UK LP IT'S ONLY ROCK 'N' ROLL: 18 October 1974: No **2** – 9 weeks*
*USA LP IT'S ONLY ROCK 'N' ROLL: 18 October 1974: No **1** – 11 weeks*
UK Compilation LP TIME WAITS FOR NO ONE – ANTHOLOGY 1971 – 1977: May 1978
UK Compilation LP SUCKING IN THE SEVENTIES: May 1981
*USA Compilation LP SUCKING IN THE SEVENTIES: May 1981: No **15** – 5 weeks*
Rolling Stones with Nicky Hopkins, Ray Cooper.

If artifacts are required to immortalize an individual then the guitar virtuoso performance by Mick Taylor on *Time Waits For No One* is his vinyl *pièce de résistance*. (Carlos Santana has been trying to copy the style displayed ever since!?) The Stones were later to honour this distinction by releasing a compilation of works called TIME WAITS FOR NO ONE–ANTHOLOGY 1971–1977 in May 1978. *Time Waits For No One* took prime spot on side one and was the only track to come from the 1974 era, hence stating its importance. In the 'eighties another compilation SUCKING IN THE SEVENTIES, also included *Time Waits For No One*. Mick Taylor, frustrated at the lack of credence given to his song-writing talents, was beginning to show signs that the domination by Jagger and Richards was stultifying his ability.

365. LUXURY (Jagger, Richard)

March–April 1974: Musicland, Munich, West Germany. Producer: The Glimmer Twins. Engineer: Andy Johns, Keith Harwood. Assistant Engineers: Tapani Tapanainen, Rod Thear, Howard Kilgour, Mac 'Munich', George Chkiantz.
*UK LP IT'S ONLY ROCK 'N' ROLL: 18 October 1974: No **2** – 9 weeks*
*USA LP IT'S ONLY ROCK 'N' ROLL: 18 October 1974: No **1** – 11 weeks*
Rolling Stones with Nicky Hopkins, Ray Cooper.

The engineering exploits of Andy Johns and Co. were well displayed on IT'S ONLY ROCK 'N' ROLL as more sophisticated studio electronics (the gimmick tactics) played a more prominent rôle. The new credits on album covers underline this. George Chkiantz, the Stones over-dub engineer, was not new to the band. At the instigation of Brian Jones he had engineered the tapes recorded in 1968 of the Marakesh Gnaoua'n musicians and had also assisted on the 1969 LET IT BLEED album. His engineering works also linked him with the 1973 Led Zeppelin album, HOUSES OF THE HOLY, hence the introduction to the band of his co-conspirator, Keith Harwood. *Luxury* is a slick jibe (with a reggae beat) at all those who work so hard in offices to keep the wives back home in luxury. Keith Richards joins in on the middle-class theme, supporting Mick Jagger's vocals, while the band rock adequately on this mid-paced track.

366. LIVING IS A HARDER LOVE (Jagger, Richard)
March–April 1974: Musicland, Munich, West Germany.
Bootleg only.

This track was possibly a forerunner lyric-wise for *Luxury*. It is a classy number which certainly could have been worked on for release. The content is good enough.

367. DANCE LITTLE SISTER (Jagger, Richard)
March–April 1974: Musicland, Munich, West Germany. Producer: The Glimmer Twins. Engineer: Andy Johns, Keith Harwood. Assistant Engineers: Tapani Tapanainen, Rod Thear, Howard Kilgour, Mac 'Munich', George Chkiantz.
*UK LP IT'S ONLY ROCK 'N' ROLL: 18 October 1974: No **2** – 9 weeks*
*USA LP IT'S ONLY ROCK 'N' ROLL: 18 October 1974: No **1** – 11 weeks*
USA B-side Ain't Too Proud To Beg: October 1974.
*UK Compilation LP MADE IN THE SHADE: 6 June 1975: No **14** – 12 weeks*
*USA Compilation LP MADE IN THE SHADE: 6 June 1975: No **6** – 9 weeks*
Rolling Stones with Ray Cooper.

The American single featuring *Ain't Too Proud To Beg* and *Dance Little Sister*, released in October 1974, deserved to be credited as a double A-side. They were both foot-tapping dance-orientated numbers. *Dance Little Sister* is a typical Keith Richards rocker, cruising at road-running pace with twin guitar riffs under the bonnet. Ian Stewart confirms the song's rock 'n' roll origin capturing a bar-room piano feel.

368. SHORT AND CURLIES (Jagger, Richard)
March–April 1974: Musicland, Munich, West Germany. Producer: The Glimmer Twins. Engineer: Andy Johns, Keith Harwood. Assistant Engineers: Tapani Tapanainen, Rod Thear, Howard Kilgour, Mac 'Munich', George Chkiantz.
*UK LP IT'S ONLY ROCK 'N' ROLL: 18 October 1974: No **2** – 9 weeks*
*USA LP IT'S ONLY ROCK 'N' ROLL: 18 October 1974: No **1** – 11 weeks*
Rolling Stones with Ray Cooper.

Ian Stewart continues his bar-room piano display. It is the shortest track on the album and lacks conviction and R 'n' B guts. The lyrics describe a woman's firm upper hand. The album was released in October 1974 only six months after the sessions had finished and received relatively good reviews. The record-buying public responded to create a very luke-warm hit. It remained in the charts for only nine weeks becoming their least successful chart album. It certainly signified a lean period for the Stones.

8

HAND OF FATE ENDS
GUITARIST HUNT

DECEMBER 1974 – AUGUST 1976

369. FOOL TO CRY (Jagger, Richard)
*12 December 1974: Musicland, Munich, West Germany. Producer: The
Glimmer Twins. Engineer: Keith Harwood, Glyn Johns, Phil McDonald,
Lew Hahn. Assistant Engineer: Jeremy Gee, Dave Richards, Tapani
Tapanainen, Steve Dowd, Gene Paul, Lee Hulko.
UK Single: 20 April 1976: No **6** – 10 weeks
USA Single: 20 April 1976: No **10** – 7 weeks
UK LP BLACK AND BLUE: 20 April 1976: No **2** – 14 weeks
USA LP BLACK AND BLUE: 20 April 1976: No **1** – 14 weeks
UK Compilation LP TIME WAITS FOR NO ONE – ANTHOLOGY 1971
– 1977: May 1978
UK Compilation LP SUCKING IN THE SEVENTIES: May 1981
USA Compilation LP SUCKING IN THE SEVENTIES: May 1981: No **15**
– 5 weeks
Rolling Stones with Wayne Perkins, Nicky Hopkins.*

On the day that the Stones returned to the Musicland Studios an official
press release announced the departure of Mick Taylor who had only told
the band a few days previously that he did not wish to join them in
Munich. A contributory cause was certainly the song-writing upsets, but
more importantly there was a desire by Mick to broaden horizons. He
joined the Jack Bruce Band and has since lived quietly not so evidently
achieving the success he had during the five-year period with the Stones.
The band were left to find a guitarist and the so-called 'Great Guitarists
Hunt' began. Wayne Perkins, an American, first stepped into the breach
on 12 December 1974. The accentuated high-pitch vocals of Mick Jagger
got to grips with the ballad *Fool To Cry* so much so that fans mimicked the
high notes, betraying the touching love song. Mick shares a convincing
role on the electric piano with Nicky Hopkins, who was still firmly
entrenched in the Stones' scene. While the single reached a new audience, the regulars were a little stunned at this sentimental overdose. It
was certainly Mick's creation, Keith Richards preferring to humour its
success. Keith wryly recalls falling asleep during the number when they
toured with the BLACK AND BLUE set later in the year.

370. CHERRY OH BABY (Donaldson)
*15 December 1974: Musicland, Munich, West Germany. Producer: The
Glimmer Twins. Engineer: Keith Harwood, Glyn Johns, Phil McDonald,
Lew Hahn. Assistant Engineer: Jeremy Gee, Dave Richards, Tapani*

Tapanainen, Steve Dowd, Gene Paul, Lee Hulko.
UK LP BLACK AND BLUE: 20 April 1976: No 2 – 14 weeks
USA LP BLACK AND BLUE: 20 April 1976: No 1 – 14 weeks
Rolling Stones with Nicky Hopkins, Ron Wood.

A studio out-take version illustrates the problems associated with recording different music styles. Reggae needs to be delivered with passion. On this occasion it lacks both the subtle rhythm and the required vocal graces. With the vocals on the released version improved, the danger of contrivance is removed. Reggae music in the mid-'seventies was beginning to capture the public's taste with such talents as Bob Marley and Peter Tosh emerging from Jamaica and leading the crossover to chart compromise. It was natural that the Stones would try an odd delivery or two. The feigned deliverance of Eric Donaldson's *Cherry Oh Baby* unfortunately falls at the first hurdle. Guest guitarist Ron Wood's contribution is noted since it was his first official appearance with the Stones – his work on *It's Only Rock 'N' Roll* was not acknowledged officially. Ron must have been delighted to work with his old colleague, Nicky Hopkins from the Jeff Beck days. Perhaps Ronnie and Nicky had found the 'truth' about rock at long last!

371. SLAVE (a.k.a. BLACK AND BLUE JAM) (Jagger, Richards)
December 1974–March 1975: Musicland, Munich, West Germany.
Producer: The Glimmer Twins.
UK LP TATTOO YOU: 24 August 1981: No 2 – 29 weeks
USA LP TATTOO YOU: 24 August 1981: No 1 – 30 weeks
Rolling Stones with Ron Wood, Pete Townshend, Sonny Rollins.

Slave is a BLACK AND BLUE session out-take, widely titled *Black and Blue Jam*. It was taken down from the shelves, dusted and remixed by Bob Clearmountain and Gary Lyons for inclusion on the 1981 TATTOO YOU album. The unknown contributor on keyboards (probably Nicky Hopkins) and the illustrious sax talents of Sonny Rollins help to formulate quite a composition of rhythm and funk. Pete Townshend performs backing vocals. The original *Black And Blue Jam* contains the guitar work of Jeff Beck, an opportunity for him to display his wares.

372. WORRIED ABOUT YOU (Jagger, Richards)
December 1974–March 1975: Musicland, Munich, West Germany.
Producer: The Glimmer Twins.
UK LP TATTOO YOU: 24 August 1981: No 2 – 29 weeks
USA LP TATTOO YOU: 24 August 1981: No 1 – 30 weeks
Rolling Stones with Ron Wood.

Provisionally *Worried About You* was also lined up for the BLACK AND BLUE album. Its release was, however, held over until the TATTOO YOU album. This was certainly an indication of the band's liking for the track but it also showed up a weak foundation of available material for TATTOO YOU. *Worried About You* is a soft, melodious venture into the *Fool To Cry* land of falsetto vocals (with the exception of Keith's backing vocals). A piercing guitar solo is delivered mid-way through, an attempt at glossing over the loss of Mick Taylor. A long version was recorded at the Pathé Marconi Studios in July/August 1979 and this was edited for TATTOO YOU.

373. MELODY (Jagger, Richard)
23 January 1975: Mobile Studio, Rotterdam, Holland. Producer: The Glimmer Twins. Engineer: Keith Harwood, Glyn Johns, Phil McDonald, Lew Hahn. Assistant Engineer: Jeremy Gee, Dave Richards, Tapani Tapanainen, Steve Dowd, Gene Paul, Lee Hulko. Horns arrangement: Arif Mardin.
UK LP BLACK AND BLUE: 20 April 1976: No 2 – 14 weeks
USA LP BLACK AND BLUE: 20 April 1976: No 1 – 14 weeks
Rolling Stones with Billy Preston.

Inspired and collaborated by Billy Preston, *Melody* is a pseudo 'twenties jazz song. Bill Wyman and Charlie Watts are evidently familiar and at home in jazz/blues territory. Keith Richards exudes confidence, licks complementing the swing style of Billy Preston's piano and organ playing. The long track is an inspired transgression and perhaps the album's most original and strongest cut.

374. SEXY NIGHT (a.k.a. **LOVELY LADY**) (Jagger, Richard)
March 1975: Musicland, Munich, West Germany. Producer: The Glimmer Twins.
Bootleg only.
Rolling Stones with Jeff Beck.

Sexy Night is an out-take in the vein of *Fool To Cry* complete with Mick Jagger's high pitched vocals. *Sexy Night* or *Lovely Lady* is a soft ballad which rises and falls in unconvincing manner. A funky guitar accompanies the tune and this is likely to be provided by Jeff Beck, who (rumour has it) rejected the Stones because Bill Wyman and Charlie Watts could not funk it up (or Jeff could not rock it up!).

375. COME ON SUGAR (a.k.a. **LET'S DO IT RIGHT**) (Jagger, Richard)
March 1975: Musicland, Munich, West Germany. Producer: The Glimmer Twins.
Bootleg only.
Rolling Stones with Jeff Beck.

A more intense funk number which was unfinished lyrically. However, it provided Jeff Beck the opportunity to groove again on the funk express. (Jeff Beck was a very experienced lead guitarist who had fronted his own group since the end of The Yardbirds in the mid-'sixties. During the period 1967–69, a young Ron Wood played with Jeff Beck prior to joining The Small Faces and then instigating the formation of Rod Stewart and The Faces).

376. HAND OF FATE (Jagger, Richard)
25 March 1975: Musicland, Munich, West Germany. Producer: The
Glimmer Twins. Engineer: Keith Harwood, Glyn Johns, Phil McDonald,
Lew Hahn. Assistant Engineer: Jeremy Gee, Dave Richards, Tapani
Tapanainen, Steve Dowd, Gene Paul, Lee Hulko.
UK LP BLACK AND BLUE: 20 April 1976: No 2 – 14 weeks
USA LP BLACK AND BLUE: 20 April 1976: No 1 – 14 weeks
UK Compilation LP TIME WAITS FOR NO ONE – ANTHOLOGY 1971
– 1977: May 1978
Rolling Stones with Wayne Perkins, Ron Wood, Ollie Brown, Billy
Preston.

A return to an up-beat number, *Hand of Fate* rears its ugly head. Mick
Jagger relates a tale of a fugitive running out of luck from a crime of
passion. Although a faster track, it is played in a lazy manner. The guitar
solo is performed by Wayne Perkins, Ronnie Wood's rôle being restricted to backing vocals. Keith Richards provides the rhythm guitar and
Ollie Brown, formerly a Stevie Wonder side-kick, helps Charlie Watts on
percussion.

377. CRAZY MAMA (Jagger, Richard)
29 March 1975: Musicland, Munich, West Germany. Producer: The
Glimmer Twins. Engineers: Keith Harwood, Glyn Johns, Phil
McDonald, Lew Hahn. Assistant Engineer: Jeremy Gee, Dave
Richards, Tapani Tapanainen, Steve Dowd, Gene Paul, Lee Hulko.
UK B-side Fool to Cry: 20 April 1976
UK LP BLACK AND BLUE: 20 April 1976: No 2 – 14 weeks
USA LP BLACK AND BLUE: 20 April 1976: No 1 – 14 weeks
UK Compilation LP TIME WAITS FOR NO ONE – ANTHOLOGY 1971
– 1977: May 1978
UK Compilation LP SUCKING IN THE SEVENTIES: May 1981
USA Compilation LP SUCKING IN THE SEVENTIES: May 1981: No 15
– 5 weeks
Rolling Stones with Billy Preston, Ron Wood, Ollie Brown.

The extensive details on the inner cover of BLACK AND BLUE give a
valuable insight into the make-up of a Rolling Stones track. One learns
that Bill Wyman is removed from the line-up on *Crazy Mama* and that the
lead and bass guitars are played by Keith Richards, with the exception of
a rhythm piece by Mick Jagger. Ronnie Wood and Billy Preston contribute backing vocals. *Crazy Mama* is a strong track in the mould of a typical
sleaze rocker. It was featured on the British flip-side of *Fool To Cry*, the
Americans preferring the funky *Hot Stuff.*

378. HOT STUFF (Jagger, Richard)
30 March 1975: Musicland, Munich, West Germany. Producer: The
Glimmer Twins. Engineers: Keith Harwood, Glyn Johns, Phil
McDonald, Lew Hahn. Assistant Engineer: Jeremy Gee, Dave
Richards, Tapani Tapanainen, Steve Dowd, Gene Paul, Lee Hulko.
USA B-side Fool to Cry: 20 April 1976.

*UK LP BLACK AND BLUE: 20 April 1976: No **2** – 14 weeks*
*USA LP BLACK AND BLUE: 20 April 1976: No **1** – 14 weeks*
UK Compilation LP SUCKING IN THE SEVENTIES: May 1981
*USA Compilation LP SUCKING IN THE SEVENTIES: May 1981: No **15***
– 5 weeks
Rolling Stones with Harvey Mandel, Billy Preston, Ron Wood, Ollie Brown.

Hot Stuff is one of the two tracks on which noted American virtuoso Harvey Mandel played lead guitar. His solo guitar work on *Hot Stuff* is certainly vigorous. The track encircles the disco format of funk. Mick Jagger lays down some rap jive, popularizing the track into an underground clubland hit, the probable reason for its American single release. *Hot Stuff* was, at one time, a working title for the album.

379. **MEMORY MOTEL** (Jagger, Richard)
31 March 1975: Musicland, Munich, West Germany. Producer: The Glimmer Twins. Engineers: Keith Harwood, Glyn Johns, Phil McDonald, Lew Hahn. Assistant Engineer: Jeremy Gee, Dave Richards, Tapani Tapanainen, Steve Dowd, Gene Paul, Lee Hulko.
*UK LP BLACK AND BLUE: 20 April 1976: No **2** – 14 weeks*
*USA LP BLACK AND BLUE: 20 April 1976: No **1** – 14 weeks*
Rolling Stones with Wayne Perkins, Harvey Mandel, Billy Preston, Ron Wood.

With the formidable keyboard line-up of Mick Jagger on concert piano, Keith Richards performing electric piano and Billy Preston on the string synthesizer, *Memory* is a lengthy sojourn into life on the road. Keith Richards features heavily on vocals leaving the acoustic guitar to Wayne Perkins and the electric guitar to Harvey Mandel. A meandering song, slightly below par.

380. **HEY NEGRITA** (Jagger, Richard)
2 April 1975: Musicland, Munich, West Germany. Producer: The Glimmer Twins. Engineers: Keith Harwood, Glyn Johns, Phil McDonald, Lew Hahn. Assistant Engineer: Jeremy Gee, Dave Richards, Tapani Tapanainen, Steve Dowd, Gene Paul, Lee Hulko.
*UK LP BLACK AND BLUE: 20 April 1976: No **2** – 14 weeks*
*USA LP BLACK AND BLUE: 20 April 1976: No **1** – 14 weeks*
Rolling Stones with Ron Wood, Billy Preston, Ollie Brown.

Fittingly, from the BLACK AND BLUE sessions, the last guitar 'audition' was left to Ronnie Wood. It seems that above all the other guitarists he was most suited to the spare axe position and most at ease with the Stones' ambience. Little did Ronnie know that in 1969, shortly after Brian Jones' death, Ian Stewart rang the studio, where The Small Faces were recording and asked if Woody would want to join the Stones. Ronnie Lane answered 'No', not even giving Ron Wood the chance to answer for himself. Other stories believe that Ian called the studio and asked to speak to Ronnie. Ronnie Lane believed they meant him and responded that he did not feel he was suited for the Stones' spare guitarist role. In 1975 the only other serious contender was Wayne Perkins but for various reasons his signing was not agreed. If you believe certain sources (some are confirmed sightings), the merits of Rory Gallagher, Shuggie Otis, Max Middleton, Chris Spedding, Peter Frampton, Jeff Beck, Nils Lofgren, Robert Johnson, Steve Marriott, Jimmy Page, Wilko Johnson and Harvey Mandel were considered. Pete Townshend managed to keep a low profile and avoided inclusion on the hit list. Most of the aforementioned are essentially lead guitarists. What was needed was a return to the dual rhythm thrust of the early Richards/Jones days, hence Keith Richards' natural choice of honest mate, Ron Wood. This position was formally confirmed in the press in December 1975. *For sessionography purposes Ron Wood is in future Rolling Stones 'personnel'. Hey Negrita* ran the risk of incensing racial harmony. Mick Jagger fondly termed Bianca as a 'Negrita' – she thought it would make a good song title. Further risk was run once the album was released – posters with a sado-masochistic streak displayed a girl, roped and beaten, sitting on an enlarged album cover. The cover also confirmed Ron Wood's position as Stones' hench-man. He joined the rest of the band on the album cover, although his guitar had only featured on two tracks.

381. **SURE THE ONE YOU NEED** (Richard)
6 June 1975: Arrowhead Stadium, Kansas City.
Bootleg only.

This track originates from the September 1974 Ron Wood solo project I'VE GOT MY OWN ALBUM TO DO. Keith Richards had performed on several of the album's tracks and had written this one and also *Act Together*. The tour of the Americas (both North and South) commenced in June 1975 and intended to wind up at the end of August in, of all places, Venezuela. *Sure The One You Need* was performed on this tour, a rarity since this is its one and only recording by the full Stones' line-up. It became an outlet for Keith and Ron to jam together. Mick Jagger was permitted a vocal line or two – who could suppress him? The Tour undoubtedly confirmed Ron Wood's position as the new Stones' rhythm guitarist.

382. **HONKY TONK WOMEN** (Jagger, Richard)
4/7 June 1976: Avetoire, Paris, France. Producer: The Glimmer Twins.
Engineer: Keith Harwood, Eddie Kramer, Ron Nevison, Dave Jordan,
Jimmy Douglass. Assistant Engineer: Mick McKenna, Tom Heid,
Randy Hason, Bobby Warner, Lew Hahn, Tapani Tapanainen, Lee
Hulko.
*UK LP LOVE YOU LIVE: September 1977: No **3** – 8 weeks*
*USA LP LOVE YOU LIVE: September 1977: No **5** – 7 weeks*
Rolling Stones with Billy Preston, Ollie Brown.

383. **IF YOU CAN'T ROCK ME** (Jagger, Richard)
4/7 June 1976: Avetoire, Paris, France. Producer: The Glimmer Twins.
Engineer: Keith Harwood, Eddie Kramer, Ron Nevison, Dave Jordan,

Jimmy Douglass. Assistant Engineer: Mick McKenna, Tom Heid,
Randy Hason, Bobby Warner, Lew Hahn, Tapani Tapanainen, Lee
Hulko.
UK LP LOVE YOU LIVE: September 1977: No **3** *– 8 weeks*
USA LP LOVE YOU LIVE: September 1977: No **5** *– 7 weeks*
UK Compilation LP TIME WAITS FOR NO ONE – ANTHOLOGY 1971
– 1977: May 1978
Rolling Stones with Billy Preston, Ollie Brown.

384. GET OFF MY CLOUD (Jagger, Richard)
4/7 June 1976: Avetoire, Paris, France. Producer: The Glimmer Twins.
Engineer: Keith Harwood, Eddie Kramer, Ron Nevison, Dave Jordan,
Jimmy Douglass. Assistant Engineer: Mick McKenna, Tom Heid,
Randy Hason, Bobby Warner, Lew Hahn, Tapani Tapanainen, Lee
Hulko.
UK LP LOVE YOU LIVE: September 1977: No **3** *– 8 weeks*
USA LP LOVE YOU LIVE: September 1977: No **5** *– 7 weeks*
UK Compilation LP TIME WAITS FOR NO ONE – ANTHOLOGY 1971
– 1977: May 1978
Rolling Stones with Billy Preston, Ollie Brown.

385. HAPPY (Jagger, Richard)
4/7 June 1976: Avetoire, Paris, France. Producer: The Glimmer Twins.
Engineer: Keith Harwood, Eddie Kramer, Ron Nevison, Dave Jordan,
Jimmy Douglass. Assistant Engineer: Mick McKenna, Tom Heid,
Randy Hason, Bobby Warner, Lew Hahn, Tapani Tapanainen, Lee
Hulko.
UK LP LOVE YOU LIVE: September 1977: No **3** *– 8 weeks*
USA LP LOVE YOU LIVE: September 1977: No **5** *– 7 weeks*
Rolling Stones with Billy Preston, Ollie Brown.

386. HOT STUFF (Jagger, Richard)
4/7 June 1976: Avetoire, Paris, France. Producer: The Glimmer Twins.
Engineer: Keith Harwood, Eddie Kramer, Ron Nevison, Dave Jordan,
Jimmy Douglass. Assistant Engineer: Mick McKenna, Tom Heid,
Randy Hason, Bobby Warner, Lew Hahn, Tapani Tapanainen, Lee
Hulko.
UK LP LOVE YOU LIVE: September 1977: No **3** *– 8 weeks*
USA LP LOVE YOU LIVE: September 1977: No **5** *– 7 weeks*
Rolling Stones with Billy Preston, Ollie Brown.

387. STAR STAR (Jagger, Richard)
4/7 June 1976: Avetoire, Paris, France. Producer: The Glimmer Twins.
Engineer: Keith Harwood, Eddie Kramer, Ron Nevison, Dave Jordan,
Jimmy Douglass. Assistant Engineer: Mick McKenna, Tom Heid,
Randy Hason, Bobby Warner, Lew Hahn, Tapani Tapanainen, Lee
Hulko.
UK LP LOVE YOU LIVE: September 1977: No **3** *– 8 weeks*

USA LP LOVE YOU LIVE: September 1977: No **5** *– 7 weeks*
Rolling Stones with Billy Preston, Ollie Brown.

388. TUMBLING DICE (Jagger, Richard)
4/7 June 1976: Avetoire, Paris, France. Producer: The Glimmer Twins.
Engineer: Keith Harwood, Eddie Kramer, Ron Nevison, Dave Jordan,
Jimmy Douglass. Assistant Engineer: Mick McKenna, Tom Heid,
Randy Hason, Bobby Warner, Lew Hahn, Tapani Tapanainen, Lee
Hulko.
UK LP LOVE YOU LIVE: September 1977: No **3** *– 8 weeks*
USA LP LOVE YOU LIVE: September 1977: No **5** *– 7 weeks*
Rolling Stones with Billy Preston, Ollie Brown.

389. FINGERPRINT FILE (Jagger, Richard)
4/7 June 1976: Avetoire, Paris, France. Producer: The Glimmer Twins.
Engineer: Keith Harwood, Eddie Kramer, Ron Nevison, Dave Jordan,
Jimmy Douglass. Assistant Engineer: Mick McKenna, Tom Heid,
Randy Hason, Bobby Warner, Lew Hahn, Tapani Tapanainen, Lee
Hulko.
UK LP LOVE YOU LIVE: September 1977: No **3** *– 8 weeks*
USA LP LOVE YOU LIVE: September 1977: No **5** *– 7 weeks*
Rolling Stones with Billy Preston, Ollie Brown.

390. YOU GOTTA MOVE (McDowell)
4/7 June 1976: Avetoire, Paris, France. Producer: The Glimmer Twins.
Engineer: Keith Harwood, Eddie Kramer, Ron Nevison, Dave Jordan,
Jimmy Douglass. Assistant Engineer: Mick McKenna, Tom Heid,
Randy Hason, Bobby Warner, Lew Hahn, Tapani Tapanainen, Lee
Hulko.
UK LP LOVE YOU LIVE: September 1977: No **3** *– 8 weeks*
USA LP LOVE YOU LIVE: September 1977: No **5** *– 7 weeks*
Rolling Stones with Billy Preston, Ollie Brown.

391. YOU CAN'T ALWAYS GET WHAT YOU WANT (Jagger, Richard)
4/7 June 1976: Avetoire, Paris, France. Producer: The Glimmer Twins.
Engineer: Keith Harwood, Eddie Kramer, Ron Nevison, Dave Jordan,
Jimmy Douglass. Assistant Engineer: Mick McKenna, Tom Heid,
Randy Hason, Bobby Warner, Lew Hahn, Tapani Tapanainen, Lee
Hulko.
UK LP LOVE YOU LIVE: September 1977: No **3** *– 8 weeks*
USA LP LOVE YOU LIVE: September 1977: No **5** *– 7 weeks*
Rolling Stones with Billy Preston, Ollie Brown.

392. IT'S ONLY ROCK 'N' ROLL (Jagger, Richard)
4/7 June 1976: Avetoire, Paris, France. Producer: The Glimmer Twins.
Engineer: Keith Harwood, Eddie Kramer, Ron Nevison, Dave Jordan,
Jimmy Douglass. Assistant Engineer: Mick McKenna, Tom Heid,
Randy Hason, Bobby Warner, Lew Hahn, Tapani Tapanainen, Lee
Hulko.

UK LP LOVE YOU LIVE: September 1977: No **3** *– 8 weeks*
USA LP LOVE YOU LIVE: September 1977: No **5** *– 7 weeks*
Rolling Stones with Billy Preston, Ollie Brown.

393. **BROWN SUGAR** (Jagger, Richard)
4/7 June 1976: Avetoire, Paris, France. Producer: The Glimmer Twins.
Engineer: Keith Harwood, Eddie Kramer, Ron Nevison, Dave Jordan,
Jimmy Douglass. Assistant Engineer: Mick McKenna, Tom Heid,
Randy Hason, Bobby Warner, Lew Hahn, Tapani Tapanainen, Lee
Hulko.
UK LP LOVE YOU LIVE: September 1977: No **3** *– 8 weeks*
USA LP LOVE YOU LIVE: September 1977: No **5** *– 7 weeks*
Rolling Stones with Billy Preston, Ollie Brown.

394. **JUMPIN' JACK FLASH** (Jagger, Richard)
4/7 June 1976: Avetoire, Paris, France. Producer: The Glimmer Twins.
Engineer: Keith Harwood, Eddie Kramer, Ron Nevison, Dave Jordan,
Jimmy Douglass. Assistant Engineer: Mick McKenna, Tom Heid,
Randy Hason, Bobby Warner, Lew Hahn, Tapani Tapanainen, Lee
Hulko.
UK LP LOVE YOU LIVE: September 1977: No **3** *– 8 weeks*
USA LP LOVE YOU LIVE: September 1977: No **5** *– 7 weeks*
Rolling Stones with Billy Preston, Ollie Brown.

395. **SYMPATHY FOR THE DEVIL** (Jagger, Richard)
4/7 June 1976: Avetoire, Paris, France. Producer: The Glimmer Twins.
Engineer: Keith Harwood, Eddie Kramer, Ron Nevison, Dave Jordan,
Jimmy Douglass. Assistant Engineer: Mick McKenna, Tom Heid,
Randy Hason, Bobby Warner, Lew Hahn, Tapani Tapanainen, Lee
Hulko.
UK LP LOVE YOU LIVE: September 1977: No **3** *– 8 weeks*
USA LP LOVE YOU LIVE: September 1977: No **5** *– 7 weeks*
Rolling Stones with Billy Preston, Ollie Brown.

The demand for the Stones as a performing group was at a peak. The heavy schedule of a three-month tour of America in 1975 was followed by a three-month jaunt around Europe in April, May and June, 1976. When the British leg of the tour was announced a cool one million postal applications were received at an average request of four tickets each. An estimated four million Britons wanted to see a performance by 'the greatest rock and roll band in the world'. Many would be disappointed, since only fifteen shows at small venues were performed in the UK. A prerequisite of the tour was that the Stones would put on a performance previously unequalled. A unique stage was built covering 500 square yards and various theatrical gimmicks were used. Clowns and African drummers roamed the auditorium enhancing the atmosphere, then, from the PA, Aaron Copeland's *Fanfare For The Common Man* was heard, building the crowd to a higher level of excitement. As the fanfare subsided and the compere announced the Rolling Stones, the leaves of a massive crown began to unfurl and the strains of the *Honky Tonk* riff began to belch from Keith Richards' guitar. The show had started, and by the time the stage was fully revealed, Mick Jagger had commenced the bar-room inspired lyrics. *If You Can't Rock Me* seems to breathe new life, it segues into *Get Off My Cloud*, Mick Jagger playing off Billy Preston's vocals. Keith Richards is brought to the front of the stage to perform *Happy*. A few songs later the show returns to a degree of normality, an adventurous version of *Fingerprint File* is tackled and also the late 'sixties song, *You Can't Always Get What You Want*, a permanent feature of a Stones' gig. The finale incorporates a raunchy *It's Only Rock 'n' Roll*, old favourites *Brown Sugar* and *Jumpin' Jack Flash* and a superb encore of *Sympathy For The Devil*. It was the first occasion *Sympathy* had been attempted on tour since the fatal Altamont incident. It provided Ron and Keith with a chance to trade guitar solos like long lost brothers. The LOVE YOU LIVE double album used three sides of the shows recorded by Keith Harwood at the Paris concerts in June 1976. The quality is high but the atmosphere of Jagger swinging on ropes, riding a blow-up phallic shape during *Star Star* and dousing hot fans with buckets of water at the show's end are lost forever. They are untenable and remain solely with the memories of the witnesses of the band's performance. An EP was produced for promotional purposes in the States. It contained *If You Can't Rock Me, Get Off My Cloud, Hot Stuff, Brown Sugar* and *Jumping Jack Flash* (note the 'g', unlike the 1968 original). LOVE YOU LIVE was dedicated to the memory of Keith Harwood who died in a car accident in 1977.

396. STRAY CAT BLUES (Jagger, Richard)
21 August 1976: Knebworth, England.
Bootleg only.

An all-day rock festival enabled the Stones to thank British fans for their past support. Over a quarter of a million troops responded and witnessed a day of rock and blues set in the illustrious Knebworth country estate. The Don Harrison Band, Hot Tuna, Todd Rundgren, Lynyrd Skynyrd and 10 cc were the support acts. Late afternoon, Lynyrd Skynyrd took the tongue-shaped stage and introduced to English soils a set of magic, southern blues boogie, *Freebird* being one of the most inspired performances ever viewed on a British stage. The crowd, some perched precariously in oak trees, were ecstatic, rebel flags waved furiously. 10 cc had a hard job to follow this and after a two-hour delay hit the stage to a by-now sour, sun-blistered crowd. They were unable to recapture the atmosphere founded by Lynyrd Skynyrd and so the stage awaited the old hands. The Stones performed a lengthy set of over two hours, drawing material from the early 'sixties with *Little Red Rooster* and *Around And Around* and from the late 'sixties with the unfamiliar *Stray Cat* and up to date material including *Fool To Cry* and *Hey Negrita*. The day was a mark of respect to hippiedom, but the tide was turning.

9

PUNK AND THE EMOTIONAL YEARS

MARCH 1977 – JUNE 1982

397. MANNISH BOY (London, McDaniel, Morganfield)
*4/5 March 1977: El Mocambo, Toronto, Canada. Producer: The
Glimmer Twins. Engineer: Keith Harwood, Eddie Kramer, Ron
Nevison, Dave Jordan, Jimmy Douglass. Assistant Engineer: Mick
McKenna, Tom Heid, Randy Hason, Bobby Warner, Lew Hahn, Tapani
Tapanainen, Lee Hulko.*
UK LP LOVE YOU LIVE: September 1977: No **3** *– 8 weeks*
USA LP LOVE YOU LIVE: September 1977: No **5** *– 7 weeks*
UK Compilation LP SUCKING IN THE SEVENTIES: May 1981.
USA Compilation LP SUCKING IN THE SEVENTIES: May 1981: No **15**
– 5 weeks
Rolling Stones with Billy Preston, Ollie Brown.

398. CRACKIN' UP (McDaniel)
*4/5 March 1977: El Mocambo, Toronto, Canada. Producer: The
Glimmer Twins. Engineer: Keith Harwood, Eddie Kramer, Ron
Nevison, Dave Jordan, Jimmy Douglass. Assistant Engineer: Mick
McKenna, Tom Heid, Randy Hason, Bobby Warner, Lew Hahn, Tapani
Tapanainen, Lee Hulko.*
UK LP LOVE YOU LIVE: September 1977: No **3** *– 8 weeks*
USA LP LOVE YOU LIVE: September 1977: No **5** *– 7 weeks*
Rolling Stones with Billy Preston, Ollie Brown.

399. LITTLE RED ROOSTER (Dixon)
*4/5 March 1977: El Mocambo, Toronto, Canada. Producer: The
Glimmer Twins. Engineer: Keith Harwood, Eddie Kramer, Ron
Nevison, Dave Jordan, Jimmy Douglass. Assistant Engineer: Mick
McKenna, Tom Heid, Randy Hason, Bobby Warner, Lew Hahn, Tapani
Tapanainen, Lee Hulko.*
UK LP LOVE YOU LIVE: September 1977: No **3** *– 8 weeks*
USA LP LOVE YOU LIVE: September 1977: No **5** *– 7 weeks*
Rolling Stones with Billy Preston, Ollie Brown.

400. AROUND AND AROUND (Berry)
*4/5 March 1977: El Mocambo, Toronto, Canada. Producer: The
Glimmer Twins. Engineer: Keith Harwood, Eddie Kramer, Ron
Nevison, Dave Jordan, Jimmy Douglass. Assistant Engineer: Mick*

McKenna, Tom Heid, Randy Hason, Bobby Warner, Lew Hahn, Tapani Tapanainen, Lee Hulko.
UK LP LOVE YOU LIVE: September 1977: No **3** *8 weeks*
USA LP LOVE YOU LIVE: September 1977: No **5** – *7 weeks*
Rolling Stones with Billy Preston, Ollie Brown.

Mick Jagger planned a quiet stay in Toronto, the intention being to record five gigs at the snug El Mocambo Club (capacity 500) and place some of the tracks on the forthcoming live, double album. Having (eventually) persuaded Keith Richards to join the band in Canada after a series of pleading 'phone calls coupled with threatening telegrams, the band set about rehearsing for a reduced two gigs at the El Mocambo. Plans were disrupted on 28 February when the Mounties visited Keith's hotel suite. Search and arrest warrants in hand, they discovered a bountiful supply of hallucinogens. Keith was charged with possession of cocaine and more seriously, a charge of intent to traffic. The consequences were grave. Trafficking in Canada carried a life sentence. Meanwhile, brave Ronnie Wood was seen on the boulevard cohorting with the Prime Minister's wife, Margaret Trudeau. The insignificant visit to Canada became a major incident and the world press had a field day. Margaret's escapades at the El Mocambo Club and various hotel suites prompted the press to launch an attack on the credibility of the Canadian Government while the future of Keith jeopardized the very existence of the Stones. These events were temporarily put aside for their performances at the El Mocambo Club. Keith likened the cosy atmosphere to the Crawdaddy Club in Richmond. The band were inspired and performed two electrifying sets. The tracks on the album are oldies conjured from the past. *Crackin' Up*, a Bo Diddley number, was recalled from the murky depths and at last was given an official release following the January 1963 IBC sessions. *Around And Around* with Mick's humorous introduction has Keith riff-playing flawlessly. It would have made a perfect single release in late 1977 amid the furore of the punk music scene emanating from Britain. 'No more, Elvis, Beatles or Rolling Stones in 1977' cried angry Joe Strummer, ironically.

401. APARTMENT NO. 9 (Sherrill)
12/13 March 1977: Sounds Interchange, Toronto, Canada.
Bootleg only. Keith Richards, Ian Stewart.

402. WORRIED LIFE BLUES (Merryweather)
12/13 March 1977: Sounds Interchange, Toronto, Canada.
Bootleg only.
Keith Richards, Ian Stewart.

These gems were recorded while Keith was technically detained in Canada pending a decision on the drugs bust. The vocals are a shade rusty, but for pure authenticity they are great collectors' items. Backed by Ian Stewart, Keith sings his heart out epitomizing his then current situation – my friends have all left me. *Worried Life Blues*, a traditional standard, was originally performed by the king of Chicago blues piano,

Big Maceo Merryweather. *Apartment No 9*, a Tammy Wynette song, was rerecorded in 1981 but failed to capture the poignancy of the Toronto session. When Keith toured with the New Barbarians – Ron Wood's touring band – *Apartment No 9* was a stage favourite.

403. BLACK LIMOUSINE (Jagger, Richard, Wood)
October 1977–March 1978: EMI, Pathé Marconi, Paris. Producer: The Glimmer Twins. Engineer: Chris Kimsey, Bob Clearmountain, Gary Lyons, Bob Ludwig.
*UK LP TATTOO YOU: 24 August 1981: No **2** – 29 weeks*
*USA LP TATTOO YOU: 24 August 1981: No **1** – 30 weeks*

Following the drug bust in Canada the relationship between Keith Richards and Mick Jagger reached a low ebb. Mick quietly retreated from Toronto leaving Keith confined by the authorities until a decision was reached on the charges. Eventually, a date for trial was set for December 1977 and Keith was bailed and free to leave. He journeyed to New York in April 1977 for drug addiction treatment, and in September 1977 he and Ron Wood travelled to Paris to start recording the new album. The members of the band rekindled their friendship, but it was evident that Keith and Mick were still slightly distanced. *Black Limousine* was a departure in style from their previously recorded outings. A renewed vigour symbolized a return to basics, but the guitar sound was distinctly modern, or as Ian Stewart was heard to say: 'Bloody Status Quo music'. It is, however, a good boogie song, complete with harp work. *Black Limousine* was left off the SOME GIRLS album, but thought suitable for the generally incohesive TATTOO YOU long player. Ron Wood is co-credited on his first Stones' composition.

404. MUNICH HILTON (a.k.a. ROTTEN ROLL) (Jagger, Richard)
October 1977–March 1978: EMI, Pathé Marconi, Paris. Producer: The Glimmer Twins.
Bootleg only.

'The No More Fast Numbers' sessions (as they soon became known) produced a plentiful crop of songs requiring a wily selection process in order to cut them down to the standard single album format of ten tracks. *Munich Hilton*, inspired by the 1974/75 München recording period and the town's Hilton Hotel, is a lengthy number centred around one of Keith's guitar riffs. Similar in style to *Tumbling Dice*, it raunches and rolls; out-takes, some under the title *Rotten Roll*, feature an instrumental mix and also a rarer vocal mix. *Munich Hilton* evidently strained on Keith's imagination, because it was included on an unofficial album featuring his solo electric guitar work recorded during rehearsals for the 1981 US tour.

405. WHEN THE WHIP COMES DOWN (Jagger, Richards)
October 1977–March 1978: EMI, Pathé Marconi, Paris. Producer: The Glimmer Twins. Engineer: Chris Kimsey. Assistant Engineer: Barry Sage, Dave Jordan, Ben King, Philippe.
*UK LP SOME GIRLS: 9 June 1978: No **2** – 25 weeks*

*USA LP SOME GIRLS: 9 June 1978: No **1** – 32 weeks*
UK B-side Respectable: 15 September 1978
USA B-side Beast Of Burden: September 1978

This is a harsh song about a gay learning the ropes in New York City. The music is equally punishing: raunchy, hard driving, no nonsense boogie. The guitars thrash and writhe, Jagger's included, while Ron Wood can be heard on the pedal steel. Coupled with *Respectable* in Britain it provided a double slice of hard rock 'n' roll. An out-take version obtainable on bootleg is a lengthy ten minute rendition, the tempo changes, at one stage simmering down before boisterously building up again, the three guitars and Bill Wyman's bass literally panting for attention.

406. RESPECTABLE (Jagger, Richards)

October 1977–March 1978: EMI, Pathé Marconi, Paris. Producer: The Glimmer Twins. Engineer: Chris Kimsey. Assistant Engineer: Barry Sage, Dave Jordan, Ben King, Philippe.
*UK LP SOME GIRLS: 9 June 1978: No **2** – 25 weeks*
*USA LP SOME GIRLS: 9 June 1978: No **1** – 32 weeks*
*UK Single: 15 September 1978: No **23** – 9 weeks*

Viewed by fans as a tongue-in-cheek prod at their own social status, *Respectable* streaks along at an energetic pace. Reference in the lyrics is made to Bianca Jagger's meeting with the then President's son, Jack Ford, at the White House: 'We're talking heroin with the President!' Keith Richards and Ron Wood lay claim to another volume in their guitar solo autobiography as they weave their way, Ronnie Wood being so at home on his first official sessions as a band member. *Respectable* was released as the second single from the SOME GIRLS album in Britain, but it failed to make a strong impact, only charting at Number 23. An out-take can be heard with Mick Jagger issuing instructions to the rest of the band on tempo and guitar breaks.

407. I NEED YOU (a.k.a. I LIKE IT TOO MUCH) (Jagger, Richards)

October 1977–March 1978: EMI, Pathé Marconi, Paris. Producer: The Glimmer Twins.
Bootleg only.

For Keith Richards March 1977 was spent in Toronto waiting for the Canadian trial verdict. He tried to use the time industriously recording several tracks, mostly of a country nature, such as *She Still Comes Around* and a Merle Haggard song *Sing Me Back Home*. With these tracks still in mind some of the SOME GIRLS sessions included a few country outings. *I Need You* was in an early stage, but the country steel guitar shines through while Jagger struggles with what seems unfinished lyrics. Keith is featured prominently on vocals.

408. HANG FIRE (a.k.a. LAZY BITCH) (Jagger, Richards)

October 1977–March 1978: EMI, Pathé Marconi, Paris. Producer: The Glimmer Twins. Engineer: Chris Kimsey, Bob Clearmountain, Gary Lyons, Bob Ludwig.

*UK LP TATTOO YOU: 24 August 1981: No **2** – 29 weeks*
*USA LP TATTOO YOU: 24 August 1981: No **1** – 30 weeks*
*USA Single: April 1982: No **20** – 6 weeks*

A band favourite, this song is characterized by innocent-sounding harmony vocals. The track portrays the depressing state of a country racked by unemployment and poverty. It has a cynical ring since the people described seem content to remain faltering at the bottom of the social pile – the working title (*Lazy Bitch*) confirms these suspicions. 'The country dear friends is one where I used to come from', sings Jagger. The single release was only made in the States, the insinuations perhaps too strong for an upfront single release on home territory. *Hang Fire's* mood is uptempo. Yet another fast number and since the SOME GIRLS quota was full it was not released until the TATTOO YOU album. It was recorded originally at the Paris 'More Girls' sessions, under the title *Lazy Bitch.* (An out-take from those sessions lasts for six minutes – a true opus!)

409. START ME UP (Jagger, Richards)

October 1977–March 1978: EMI, Pathé Marconi, Paris. Producer: The Glimmer Twins. Engineer: Chris Kimsey, Bob Clearmountain, Gary Lyons, Bob Ludwig.
*UK Single: 17 August 1981: No **7** – 9 weeks*
*USA Single: 17 August 1981: No **2** – 18 weeks*
*UK LP TATTOO YOU: 24 August 1981: No **2** – 29 weeks*
*USA LP TATTOO YOU: 24 August 1981: No **1** – 30 weeks*

The sound and feel of *Start Me Up* right from the slightly echoed opening guitar chords is instantaneous and proved the Stones' mettle was not broken. Originally recorded during the 1977/78 Paris sessions as a reggae number, it was rerecorded and remixed from January to June 1981 for the TATTOO YOU album. Keith Richards lays down another classic Stones' riff reminiscent of some of their hottest singles. Charlie Watts is a co-conspirator in the track's attack, his drum-sound inducing the infectious head-banging syndrome. It certainly reaffirmed the Stones' chart presence, becoming their biggest chart topper of the 'eighties both sides of the Atlantic. Such has been its popularity that in recent stage shows it has been included in finale material with the likes of *Brown Sugar*, *Jumpin' Jack Flash*, *Street Fighting Man* and *Satisfaction*. The Cult's lead guitarist Billy Duffy reproduced the main riff from *Start Me Up* for the 1987 chart hit *Love Removal Machine*.

410. YELLOW CAB (a.k.a. DO YOU THINK I CARE?) (Jagger, Richards)

October 1977–March 1978: EMI, Pathé Marconi, Paris, France.
Producer: The Glimmer Twins.
Bootleg only.
Rolling Stones with Ian McLagan.

Most of the SOME GIRLS tracks were recorded in a two month stint in October and November 1977. One of the many out-takes from these sessions is *Yellow Cab*, which features a slide (almost Hawaiian sounding) country steel guitar and the reputed piano playing of Ian McLagan who had been introduced by Ron Wood to the band. His rock pedigree included membership of The Small Faces and also The Faces. The unofficial piano seat previously filled by Nicky Hopkins was about to be taken over.

411. I THINK I'M GOING MAD (Jagger, Richards)
October 1977–August 1979: EMI, Pathé Marconi, Paris, France.
Producer: The Glimmer Twins. Engineer: Chris Kimsey, Bob Clearmountain.
UK B-side She Was Hot: February 1984
USA B-side She Was Hot: February 1984
Rolling Stones with Mel Collins.

First discarded as an out-take and bootlegged widely, *Going Mad* was finally released in 1984 as the flip-side of *She Was Hot*, having been remixed at the Right Track Studios in New York. The reason for this tardy release is unknown, but it was a welcome change from the usual B-side from the album rip off. A slow, self-ridiculing number, it includes the saxophone playing of Mel Collins who also contributed the sax on the *Miss You* single. The country steel guitars and the piano are, again, the track's prominent instruments. The original take, which can be found on bootleg, has an extended piano section. Some copies of these were heard on American radio stations when the official version was released.

412. BEAST OF BURDEN (Jagger, Richards)
October 1977–March 1978: EMI, Pathé Marconi, Paris, France.
Producer: The Glimmer Twins. Engineer: Chris Kimsey. Assistant Engineer: Barry Sage, Dave Jordan, Ben King, Philippe.
*UK LP SOME GIRLS: 9 June 1978: No **2** – 25 weeks*
*USA LP SOME GIRLS: 9 June 1978: No **1** – 32 weeks*
*USA Single: September 1978: No **8** – 9 weeks.*
UK Compilation LP SUCKING IN THE SEVENTIES: May 1981
*USA Compilation LP SUCKING IN THE SEVENTIES: May 1981: No **15***
– 5 weeks

The spirits invoked on numbers such as *Under My Thumb* winced at the imagery of *Beast Of Burden*. 'I've walked miles for your loving and my feet are hurting' was the picture painted. Jagger obviously thought hard before singing the vocals true to their context in solemn tones. Bootlegged out-takes (one lasting six and a half minutes) suggest that high falsetto vocals were also attempted but these would have given a soft wry edge to the track. Ron Wood and Keith Richards lay down an acoustic tracking and also overdub electric guitars. Their lead solos, which require an attentive ear, are particularly pleasing. Selected as the second American single, it charted in September 1978 attaining a very respectable Number 8 position. The original USA picture sleeve was a possible EXILE album cover but was withdrawn; it represented 'A lion sitting on a woman' – who's your beast of burden?

413. LIES (Jagger, Richards)
October 1977–March 1978: EMI, Pathé Marconi, Paris, France.
Producer: The Glimmer Twins. Engineer: Chris Kimsey. Assistant
Engineer: Barry Sage, Dave Jordan, Ben King, Philippe.
*UK LP SOME GIRLS: 9 June 1978: No **2** – 25 weeks*
*USA LP SOME GIRLS: 9 June 1978: No **1** – 32 weeks*

SOME GIRLS was predominantly an album conceived and inspired by Mick Jagger. He was very conscious of the young British bands springing up in 'Garage Land' and was inspired by the refreshing punk rock scene. Mick seemed to want to prove that he too could relive his past and sing in an 'angry young man' stance but could he persuade the band to join in on a derivative musical thrash? Evidently *Lies* is in this turion mould, but the Stones' R 'n' B formula was not easily forgotten; the pace quickened, but the end product was distinctively The Rolling Stones. Two recorded out-takes highlight Jagger's fervour as he whips the band into a rock and roller coaster, his guitar work, as tutored by Ron Wood, becoming more than just a few rhythm chords.

414. SHAVED STONE (a.k.a. **I CAN'T HELP IT**) (Jagger, Richards)
October 1977–March 1978: EMI, Pathé Marconi, Paris, France.
Producer: The Glimmer Twins.
Bootleg only.

Mick Jagger's vocals on *Shaved Stone* were a touch too much Johnny Rotten in both style and in performing antics. The band were also stripped to the bare essentials and sounded as if they were recording in a back street garage. The line had to be drawn, and Keith Richards, determined to keep the Stones within their own well-found limits, argued with Mick about the character and tempo of some of the session material. As Barbara Charone confirms, Keith Richards put it a little more bluntly 'What the fuck do we need to try and sound like the Sex Pistols for?'. *Shaved Stone*, alias *I Can't Help It*, remained on the cutting room floor, Keith Richards ensuring the *entente diplomatique*.

415. FIJI JIM (Jagger, Richards)
October 1977–March 1978: EMI, Pathé Marconi, Paris, France.
Producer: The Glimmer Twins.
Bootleg only.

Keith's favourite Scotty Moore guitar riffs were extracted from the all-time rock 'n' roll sound-track of guitar breaks and used on this pseudo 'fifties rocker. The country connection was not disregarded and the band are literally propelled forward on collision course with Fiji Jim, or was it all due to the spirits of Pacific Gin?

416. SOME GIRLS (a.k.a. **SOME MORE GIRLS**) (Jagger, Richards)
October 1977–March 1978: EMI, Pathé Marconi, Paris, France.
Producer: The Glimmer Twins. Engineer: Chris Kimsey. Assistant
Engineer: Barry Sage, Dave Jordan, Ben King, Philippe.
*UK LP SOME GIRLS: 9 June 1978: No **2** – 25 weeks*

*USA LP SOME GIRLS: 9 June 1978: No **1** – 32 weeks*
Rolling Stones with Sugar Blue.

Some Girls, the album's eventual title track, featured the harmonica work of Sugar Blue, which inspired the almost sardonic working title for the album of 'Sugar Blue And His Fabulous Rolling Stones'. It also featured Bill Wyman who shed his bass guitar for the synthesizer. Keith Richards was an eager debutante for the bass guitar role. *Some Girls* became a contentious number due to a one-liner proclaiming that black girls have athletic nocturnal habits. Atlantic Records tried to ensure that the line was rewritten, but the band refused. This ensured that, although released, it would not become a radio hit. The concept and design by Peter Corriston of the album cover also created problems because some of the girls depicted were less than happy at being fronted on a Rolling Stones album cover with rouged lips together with the Stones in drag. Lucille Ball's legal action not long after the album's release forced a change to the sleeve work. The original covers became collectors' items.

417. EVERYTHING IS TURNING TO GOLD (a.k.a. TIME TO GO)
(Jagger, Richards, Wood)
October 1977–March 1978: EMI, Pathé Marconi, Paris, France.
Producer: The Glimmer Twins.
USA B-side Shattered: December 1978.
UK Compilation LP SUCKING IN THE SEVENTIES: May 1981
*USA Compilation LP SUCKING IN THE SEVENTIES: May 1981: No **15***
– 5 weeks
Rolling Stones with Mel Collins.

The distractions of superstars trouncing in on the band's sessions were deliberately avoided on SOME GIRLS. The band performed as a unit and guests appeared strictly by invitation only. Most tracks were, therefore, Jagger, Richards compositions just involving the five instrumentalists. Ron Wood's co-composition of *Everything Is Turning To Gold* evaded album recognition, the Mel Collins saxophone work being again destined only to appear as a single flip-side (like *Going Mad*). In Britain, the track was not released until the 1981 collection of 'seventies material SUCKING IN THE SEVENTIES. Out-takes of this track from the sessions are titled *Time To Go*.

418. SHATTERED (Jagger, Richards)
October 1977–March 1978: EMI, Pathé Marconi, Paris, France.
Producer: The Glimmer Twins. Engineer: Chris Kimsey. Assistant
Engineer: Barry Sage, Dave Jordan, Ben King, Philippe.
*UK LP SOME GIRLS: 9 June 1978: No **2** – 25 weeks*
*USA LP SOME GIRLS: 9 June 1978: No **1** – 32 weeks*
*USA Single: December 1978: No **31** – 4 weeks*
UK Compilation LP SUCKING IN THE SEVENTIES: May 1981
*USA Compilation LP SUCKING IN THE SEVENTIES: May 1981: No **15***
– 5 weeks
Rolling Stones with 1 Moroccan, 1 Jew, 1 Wasp.

Apparently, a long time in the making, *Shattered* is a percussive assault on the senses. Bill Wyman is removed from the proceedings again. Ron Wood (modesty forbid) performs on bass, pedal steel guitar, bass drum and backing vocals. Other percussive sounds are made by a foreign legion of Moroccans, Jews and Wasps. Released as a single in the States, it struggled up the charts as it related the seediness of New York. Mick Jagger's vocals saved the grace on an otherwise over-baked number.

419. FAR AWAY EYES (a.k.a. **TRUCKDRIVER BLUES**) (Jagger, Richards)
October 1977-March 1978: EMI, Pathé Marconi, Paris, France.
Producer: The Glimmer Twins. Engineer: Chris Kimsey. Assistant
Engineer: Barry Sage, Dave Jordan, Ben King, Philippe.
UK B-side Miss You: 19 May 1978: No. 3 – 13 weeks
USA B-side Miss You: 19 May 1978
UK LP SOME GIRLS: 9 June 1978: No. 2 – 25 weeks
USA LP SOME GIRLS: 9 June 1978: No. 1 – 32 weeks

Mick Jagger, stetson in hand, turns on a Bakersfield accent and preaches the optimistic teachings of the Sacred Bleeding Heart of Jesus. The lyrics are perhaps the best, certainly the most humorous, on the album. Mick's delivery is staged convincingly. Keith Richards thought the final take was too affected. He preferred a straighter approach with just a touch of satirical flavour. The release on the flipside of *Miss You* preceded the album release. In Britain, due to significant radio air-play, it became a double A-side and at one stage was credited in the charts as *Far Away Eyes*, taking over from its flip, the disco orientated *Miss You*. *Far Away Eyes* also had the distinction of being the first Stones release on the new marketing phenomenon – the twelve inch single – notwithstanding that the release on 2 June 1978 was a limited edition in gaudy pink vinyl. Collectors can still find the product in back-street second-hand shops fetching rather more than the original cost.

420. CLAUDINE (Jagger, Richards)
November 1977: EMI, Pathé Marconi, Paris, France. Producer: The Glimmer Twins.
Bootleg only.

An instantaneous uptempo country track which relates the tale of Claudine Longet, former wife of celebrity Andy Williams. She was convicted of murdering her lover Spider Sabach, the sentence being moderated to allow her family rights during the week meaning she was only imprisoned at week-ends. *Claudine* is played at a striking pace, governed by an uncredited boogie piano player who was either road/studio manager Ian Stewart or current piano session player Ian 'McHooligan' McLagan. Keith Richards is in electrifying form soloing on guitar. Destined possibly for the EMOTIONAL RESCUE album, *Claudine's* release was prevented due to the inherent litigation threat.

421. MISTY ROADS (a.k.a. WHEN SHE HELD ME TIGHT) (Jagger, Richards)
October 1977–March 1978: EMI, Pathé Marconi, Paris, France.
Producer: The Glimmer Twins.
Bootleg only.

Another excursion into the Nashville land of tinkling piano and country guitar licks. Ron Wood plugs in a pedal steel and Keith Richards the lead guitar. The sound is not as clinical as *Claudine*, meaning that *Misty Roads* was soon banished as an out-take, despite the ever-popular falsetto 'ooh-ooh-oohs'.

422. MISS YOU (a.k.a. I MISS YOU) (Jagger, Richards)
October 1977–March 1978: EMI, Pathé Marconi, Paris, France.
Producer: The Glimmer Twins. Engineer: Chris Kimsey. Assistant
Engineer: Barry Sage, Dave Jordan, Ben King, Philippe.
UK Single: 19 May 1978: No. 3 – 13 weeks
USA Single: 19 May 1978: No. 1 – 16 weeks
UK LP SOME GIRLS: 9 June 1978: No. 2 – 25 weeks
USA LP SOME GIRLS: 9 June 1978: No. 1 – 32 weeks
Rolling Stones with Ian McLagan, Mel Collins, Sugar Blue.

423. MISS YOU (a.k.a. I MISS YOU) (Jagger, Richards)
October 1977–March 1978: EMI, Pathé Marconi, Paris, France.
Producer: The Glimmer Twins. Engineer: Bob Clearmountain.
UK twelve-inch Single: 19 May 1978: No. 3 – 13 weeks
USA twelve-inch Single: 19 May 1978: No. 1 – 16 weeks
Rolling Stones with Ian McLagan, Mel Collins, Sugar Blue.

The disco-entrenched beat of *Miss You*, more than any other 'seventies track, opened avenues only Mick Jagger had ever thought the band were capable of exploring. It provided them with their most contemporary and distinctive sound since the chart-topping *Brown Sugar* and in the States became their most successful Number 1 ever, even out-pacing the monumental *Honky Tonk Women*. The latter had a run of 14 weeks in the charts while the media-catapulted *Miss You* managed 16 weeks. Time was certainly on the Stones' side. The single release was made in the usual seven-inch format but also for the first time on glorious twelve-inch where it was remixed by Bob Clearmountain to eight and a half minutes. Various out-takes of this prolonged *Miss You* have surfaced on bootlegs. The finished article was an inspired and calculated attempt to reach a new audience, significantly promoting the SOME GIRLS album. Joining the band were harpist Sugar Blue, Mac on piano and Mel Collins the saxophonist. A dull video accompanied the release. It was produced by promo stalwart Michael Lindsay-Hogg, the Stones mimed to the lyrics while Charlie Watts showed off his new GI hair-crop. (Ironically, for an R 'n' B originated band with new disco success, Chicago blues guitarist Phil Guy (and brother of Keith's sparring partner Buddy) used it in 1988–89 to close his totally blues act!)

424. JUST MY IMAGINATION (RUNNING AWAY WITH ME) (Whitfield, Strong)
October 1977–March 1978: EMI, Pathé Marconi, Paris, France.
Producer: The Glimmer Twins. Engineer: Chris Kimsey. Assistant
Engineer: Barry Sage, Dave Jordan, Ben King, Philippe.
*UK LP SOME GIRLS: 9 June 1978: No. **2** – 25 weeks*
*USA LP SOME GIRLS: 9 June 1978: No. **1** – 32 weeks*
Rolling Stones with Ian McLagan.

Definitely a highlight of the album, this Temptations Motown hit was moulded into the Stones' slick R 'n' B format, and the band cruise along – after all, 'Papa was a Rolling Stone'. Ron Wood epitomized a new-found freshness in the Stones' studio performance. He inspired Mick Jagger to play guitar on a number of tracks and moulded a contemporary rock sound and was an integral additive to the band. Even Bill Wyman commented on how much he enjoyed the SOME GIRLS recordings due to Ronnie's presence. The ultimate accolade, however, is the camaraderie he instinctively struck with inmate Keef the Riff. The guitar rhapsody charge during the last few minutes 'runs away with me'. An out-take also illustrates frenzied guitar playing. *Just My Imagination* should have been a single!

425. JAH IS NOT DEAD (a.k.a. JAH IS WONDERFUL) (Jagger, Richards)
November 1977: EMI, Pathé Marconi, Paris, France. Producer: The
Glimmer Twins.
Bootleg only.

The winsome rhythm sounds of *Jah Is Not Dead* emanate powerfully onto the hi-fi. The song's main guitar riff, however, is so typically white that Jamaican creditability is soon lost. The track may have originated from the BLACK AND BLUE sessions in Munich. A humorous story, courtesy of journalist Barbara Charone, indicates a fifty-minute version was recorded. Two senior EMI executives arrived to hear how the new album was progressing and Mick Jagger, in a buoyantly mischievous mood, played them the track in its entirety, seriously insisting that *Jah* was the album, though offering that it could be cut down to the usual forty-five minute album format. Exit two worried execs. In August, later that year, Keith continued his solo recordings and recorded Jimmy Cliffs' *The Harder They Come* in true reggae style. This recording was released with *Run Rudolph Run* as Keith's first solo single in 1978. *Run Rudolph Run* was originally recorded on 10 December 1976 in London with Mike Driscoll and Ian Stewart.

426. BEFORE THEY MAKE ME RUN (Jagger, Richards)
March 1978: EMI, Pathé Marconi, Paris, France. Producer: The
Glimmer Twins. Engineer: Dave Jordan.
*UK LP SOME GIRLS: 9 June 1978: No. **2** – 25 weeks*
*USA LP SOME GIRLS: 9 June 1978: No. **1** – 32 weeks*

Not since *Happy* was recorded in 1971 had Keith Richards sung the lead vocals on an album cut. *Before They Make Me Run*, a Keith Richards' penned track, autobiographical in lyrical message, was recorded while Mick Jagger was away from the Paris sessions and had to meet with his approval when he returned. *Before They Make Me Run* was engineered by Dave Jordan, the only time on the album when Chris Kimsey was not at the mastering desk. It is a high-energy rock 'n' roller proving that Keith's unique guitar playing was 'Almost Grown'! A US promo release differs slightly from the album version including minor lyrical changes. Anne Liebovitz's excellent colour sleeve is frameable!

427. EVERLASTING IS MY LOVE (a.k.a. NANKER PHELGE) (Jagger, Richards)
October 1977–March 1978: EMI, Pathé Marconi, Paris, France.
Producer: The Glimmer Twins.
Bootleg only.

The Stones perform a country ballad and show the softer side of life in a studio. Many out-takes from the Paris sessions for SOME GIRLS were in this mould and as such DON'T STEAL MY GIRLFRIEND (an original working title for the album) recording sessions produced a prodigious crop of out-takes. It should be noted that some of the 'also known as' titles originate from bootleggers' less inspired guesswork, such as the other title for *Everlasting – Nanker Phelge*.

428. WHERE THE BOYS GO (Jagger, Richards)
October 1977–March 1978: EMI, Pathé Marconi, Paris, France.
Producer: The Glimmer Twins. Associate Producer: Chris Kimsey.
Engineer: Sean Fullan, Brad Samuelsohn, 'Snake' Reynolds, Jon Smith.
UK LP EMOTIONAL RESCUE: 22 June 1980: No. 1 – 18 weeks
USA LP EMOTIONAL RESCUE: 22 June 1980: No. 1 – 20 weeks

Recorded initially at the SOME GIRLS sessions, *Where The Boys Go* was hung over for use on the next studio album, EMOTIONAL RESCUE. It is an up-tempo Saturday-night-out rocker. The band sounded tight: Charlie Watts' drum sounds just right, Mick Jagger particularly wry on cockney vocals, while Keith Richards and Ron Wood delivered the lead solos. Ian Stewart boogies on piano, Bill Wyman stands upright and certain uncredited females join in on Travolta/Newton-John backing vocals at the song's climax.

429. SUMMER ROMANCE (Jagger, Richards)
October 1977–March 1978: EMI, Pathé Marconi, Paris, France.
Producer: The Glimmer Twins. Associate Producer: Chris Kimsey.
Engineer: Sean Fullan, Brad Samuelsohn, 'Snake' Reynolds, Jon Smith.
UK LP EMOTIONAL RESCUE: 22 June 1980: No. 1 – 18 weeks
USA LP EMOTIONAL RESCUE: 22 June 1980: No. 1 – 20 weeks

Another pacey number with Ian Stewart accompanying them as the band members strain to recollect those 'Butlins Holiday Romances'. Keith Richards and Ron Wood intuitively wind up their guitars to produce a number which is essentially lead guitar orientated. A guitar-picking sound fills in when the leads fuse out. Recorded in Paris, it was later remixed for the EMOTIONAL RESCUE album. And so the Paris sessions finally expired in March 1978 having produced some good sounds and a highly respectable album.

430. SWEET LITTLE SIXTEEN (Berry)
14 June 1978: Passaic Theatre, New York, USA.
Bootleg only.
Rolling Stones with Ian McLagan.

431. WHEN THE WHIP COMES DOWN (LIVE VERSION) (Jagger, Richards)
14 June 1978: Passaic Theatre, New York, USA.
UK Compilation LP SUCKING IN THE SEVENTIES: May 1981
USA Compilation LP SUCKING IN THE SEVENTIES: May 1981: No. **15**
– 5 weeks
Rolling Stones with Ian McLagan.

432. HOUND DOG (Leiber, Stoller)
28 June 1978: Memphis, Tennessee, USA.
Bootleg only.
Rolling Stones with Ian McLagan.

With memories of *Parisienne* recording days fading, the Stones embarked in the Summer of 1978 on the well-practised United States tour. Two months of dates enabled them to promote the SOME GIRLS album and play some more fast numbers. The set was mostly made up of 'seventies material but the finale included 'sixties favourites *Jumpin' Jack Flash* and *Street Fighting Man.* Collectors will be interested in the detours from the standard album material, such as the Memphis (roots music) *Hound Dog* and a version of Chuck Berry's *Sweet Lil' Sixteen.* The 1978 tour was enthusiastically bootlegged. Many were of a high stereo quality perpetuated by local FM radio stations. *When The Whip Comes Down* originated from such a recording and was released without any explanation of its origin except for the track title (live version) on the tongue twisting 1981 compilation SUCKING IN THE SEVENTIES.

433. BEFORE THEY MAKE ME RUN (Jagger, Richards)
22 April 1979: Oshawa Civic Auditorium, Toronto, Canada.
Bootleg only.

434. PRODIGAL SON (Wilkins)
22 April 1979: Oshawa Civic Auditorium, Toronto, Canada.
Bootleg only.

On 24 October 1978 Keith Richards' fracas with the Canadian authorities was finally settled. His sentence was to play to the Toronto public in aid of the Canadian National Institute for The Blind, among other conditions set by the authorities. Ron Wood's touring band for his solo activities, The New Barbarians, of which Keith was a guest guitarist, provided the basis of the free concert, held on 22 April 1979. The above two tracks are quite apt in their titles and were the climax of the Barbarians' set –with Keith on vocals and a duet by Mick Jagger and Keith signifying the entrance of the full Rolling Stones line-up on stage, a surprise to the ecstatic Canadian crowd.

435. WE HAD IT ALL (Seal, Fritts)
May 1979–May 1980: Compass Point Studio, Nassau, Bahamas.
Producer: The Glimmer Twins.
Bootleg only.

The RCA territory of Hollywood and, more predominantly, the Compass Point Studios in Nassau were the recording bases for the remaining tracks necessary for the completion of the EMOTIONAL RESCUE album. These tracks were recorded over a number of years and some may have even originated from the Paris sessions in 1977/78. *We Had It All* is an out-take from these recordings being a solo recording by Keith Richards. His gold-labelled vocals glide competently over what is quite a sentimental song.

436. EMOTIONAL RESCUE (Jagger, Richards)
May 1979–May 1980: Compass Point, Nassau, Bahamas. Producer: The Glimmer Twins. Associate Producer: Chris Kimsey. Engineer: Sean Fullan, Brad Samuelsohn, 'Snake' Reynolds, Jon Smith.
UK Single: 20 June 1980: No. 9 – 8 weeks
USA Single: 20 June 1980: No. 3 – 14 weeks
UK LP EMOTIONAL RESCUE: 22 June 1980: No. 1 – 18 weeks
USA LP EMOTIONAL RESCUE: 22 June 1980: No. 1 – 20 weeks
Rolling Stones with Bobby Keys.

This is the album title track and another number formulated in the disco mould, reminiscent of the hit single *Miss You* (remember the falsetto vocals?). Mick Jagger takes the centre stage unfurling, rap-style, the message of chivalry: rescuing the screwed-up chick. Written by Mick Jagger on the electric piano, the initial backing track was recorded simply with Ron Wood on bass and Charlie Watts on drums. The saxophone was added by Bobby Keys and guitar parts overlaid at the mixing stage. A dub version of the song was mixed, but has never been given the luxury of public release. *Emotional Rescue* did not exactly emulate the success of *Miss You*, but consolidated their contemporary position as they again achieved Top 10 positions and entered yet another decade, the 'eighties, in chart form. To accompany the single, a video was produced by David Mallett. The film, in parts, uses the same techniques of heat-image camera work that appeared on the front and rear sleeves of the album cover and also the freebie inner poster of 15 similar works. Roy Adzak was the inspirer of the idea which is known as thermographics. The video, as a piece of imagery, was a step up from the previous *Miss You* promotion.

437. GANGSTERS MAUL (Jagger, Richards)
May 1979–May 1980: Compass Point, Nassau, Bahamas. Producer: The Glimmer Twins.
Bootleg only.

Mick Jagger can be heard directing *Gangsters Maul*, uttering the different scales for the band to play. It has quite a catchy 'lick' and could have made the grade to an official release.

438. SWEET HOME CHICAGO (Johnson)
May 1979–May 1980: Compass Point, Nassau, Bahamas. Producer: The Glimmer Twins.
Bootleg only.

A slow Chicago blues which the band seem to enjoy. Keith is at home meandering along the fret-board. Well worth a listen!

439. DANCE (Jagger, Richards, Wood)
May 1979–May 1980: Compass Point, Nassau, Bahamas. Producer: The Glimmer Twins. Associate Producer: Chris Kimsey. Engineer: Sean Fullan, Brad Samuelsohn, 'Snake' Reynolds, Jon Smith.
UK LP EMOTIONAL RESCUE: 22 June 1980: No. 1 – 18 weeks
USA LP EMOTIONAL RESCUE: 22 June 1980: No. 1 – 20 weeks
Rolling Stones with Bobby Keys, Michael Shrieve, Max Romeo.

440. IF I WAS A DANCER (DANCE PART TWO) (Jagger, Richards, Wood)
May 1979–May 1980: Compass Point, Nassau, Bahamas. Producer: The Glimmer Twins. Associate Producer: Chris Kimsey. Engineer: Sean Fullan, Brad Samuelsohn, 'Snake' Reynolds, Jon Smith.
UK Compilation LP SUCKING IN THE SEVENTIES: May 1981
USA Compilation LP SUCKING IN THE SEVENTIES: May 1981: No. 15 – 5 weeks
Rolling Stones with Bobby Keys, Michael Shrieve, Max Romeo.

Here we have two variations on a theme of rhythmic mayhem instigated by Michael Shrieve on percussion and the back-up vocals of reggae artist Max Romeo. Georgian expatriate Bobby Keys, ever loyal to the Stones, supports the cause on saxophone. Ron Wood, practised at the art of deception, is credited as a co-songwriter with Jagger and Richards, although it is said the song was written courtesy of a Wood, Richards partnership. The first version, *Dance*, was recorded in one take and was subsequently released on the EMOTIONAL RESCUE album, its beat laced with funk. Different lyrics continue the story on *If I Was A Dancer*, a version which remained unreleased for almost a year until the appearance of the compilation SUCKING IN THE SEVENTIES. Prior to this *If I Was A Dancer* had been widely bootlegged. The two versions combined would have produced a worthwhile twelve-inch single.

441. DOWN IN THE HOLE (Jagger, Richards)

May 1979–May 1980: Compass Point, Nassau, Bahamas. Producer: The Glimmer Twins. Associate Producer: Chris Kimsey. Engineer: Sean Fullan, Brad Samuelsohn, 'Snake' Reynolds, Jon Smith.
UK B-side Emotional Rescue: 20 June 1980
USA B-side Emotional Rescue: 20 June 1980
UK LP EMOTIONAL RESCUE: 22 June 1980: No. 1 – 18 weeks
USA LP EMOTIONAL RESCUE: 22 June 1980: No. 1 – 20 weeks
Rolling Stones with Sugar Blue.

Something of a surprise to fans, the Stones produced a work of the blues! The blues had always been a foundation of the Stones' soul, but the style was revered to the extent that very few attempts were made at recording a modern-day blues song. Progression in sound had always been a strong theme; not to progress musically would have stopped them in their tracks in the mid 'sixties. A wailing Sugar Blue harmonica accompanies the band, Keith Richards' guitar solos being quite at ease in this laid-back frame. Derivative in sound, the lyrics were modern in contrast and incompatible – as such *Down In The Hole* misses the mark.

442. LONELY AT THE TOP (Jagger, Richards)

May 1979–May 1980: Compass Point, Nassau, Bahamas.
Bootleg only.

Mick Jagger was evidently fond of this song since he rerecorded it with Jeff Beck and Pete Townshend on his 1985 solo album SHE'S THE BOSS. The lyrics were altered and generally it received an uplift compared with this duller version.

443. INDIAN GIRL (Jagger, Richards)

May 1979–May 1980: Compass Point, Nassau, Bahamas. Producer: The Glimmer Twins. Associate Producer: Chris Kimsey. Engineer: Sean Fullan, Brad Samuelsohn, 'Snake' Reynolds, Jon Smith. Horns arrangement: Jack Nitzsche. Horns directed: Arif Mardin.
UK LP EMOTIONAL RESCUE: 22 June 1980: No. 1 – 18 weeks
USA LP EMOTIONAL RESCUE: 22 June 1980: No. 1 – 20 weeks
Rolling Stones with Nicky Hopkins.

The country-styled guitars of Keith Richards and Ron Wood glide their way into this ravaged tale of a girl's mother and father fighting Angolan guerrilla warfare on behalf of Cuba. Incongruous certainly, the pessimism of the message contrasted sharply with the optimistic feel of the Latin horns arranged by long-lost associate Jack Nitzsche, who had worked with the Stones in 1965 and 1966 when he was the arranger at RCA's studios in Los Angeles. Arif Mardin, who conducted the horns on *Melody* in January 1975, revisits the Stones to do the same on *Indian Girl.*

444. LET'S GO STEADY (Richards)
May 1979–May 1980: Compass Point, Nassau, Bahamas. Producer: The Glimmer Twins.
Bootleg only.
Rolling Stones with Bobby Keys.

A classic out-take featuring a 'one-sided duet' between Keith Richards and an unknown female artist. Seemingly written by Keith, whose output at the time was quite prodigious, it is a splendid ballad full of soulful ramblings. Keith's song-writing technique centred on playing melodies on a piano and if an inkling of inspiration was detected the track was cut onto a portable tape recorder. *Let's Go Steady* may, therefore, include the piano playing of Keith. The studio track has never been released but live versions recorded with the New Barbarians can be obtained.

445. SEND IT TO ME (Jagger, Richards)
May 1979–May 1980: Compass Point, Nassau, Bahamas. Producer: The Glimmer Twins. Associate Producer: Chris Kimsey. Engineer: Sean Fullan, Brad Samuelsohn, 'Snake' Reynolds, Jon Smith.
UK LP EMOTIONAL RESCUE: 22 June 1980: No. 1 – 18 weeks
USA LP EMOTIONAL RESCUE: 22 June 1980: No. 1 – 20 weeks
UK B-side She's So Cold: September 1980
USA B-side She's So Cold: September 1980
Rolling Stones with Bobby Keys, Sugar Blue.

Played with a reggae beat, *Send It To Me* is one of the weakest tracks included on the album. The sessions produced over 40 numbers of which approximately two dozen were shaped and recorded for possible release. Many were reclaimed from the Paris shelves but only a lucky ten were mastered for the album. An out-take of *Send It To Me* is lengthened and features more prominently the harmonica work of Sugar Blue.

446. LET ME GO (Jagger, Richards)
May 1979–May 1980: Compass Point, Nassau, Bahamas. Producer: The Glimmer Twins. Associate Producer: Sean Fullan, Brad Samuelsohn, 'Snake' Reynolds, Jon Smith.
UK LP EMOTIONAL RESCUE: 22 June 1980: No. 1 – 18 weeks
USA LP EMOTIONAL RESCUE: 22 June 1980: No. 1 – 20 weeks
Rolling Stones with Bobby Keys, Nicky Hopkins.

A typical Keith Richards' rocker on which Ron Wood also snatches a guitar line or two. But Keith is the convincing partner, his boot-laced tie retrieved from the remnants of Stones' rock 'n' roll acts of the past. The song, fast in pace, surges forward against the backbone of the song's rhythm: Charlie's frenetic hi-hat is in good form. Although not a classic, it became a popular stage favourite on the World Tour of 1981/82.

447. SHE'S SO COLD (Jagger, Richards)
May 1979–May 1980: Compass Point, Nassau, Bahamas. Producer: The Glimmer Twins. Associate Producer: Chris Kimsey. Engineer: Sean

Fullan, Brad Samuelsohn, 'Snake' Reynolds, Jon Smith.
*UK LP EMOTIONAL RESCUE: 22 June 1980: No. **1** – 18 weeks*
*USA LP EMOTIONAL RESCUE: 22 June 1980: No. **1** – 20 weeks*
*UK Single: September 1980: No. **33** – 6 weeks*
*USA Single: September 1980: No. **26** – 5 weeks*
Rolling Stones with Bobby Keys.

A mid-tempo rocker where the rhythm guitars of Keith Richards and Ron Wood jostle for attention. They hardly break sweat, relying on the dexterity of their string-driven fingers. Ron Wood felt quite at ease in this situation where neither was labelled lead guitarist. It was not constrictive and allowed the band to free-flow around the song's main structure. What was needed now was some better than average material on which to work. *She's So Cold* (to paraphrase 'frigid, like a refrigerator') was the second single from the album and was not successful. In Britain it was their worst chart position ever, remaining there for a very cool six weeks. Dave Mallett's video, shot in an ice compartment, was somewhat humorous but it did nothing to assist the defrosted music. A version was released for radio stations in the United States minus a reference to the Arctic girl being 'goddamn cold'.

448. ALL ABOUT YOU (Jagger, Richards)

May 1979–May 1980: Compass Point, Nassau, Bahamas. Producer: The Glimmer Twins. Associate Producer: Chris Kimsey. Engineer: Sean Fullan, Brad Samuelsohn, 'Snake' Reynolds, Jon Smith.
*UK LP EMOTIONAL RESCUE: 22 June 1980: No. **1** – 18 weeks*
*USA LP EMOTIONAL RESCUE: 22 June 1980: No. **1** – 20 weeks*
Rolling Stones with Nicky Hopkins, Bobby Keys.

Written by Keith Richards, release was delayed until he was convinced that the track had not been subconsciously copied from another artist. Keith performs as lead vocalist, a velvet balladeer, on some fine lyrics. A contest raged to see which of Keith's songs would be included on the album, and for the first time it was one of his 'slow' numbers. It is a pity the record company never pressed Keith to release a solo album. Works such as this and the rejected *Let's Go Steady* would have formed a good base for a solo project. When the Stones renewed their world-wide record company deals, the only solo guaranteed project was that of Mick Jagger. Keith, perhaps wisely, knew that solo projects could only disrupt the direction of the Stones.

449. LINDA LU (Jagger, Richards)

May 1979–May 1980: Compass Point, Nassau, Bahamas. Producer: The Glimmer Twins.
Bootleg only.

The Stones recorded approximately 40 songs for the EMOTIONAL RESCUE album but only 25 were of an acceptable standard. *Linda Lu* is one which did not make the mastering stage. It is a soft rock number on which Ron Wood and Keith Richards are kept employed – but only just!

450. WHAT'S THE MATTER? (Jagger, Richards)
May 1979–May 1980: Compass Point, Nassau, Bahamas. Producer: The Glimmer Twins.
Bootleg only.

Again *What's The Matter?* is noticeably an out-take. The guitar work is bluesy and is accompanied by a harp and a Nashville piano. Mick Jagger can be heard prompting the band on scale changes.

451. BULLDOG (Jagger, Richards)
May 1979–May 1980: Compass Point, Nassau, Bahamas. Producer: The Glimmer Twins.
Bootleg only.

452. LITTLE T & A (Jagger, Richards)
May 1979–May 1980: Compass Point, Nassau, Bahamas. Producer: The Glimmer Twins. Engineer: Chris Kimsey, Bob Clearmountain, Gary Lyons, Bob Ludwig.
UK LP TATTOO YOU: 24 August 1981: No 2 – 29 weeks
USA LP TATTOO YOU: 24 August 1981: No 1 – 30 weeks
UK B-side Waiting On A Friend: 30 November 1981
USA B-side Waiting On A Friend: 30 November 1981

Keith Richards takes the lead vocals on what was initially a song labelled *Bulldog.* It was recorded at the EMOTIONAL RESCUE sessions but put aside until (with slightly altered lyrics) it was remixed in 1981 by Bob Clearmountain and Gary Lyons for the rush job of an album TATTOO YOU. This does not, however, mar the song's obvious strength. From the opening guitar chords it is full of excitement. Guitar riffs and lead breaks, courtesy of Keith, abound while he twists his tongue around the vocal slang – T & A standing for 'tits and ass'. Incidentally, 'The Bulldog' was a pseudonym used by the band when mixing the UNDERCOVER album in 1983.

453. NO USE IN CRYING (Jagger, Richards)
May 1979–May 1980: Compass Point, Nassau, Bahamas. Producer: The Glimmer Twins. Engineer: Chris Kimsey, Bob Clearmountain, Gary Lyons, Bob Ludwig.
UK B-side Start Me Up: 17 August 1981
USA B-side Start Me Up: 17 August 1981
UK LP TATTOO YOU: 24 August 1981: No 2 – 29 weeks
USA LP TATTOO YOU: 24 August 1981: No 1 – 30 weeks
Rolling Stones with Nicky Hopkins.

Ain't No Use In Crying is the kind of track that the Stones could dutifully turn out at a session with monotonous regularity. It is a slow song fuelled by a piano, played possibly by Nicky Hopkins. Mick Jagger's vocals are mixed from one channel to another while occasionally the odd echo diminishes the vocal line at verse ends. Although veneered in the typical Stones' mould, it is not a classic. Recorded originally at the Pathé

Marconi Studios in July and August 1979, it was redone for the TATTOO YOU album.

454. WAITING ON A FRIEND (Jagger, Richards)
January–June 1981: Electric Ladyland, Atlantic Studio, New York.
Producer: The Glimmer Twins. Engineer: Chris Kimsey, Bob
Clearmountain, Gary Lyons, Bob Ludwig.
*UK LP TATTOO YOU: 24 August 1981: No **2** – 29 weeks*
*USA LP TATTOO YOU: 24 August 1981: No **1** – 30 weeks*
*UK Single: 30 November 1981: No **50** – 6 weeks*
*USA Single: 30 November 1981: No **13** – 12 weeks*
Rolling Stones with Sonny Rollins.

Waiting On A Friend is quite a contrast to the rather turgid *No Use In Crying.* Acoustic guitars strum and the band warm to the song's laid-back character. The saxophone work of Sonny Rollins serves to complement the easy atmosphere. This particular trait was used to good effect by Michael Lindsay-Hogg, who was back with the band to film a video to back up a chart position. Failing dismally in Britain, the song and the video were a great success in the States. Filmed on the boulevards of New York, it shows Mick Jagger and Keith Richards fraternizing with street life. Keith, tobacco reefer in hand, joins Mick and then they saunter to St Mark's Bar and Grill where the rest of the band can be found vertically aiding the bars' foundations. Bill Wyman and Charlie Watts lurk at the back on bar stools, while Mick sings the toon to bottle-toking Honest Ron.

455. HEAVEN (Jagger, Richards)
January–June 1981: Electric Ladyland, Atlantic Studio, New York.
Producer: The Glimmer Twins. Engineer: Chris Kimsey, Bob
Clearmountain, Gary Lyons, Bob Ludwig.
*UK LP TATTOO YOU: 24 August 1981: No **2** – 29 weeks*
*USA LP TATTOO YOU: 24 August 1981: No **1** – 30 weeks*

Although principally a mixing station for various numbers, New York provided an opportunity to record three new songs especially for the TATTOO YOU album. *Heaven* is a track enhanced by the studio techniques of Chris Kimsey and Co. The song's backbone is founded on whispering jangles and Charlie Watt's percussion work. Mick Jagger's vocals caress over the sensual lyrics in superb style. Given a head start the track surprisingly becomes lost in the mire of TATTOO YOU's general uncollectiveness and is now relatively unheard. An out-take lasting five and a half minutes is available on bootlegged recordings.

456. NEIGHBOURS (Jagger, Richards)
January–June 1981. Studio: Electric Ladyland, Atlantic Studio, New
York. Producer: The Glimmer Twins. Engineer: Chris Kimsey, Bob
Clearmountain, Gary Lyons, Bob Ludwig.
*UK LP TATTOO YOU: 24 August 1981: No **2** – 29 weeks*

USA LP TATTOO YOU: 24 August 1981: No **1** *– 30 weeks*
USA B-side Hang Fire: April 1982
Rolling Stones with Sonny Rollins.

Everybody can at times do without neighbours and the Michael Lindsay-Hogg video of apartment life portrays the seedy side of neighbours (note the English spelling – the album sleeve states *Neighbors*). There are, for example, the silk-laced copulating couples and the gory hacksaw disintegration of a by-now missing wife. Both figure in an unremissive manner in the video. By leaps and bounds the song ponders the subject under the twin thrust of guitars and saxophone, the latter again protagonized by jazz musician Sonny Rollins. The video including the lace-dressed prostitute and the be-devilled murder, was banned by the American Video Musical network, MTV. It is said it was filmed in one of Mick Jagger's New York apartments and was written about Keith Richards who was the most disruptive Stone. Bill Wyman, when asked if he had ever shared a room with Keith, replied, 'No, but I once tried to sleep in the same hotel!' The music is up-tempo and was included on subsequent tours.

457. WHOLE LOTTA SHAKIN' GOIN' ON (Williams, David)
August 1981: Long View Farm, Brookfield, Massachusetts, USA.
Bootleg only.
Keith Richards and his Rolling Stones!

Long View Farm was used as a rehearsal venue for the Stones 1981 tour. A bootlegged album has just Keith Richards playing solo riffs on lead guitar; the album includes Stones' numbers *Brown Sugar*, *Start Me Up* and *Munich Hilton* and Chuck Berry's *No Particular Place To Go*. *Whole Lotta Shakin' Goin' On* originates from the same one-man session but as well as Keith on piano and vocals, it contains the saxophone playing of Bobby Keys.

458. UNDER MY THUMB (Jagger, Richard)
5 November 1981: Meadowlands Arena, New Jersey, New York and
13 December 1981: Sun Devil Stadium, Tempe, Arizona. Producer:
The Glimmer Twins. Recorded: Bob Clearmountain, David Hewitt.
Engineer: Malcolm Pollack, Barry Bongiovi, Larry Alexander, Phil
Gitomer, Kooster MacAllister, David Brown, Bob Ludwig.
UK LP STILL LIFE: 1 June 1982: No **4** *– 18 weeks*
USA LP STILL LIFE: 1 June 1982: No **5** *– 10 weeks*
UK B-side twelve-inch Single: September 1982
USA B-side twelve-inch Single: September 1982
Rolling Stones with Ian McLagan, Ernie Watts.

459. LET'S SPEND THE NIGHT TOGETHER (Jagger, Richard)
5 November 1981: Meadowlands Arena, New Jersey, New York and
13 December 1981: Sun Devil Stadium, Tempe, Arizona. Producer:
The Glimmer Twins. Recorded: Bob Clearmountain, David Hewitt.
Engineer: Malcolm Pollack, Barry Bongiovi, Larry Alexander, Phil
Gitomer, Kooster MacAllister, David Brown, Bob Ludwig.

*UK LP STILL LIFE: 1 June 1982: No **4** – 18 weeks*
*USA LP STILL LIFE: 1 June 1982: No **5** – 10 weeks*
Rolling Stones with Ian McLagan, Ernie Watts.

460. SHATTERED (Jagger, Richard)
5 November 1981: Meadowlands Arena, New Jersey, New York and
13 December 1981: Sun Devil Stadium, Tempe, Arizona. Producer:
The Glimmer Twins. Recorded: Bob Clearmountain, David Hewitt.
Engineer: Malcolm Pollack, Barry Bongiovi, Larry Alexander, Phil
Gitomer, Kooster MacAllister, David Brown, Bob Ludwig.
*UK LP STILL LIFE: 1 June 1982: No **4** – 18 weeks*
*USA LP STILL LIFE: 1 June 1982: No **5** – 10 weeks*
Rolling Stones with Ian McLagan, Ernie Watts.

461. NEIGHBOURS (Jagger, Richards)
5 November 1981: Meadowlands Arena, New Jersey, New York and
13 December 1981: Sun Devil Stadium, Tempe, Arizona. Producer:
The Glimmer Twins. Recorded: Bob Clearmountain, David Hewitt.
Engineer: Malcolm Pollack, Barry Bongiovi, Larry Alexander, Phil
Gitomer, Kooster MacAllister, David Brown, Bob Ludwig.
Bootleg only.
Rolling Stones with Ian McLagan, Ernie Watts.

462. BLACK LIMOUSINE (Jagger, Richards)
5 November 1981: Meadowlands Arena, New Jersey, New York and
13 December 1981: Sun Devil Stadium, Tempe, Arizona. Producer:
The Glimmer Twins. Recorded: Bob Clearmountain, David Hewitt.
Engineer: Malcolm Pollack, Barry Bongiovi, Larry Alexander, Phil
Gitomer, Kooster MacAllister, David Brown, Bob Ludwig.
Bootleg only.
Rolling Stones with Ian McLagan, Ernie Watts.

463. JUST MY IMAGINATION (RUNNING AWAY WITH ME) (Whitfield, Strong)
5 November 1981: Meadowlands Arena, New Jersey, New York and
13 December 1981: Sun Devil Stadium, Tempe, Arizona. Producer:
The Glimmer Twins. Recorded: Bob Clearmountain, David Hewitt.
Engineer: Malcolm Pollack, Barry Bongiovi, Larry Alexander, Phil
Gitomer, Kooster MacAllister, David Brown, Bob Ludwig.
*UK LP STILL LIFE: 1 June 1982: No **4** – 18 weeks*
*USA LP STILL LIFE: 1 June 1982: No **5** – 10 weeks*
Rolling Stones with Ian McLagan, Ernie Watts.

464. TWENTY FLIGHT ROCK (Fairchild, Cochran)
5 November 1981: Meadowlands Arena, New Jersey, New York and
13 December 1981: Sun Devil Stadium, Tempe, Arizona. Producer:
The Glimmer Twins. Recorded: Bob Clearmountain, David Hewitt.
Engineer: Malcolm Pollack, Barry Bongiovi, Larry Alexander, Phil
Gitomer, Kooster MacAllister, David Brown, Bob Ludwig.

*UK LP STILL LIFE: 1 June 1982: No **4** – 18 weeks*
*USA LP STILL LIFE: 1 June 1982: No **5** – 10 weeks*
UK B-side Time Is On My Side: September 1982
USA B-side Time Is On My Side: September 1982
Rolling Stones with Ian McLagan, Ernie Watts.

465. LET ME GO (Jagger, Richards)
5 November 1981: Meadowlands Arena, New Jersey, New York and 13 December 1981: Sun Devil Stadium, Tempe, Arizona. Producer: The Glimmer Twins. Recorded: Bob Clearmountain, David Hewitt. Engineer: Malcolm Pollack, Barry Bongiovi, Larry Alexander, Phil Gitomer, Kooster MacAllister, David Brown, Bob Ludwig.
*UK LP STILL LIFE: 1 June 1982: No **4** – 18 weeks*
*USA LP STILL LIFE: 1 June 1982: No **5** – 10 weeks*
Rolling Stones with Ian McLagan, Ernie Watts.

466. TIME IS ON MY SIDE (Jagger, Richard)
5 November 1981: Meadowlands Arena, New Jersey, New York and 13 December 1981: Sun Devil Stadium, Tempe, Arizona. Producer: The Glimmer Twins. Recorded: Bob Clearmountain, David Hewitt. Engineer: Malcolm Pollack, Barry Bongiovi, Larry Alexander, Phil Gitomer, Kooster MacAllister, David Brown, Bob Ludwig.
*UK LP STILL LIFE: 1 June 1982: No **4** – 18 weeks*
*USA LP STILL LIFE: 1 June 1982: No **5** – 10 weeks*
*UK Single, UK twelve-inch Single: September 1982: No **62** – 2 weeks*
USA Single, USA twelve-inch Single: September 1982
Rolling Stones with Ian McLagan, Ernie Watts.

467. BEAST OF BURDEN (Jagger, Richards)
5 November 1981: Meadowlands Arena, New Jersey, New York and 13 December 1981: Sun Devil Stadium, Tempe, Arizona. Producer: The Glimmer Twins. Recorded: Bob Clearmountain, David Hewitt. Engineer: Malcolm Pollack, Barry Bongiovi, Larry Alexander, Phil Gitomer, Kooster MacAllister, David Brown, Bob Ludwig.
UK B-side Going To A Go-Go: June 1982
USA B-side Going To A Go-Go: June 1982
Rolling Stones with Ian McLagan, Ernie Watts.

468. WAITING ON A FRIEND (Jagger, Richards)
5 November 1981: Meadowlands Arena, New Jersey, New York and 13 December 1981: Sun Devil Stadium, Tempe, Arizona. Producer: The Glimmer Twins. Recorded: Bob Clearmountain, David Hewitt. Engineer: Malcolm Pollack, Barry Bongiovi, Larry Alexander, Phil Gitomer, Kooster MacAllister, David Brown, Bob Ludwig.
Bootleg only.
Rolling Stones with Ian McLagan, Ernie Watts.

469. GOING TO A GO-GO (Robinson, Moore, Johnson, Rogers)
5 November 1981: Meadowlands Arena, New Jersey, New York and

13 December 1981: Sun Devil Stadium, Tempe, Arizona. Producer: The Glimmer Twins. Recorded: Bob Clearmountain, David Hewitt. Engineer: Malcolm Pollack, Barry Bongiovi, Larry Alexander, Phil Gitomer, Kooster MacAllister, David Brown, Bob Ludwig. UK Single: June 1982: No **26** *– 6 weeks USA Single: June 1982: No* **25** *– 5 weeks UK LP STILL LIFE: 1 June 1982: No* **4** *– 18 weeks USA LP STILL LIFE: 1 June 1982: No* **5** *– 10 weeks Rolling Stones with Ian McLagan, Ernie Watts.*

470. YOU CAN'T ALWAYS GET WHAT YOU WANT (Jagger, Richard)
5 November 1981: Meadowlands Arena, New Jersey, New York and 13 December 1981: Sun Devil Stadium, Tempe, Arizona. Producer: The Glimmer Twins. Recorded: Bob Clearmountain, David Hewitt. Engineer: Malcolm Pollack, Barry Bongiovi, Larry Alexander, Phil Gitomer, Kooster MacAllister, David Brown, Bob Ludwig. Bootleg only. Rolling Stones with Ian McLagan, Ernie Watts.

471. LITTLE T & A (Jagger, Richards)
5 November 1981: Meadowlands Arena, New Jersey, New York and 13 December 1981: Sun Devil Stadium, Tempe, Arizona. Producer: The Glimmer Twins. Recorded: Bob Clearmountain, David Hewitt. Engineer: Malcolm Pollack, Barry Bongiovi, Larry Alexander, Phil Gitomer, Kooster MacAllister, David Brown, Bob Ludwig. Bootleg only. Rolling Stones with Ian McLagan, Ernie Watts.

472. TUMBLING DICE (Jagger, Richard)
5 November 1981: Meadowlands Arena, New Jersey, New York and 13 December 1981: Sun Devil Stadium, Tempe, Arizona. Producer: The Glimmer Twins. Recorded: Bob Clearmountain, David Hewitt. Engineer: Malcolm Pollack, Barry Bongiovi, Larry Alexander, Phil Gitomer, Kooster MacAllister, David Brown, Bob Ludwig. Bootleg only. Rolling Stones with Ian McLagan, Ernie Watts.

473. SHE'S SO COLD (Jagger, Richards)
5 November 1981: Meadowlands Arena, New Jersey, New York and 13 December 1981: Sun Devil Stadium, Tempe, Arizona. Producer: The Glimmer Twins. Recorded: Bob Clearmountain, David Hewitt. Engineer: Malcolm Pollack, Barry Bongiovi, Larry Alexander, Phil Gitomer, Kooster MacAllister, David Brown, Bob Ludwig. Bootleg only. Rolling Stones with Ian McLagan, Ernie Watts.

474. ALL DOWN THE LINE (Jagger, Richard)
5 November 1981: Meadowlands Arena, New Jersey, New York and 13 December 1981: Sun Devil Stadium, Tempe, Arizona. Producer:

The Glimmer Twins. Recorded: Bob Clearmountain, David Hewitt.
Engineer: Malcolm Pollack, Barry Bongiovi, Larry Alexander, Phil
Gitomer, Kooster MacAllister, David Brown, Bob Ludwig.
Bootleg only.
Rolling Stones with Ian McLagan, Ernie Watts.

475. HANG FIRE (Jagger, Richards)
5 November 1981: Meadowlands Arena, New Jersey, New York and
13 December 1981: Sun Devil Stadium, Tempe, Arizona. Producer:
The Glimmer Twins. Recorded: Bob Clearmountain, David Hewitt.
Engineer: Malcolm Pollack, Barry Bongiovi, Larry Alexander, Phil
Gitomer, Kooster MacAllister, David Brown, Bob Ludwig.
Bootleg only.
Rolling Stones with Ian McLagan, Ernie Watts.

476. MISS YOU (Jagger, Richards)
5 November 1981: Meadowlands Arena, New Jersey, New York and
13 December 1981: Sun Devil Stadium, Tempe, Arizona. Producer:
The Glimmer Twins. Recorded: Bob Clearmountain, David Hewitt.
Engineer: Malcolm Pollack, Barry Bongiovi, Larry Alexander, Phil
Gitomer, Kooster MacAllister, David Brown, Bob Ludwig.
Bootleg only.
Rolling Stones with Ian McLagan, Ernie Watts.

477. LET IT BLEED (Jagger, Richards)
5 November 1981: Meadowlands Arena, New Jersey, New York and
13 December 1981: Sun Devil Stadium, Tempe, Arizona. Producer:
The Glimmer Twins. Recorded: Bob Clearmountain, David Hewitt.
Engineer: Malcolm Pollack, Barry Bongiovi, Larry Alexander, Phil
Gitomer, Kooster MacAllister, David Brown, Bob Ludwig.
Bootleg only.
Rolling Stones with Ian McLagan, Ernie Watts.

478. START ME UP (Jagger, Richards)
5 November 1981: Meadowlands Arena, New Jersey, New York and
13 December 1981: Sun Devil Stadium, Tempe, Arizona. Producer:
The Glimmer Twins. Recorded: Bob Clearmountain, David Hewitt.
Engineer: Malcolm Pollack, Barry Bongiovi, Larry Alexander, Phil
Gitomer, Kooster MacAllister, David Brown, Bob Ludwig.
UK LP STILL LIFE: 1 June 1982: No **4** – 18 weeks
USA LP STILL LIFE: 1 June 1982: No **5** – 10 weeks
Rolling Stones with Ian McLagan, Ernie Watts.

479. HONKY TONK WOMEN (Jagger, Richard)
5 November 1981: Meadowlands Arena, New Jersey, New York and
13 December 1981: Sun Devil Stadium, Tempe, Arizona. Producer:
The Glimmer Twins. Recorded: Bob Clearmountain, David Hewitt.
Engineer: Malcolm Pollack, Barry Bongiovi, Larry Alexander, Phil

Gitomer, Kooster MacAllister, David Brown, Bob Ludwig.
Bootleg only.
Rolling Stones with Ian McLagan, Ernie Watts.

480. BROWN SUGAR (Jagger, Richard)
5 November 1981: Meadowlands Arena, New Jersey, New York and
13 December 1981: Sun Devil Stadium, Tempe, Arizona. Producer:
The Glimmer Twins. Recorded: Bob Clearmountain, David Hewitt.
Engineer: Malcolm Pollack, Barry Bongiovi, Larry Alexander, Phil
Gitomer, Kooster MacAllister, David Brown, Bob Ludwig.
Bootleg only.
Rolling Stones with Ian McLagan, Ernie Watts.

481. JUMPIN' JACK FLASH (Jagger, Richard)
5 November 1981: Meadowlands Arena, New Jersey, New York and
13 December 1981: Sun Devil Stadium, Tempe, Arizona. Producer:
The Glimmer Twins. Recorded: Bob Clearmountain, David Hewitt.
Engineer: Malcolm Pollack, Barry Bongiovi, Larry Alexander, Phil
Gitomer, Kooster MacAllister, David Brown, Bob Ludwig.
Bootleg only.
Rolling Stones with Ian McLagan, Ernie Watts.

482. (I CAN'T GET NO) SATISFACTION (Jagger, Richard)
5 November 1981: Meadowlands Arena, New Jersey, New York and
13 December 1981: Sun Devil Stadium, Tempe, Arizona. Producer:
The Glimmer Twins. Recorded: Bob Clearmountain, David Hewitt.
Engineer: Malcolm Pollack, Barry Bongiovi, Larry Alexander, Phil
Gitomer, Kooster MacAllister, David Brown, Bob Ludwig.
UK LP STILL LIFE: 1 June 1982: No 4 – 18 weeks
USA LP STILL LIFE: 1 June 1982: No 5 – 10 weeks
Rolling Stones with Ian McLagan, Ernie Watts.

483. CHANTILLY LACE (Richardson)
25 June 1982: Wembley Stadium, London.
Bootleg only.
Rolling Stones with Ian McLagan, Ernie Watts.

A subsequent World Tour directed by the legendary promoter Bill Graham followed the album release of TATTOO YOU in late 1981. Starting in America (spanning 51 dates) it wound up mid-summer 1982 with a spread of dates over Europe. The logistics of such a tour were immense, but Bill Graham's undoubted experience was an essential ingredient to a successful tour. Press speculation, more than ever before, fuelled stories that every gig was the penultimate venue, due to the incessant quote that band members were venturing into a hilly middle-aged era. Thankfully, the spread of gaining such years was visibly missing – apart from Charlie Watts' receding hair-line! The band decided that Hal Ashby, a renowned film director, would record the American section of the tour for a full-length cinema movie release. Keith Richards was the only band member who vehemently objected to the idea, claiming that it was not practical to make a feature film of the band on stage because you could not do justice to both the camera and the audience. He wanted the film to be interspersed with rare small club footage but the film released by Embassy Pictures in 1983 featured just two concerts, the Meadowlands Arena in New Jersey and the Sun Devil open-air stadium in Tempe, Arizona. Formatted around the stage show, it included 26 numbers and very brief back-stage clips of the band. Bob Clearmountain was tasked with recording selected venues for what was to become a single-album live souvenir of both the tour and the film release. The album titled STILL LIFE was the Stones' best live project to date, capturing perfectly the excitement of the occasion. Two tracks previously unrecorded were included on the album, the good-time Smokey Robinson, Motown song *Going To A Go-Go* and an untouched by The Who Eddie Cochran rock 'n' roll standard *Twenty Flight Rock*. The former was released in May 1982 as the band's next single, creating a modest chart entry. In Britain, the release was timed to the British leg of the tour. The demand for tickets allowed the Stones to perform for the very first time in one of the bastions of English fortification, the giant Wembley football arena. When Keith Richards was asked how he would approach this formidable gig he shrugged and muttered: 'from Heath-row'. On Friday and Saturday, 25 and 26 June 1982, more than 145,000 fans witnessed the spectacle, those distanced at the back visually aided by huge video screens. The package included the prestigious American R 'n' B artists The J. Geils Band and true rhythm exponents Sly Dunbar and Robbie Shakespeare in their Jamaican band Black Uhuru. (They were later to offer their talents on the 1983 UNDERCOVER album.) It was watched by an audience whose age-span took in the original protago-nists from the 1960s (now in their 40s) and teenage newcomers. Smaller British venues included the football stadiums of Bristol and Newcastle which were also used to good advantage during a provincial excursion of the heartland including for once a sizable Scottish section. Bootlegs of both the film sound-track and various venues allowed a glimpse of other tracks such as The Big Bopper's *Chantilly Lace* and originating from 1964, *Mona* and *Down The Road Apiece*. The tour, with the trusted band aid support of Ian Stewart, Ian McLagan and Ernie Watts, brought to life tracks such as *Black Limousine* and confirmed the introduction of *Start Me Up* as suitable finale material. It was rumoured that R 'n' B guitarist George Thorogood was about to join the Stones touring team should Ronnie be unable to take the impending strain – 'no chance!'. After a few months' rest the adrenalin flowed again when the process of creating another studio album began in earnest in Paris, France.

10

GIANTS ENTER A DEEP SLEEP

NOVEMBER 1982 – NOVEMBER 1985

484. UNDERCOVER OF THE NIGHT (Jagger, Richards)
*November 1982–August 1983: EMI, Paris and Compass Point, Nassau,
Bahamas. Producer: The Glimmer Twins, Chris Kimsey. Engineer:
Brian McGee, Rod Thear, Steve Lipson, Bobby Cohen, Benji
Armbrister.*
UK Single: October 1983: No 11 – 9 weeks
USA Single: October 1983: No 9 – 10 weeks
UK LP UNDERCOVER: 7 November 1983: No 3 – 18 weeks
USA LP UNDERCOVER: 7 November 1983: No 4 – 12 weeks
*Rolling Stones with Moustapha Cisse, Brahms Coundoul, Martin
Ditcham, Sly Dunbar, Robbie Shakespeare, Chuck Leavell.*

485. UNDERCOVER OF THE NIGHT (DUB VERSION) (Jagger, Richards)
*November 1982–August 1983: EMI, Paris and Compass Point, Nassau,
Bahamas. Producer: The Glimmer Twins, Chris Kimsey. Engineer:
Brian McGee, Rod Thear, Steve Lipson, Bobby Cohen, Benji
Armbrister.*
UK twelve-inch Single: October 1983: No 11 – 9 weeks
USA twelve-inch Single: October 1983: No 9 – 10 weeks
*Rolling Stones with Moustapha Cisse, Brahms Coundoul, Martin
Ditcham, Sly Dunbar, Robbie Shakespeare, Chuck Leavell.*

The Stones returned to the familiar territory of the EMI-owned Pathé
Marconi Studios in late 1982. The fraternization with the Paris-based
studios which had started in 1977 with the SOME GIRLS sessions had
continued on every album recorded to date. The Stones simply felt no
pressures recording in Paris and enjoyed the *Parisienne joie de vivre.*
EMI also allowed the Stones to record 'time gratis' as opposed to compet-
itor studios who would charge x pounds per hour. The first single taken
from the album was released in October 1983 and is the title and opening
track. Significantly, the song is shaped around a harsh up-front drum
sound, moulded around Charlie Watts' percussion bash. Mick Jagger
wrote the song on the guitar with Ron Wood's assistance. Ex-Allman
Brother Chuck Leavell applies an electric organ track while Chris Kimsey at the controls deploys phasing techniques on guitar and drums
which gives the song its unique rhythmic qualities. This trick is exagger-
ated on the twelve-inch dub version, alias an extended cheeky mix of
Undercover. Undercover's essential ingredient is, however, the menacing lyrics of political repression written by Mick Jagger; these were
vividly brought to life in the video. Produced by Michael Hamlin and

directed by Julian Temple, the video was shot in two stages. The first part recorded on 18 October 1983 filmed the Stones on stage at a Paris club, The Bain-Douches, in front of a bunch of extras while they mimed to the song's lyrics. The next week the story line was concluded in Mexico City; it featured the terrorist antics of Keith Richards and kidnap victim Mick Jagger. The mini-epic showed Jagger being kidnapped by arch-villain, Keith and his motley crew of gun-laden masked activists. The two talking points of the video were the shooting at close range of the kidnap victim with paper bag over his head and an ensuing shoot-out in a church. These vivid images caused the banning of the video on British television, although the more adventurous Channel 4 programme, The Tube, showed the video, but the camera moved away to show Mick and Julien Temple's reaction as they were being interviewed at the vital blood-soaked moments. They defended the video during the interview, stating it was no worse than some late-night films. As a safety measure, another version of the video using more of the Bain-Douches scenes allowed a screening on Top Of The Pops, and a healthy Number 11 hit followed.

486. ALL THE WAY DOWN (Jagger, Richards)
November 1982–August 1983: EMI, Paris and Compass Point, Nassau, Bahamas. Producer: The Glimmer Twins, Chris Kimsey. Engineer: Brian McGee, Rod Thear, Steve Lipson, Bobby Cohen, Benji Armbrister.
UK B-side Undercover Of The Night: October 1983
USA B-side Undercover Of The Night: October 1983
UK LP UNDERCOVER: 7 November 1983: No 3 – 18 weeks
USA LP UNDERCOVER: 7 November 1983: No 4 – 12 weeks
Rolling Stones with Moustapha Cisse, Brahms Coundoul, Martin Ditcham, Sly Dunbar, Robbie Shakespeare, Chuck Leavell.

'Just drop it in' cried Chris Kimsey on the studio's intercom and so the band respond on what is a mediocre rocker having left out the proposed intro to the song following Chris's advice. The rather wry-sounding vocals of Mick Jagger are quite aesthetic and there are also some nice guitar lines including an acoustic piece when the vocals are slowed down, down, down. Released as the flipside of the seven-inch version of *Undercover Of The Night*, it was a foretaste of the album. This was a pity since it is one of the album's weaker tracks.

487. FEEL ON BABY (Jagger, Richards)
November 1982–August 1983: EMI, Paris and Compass Point, Nassau, Bahamas. Producer: The Glimmer Twins, Chris Kimsey. Engineer: Brian McGee, Rod Thear, Steve Lipson, Bobby Cohen, Benji Armbrister.
UK LP UNDERCOVER: 7 November 1983: No 3 – 18 weeks
USA LP UNDERCOVER: 7 November 1983: No 4 – 12 weeks
Rolling Stones with Moustapha Cisse, Brahms Coundoul, Martin Ditcham, Sly Dunbar, Robbie Shakespeare, Chuck Leavell.

488. FEEL ON BABY (INSTRUMENTAL MIX) (Jagger, Richards)
*November 1982–August 1983: EMI, Paris and Compass Point, Nassau,
Bahamas. Producer: The Glimmer Twins, Chris Kimsey. Engineer:
Brian McGee, Rod Thear, Steve Lipson, Bobby Cohen, Benji
Armbrister.*
UK B-side twelve-inch Undercover Of The Night: October 1983
USA B-side twelve-inch Undercover Of The Night: October 1983
*Rolling Stones with Moustapha Cisse, Brahms Coundoul, Martin
Ditcham, Sly Dunbar, Robbie Shakespeare, Chuck Leavell.*

When Keith Richards dutifully appeared on BBC's radio programme My
Top Ten in 1986, he cited Jamaica as a major musical influence offering
reggae exponents Max Romeo and Gregory Isaacs. The sound of reggae
emerged on Stones' albums in a hesitant manner – they preferred not to
dupe the music form. *Feel On Baby* tackles in its two forms the rhythm
and a remixed dub version. The latter appeared on a twelve-inch
extended single format which was mixed by Chris Kimsey and assisted
by Brian McGee at the Hit Factory, New York City. The Stones were
joined in the UNDERCOVER sessions by Jamaican rhythm heroes Sly
Dunbar and Robbie Shakespeare. They fronted the Black Uhuru band
but were principally noted for their over-all involvement in the reggae
scene. Such was their esteem that they were now crossing frontiers and
being asked to perform on 'white man's' rock music. Keith recalls that the
percussion on the track is enhanced by Senegalese musicians who
played some amazing instruments brought from their villages. These can
be plainly heard on the track interspersed by Chuck Leavell's organ
playing and Charlie Watts' 'slave to the rhythm' drums.

489. PRETTY BEAT UP (a.k.a. **DOG SHIT**) (Jagger, Richards, Wood)
*November 1982–August 1983: EMI, Paris and Compass Point, Nassau,
Bahamas. Producer: The Glimmer Twins, Chris Kimsey. Engineer:
Brian McGee, Rod Thear, Steve Lipson, Bobby Cohen, Benji
Armbrister.*
*UK LP UNDERCOVER: 7 November 1983: No **3** – 18 weeks*
*USA LP UNDERCOVER: 7 November 1983: No **4** – 12 weeks*
*Rolling Stones with Moustapha Cisse, Brahms Coundoul, Martin
Ditcham, Sly Dunbar, Robbie Shakespeare, David Sanborn.*

Bill Wyman had good cause to remember *Pretty Beat Up* since he assists
Ian Stewart in the keyboards rôle by playing the Yamaha piano. Is this
why he recollected the working title of the track so vividly? Rôles
reversed, Keith Richards grabs the bass guitar while the saxophone is
performed by new sax recruit David Sanborn – Bobby Keys and Ernie
Watts were ousted for the moment. Ronnie Wood wrote the song with
some support from Jagger and Richards – his only co-composition on the
album. He also takes the lead guitar role but *Pretty Beat Up* is an average
album contribution, the subject material by now having a familiar sardonic ring.

490. WANNA HOLD YOU (Jagger, Richards)
*November 1982–August 1983: EMI, Paris and Compass Point, Nassau,
Bahamas. Producer: The Glimmer Twins, Chris Kimsey. Engineer:
Brian McGee, Rod Thear, Steve Lipson, Bobby Cohen, Benji
Armbrister.*
*UK LP UNDERCOVER: 7 November 1983: No **3** – 18 weeks*
*USA LP UNDERCOVER: 7 November 1983: No **4** – 12 weeks*
*Rolling Stones with Moustapha Cisse, Brahms Coundoul, Martin
Ditcham, Sly Dunbar, Robbie Shakespeare.*

Written by Keith Richards and performed almost exclusively by him,
Wanna Hold You is a warm uplifting number so reminiscent of the
optimistic *Happy* also sung by Keith. Prior to the UNDERCOVER sessions
Mick Jagger and Keith had met in a small basement studio to write and
perform in the old style. Out of this several worthwhile tracks originated
of which this is one. The original demo has Mick Jagger on drums while
Keith bashes out the lead guitar and adds his rough-textured vocals.
Keith has been heard to say that the song is akin to the spirit of a pop song
such as The Beatles' *I Wanna Hold Your Hand.* In other words, it could
have been a classic!

491. SHE WAS HOT (Jagger, Richards)
*November 1982–August 1983: EMI, Paris and Compass Point, Nassau,
Bahamas. Producer: The Glimmer Twins, Chris Kimsey. Engineer:
Brian McGee, Rod Thear, Steve Lipson, Bobby Cohen, Benji
Armbrister.*
*UK LP UNDERCOVER: 7 November 1983: No **3** – 18 weeks*
*USA LP UNDERCOVER: 7 November 1983: No **4** – 12 weeks*
*UK Single: February 1984: No **42** – 4 weeks*
USA Single: February 1984
*Rolling Stones with Moustapha Cisse, Brahms Coundoul, Martin
Ditcham, Sly Dunbar, Robbie Shakespeare, Chuck Leavell.*

Released as the follow up to the UNDERCOVER single *She Was Hot*,
politics forgotten, is a guitar laden boogie-woogie song with more than a
tinge of typical Jagger humour. This was evidently portrayed on the
video, directed by Julien Temple, at yet another Mexican location. Anita
Morris is the red-headed girl with heated aspirations. Employed by the
Stones, she seduces Mick Jagger in the first verse in cold and damp New
York and then her attentions turn to Keith Richards in smokey grey
Detroit. Still not de-fused, Anita is then thrust into a scene with the whole
band, which is a basic rip-off from the Jayne Mansfield film, *The Girl Can't
Help It,* complete with instruments hanging from the ceiling. Other
choice moments in the video include Charlie Watts convincingly playing
a showbiz agent and Bill Wyman and Jo Howard (Ron Wood's confidante)
made up like hillbilly geriatrics, being deluged by gallons of water. Four
company executives who are watching Anita Morris pose provocatively
cannot control themselves and buttons burst on one man's trousers. This
last shot caused the banning of the video on the American MTV network,
a by-now familiar fate. It was later re-edited to MTV's satisfaction. The

music is a mid-tempo rocker: Chuck Leavell plays keyboards and Ian Stewart tinkers in boogie fashion on the piano. Keith and Ronnie Wood's guitars flash angrily as they play rhythm riffs – solos temporarily put asunder.

492. TIE YOU UP (THE PAIN OF LOVE) (Jagger, Richards)

November 1982–August 1983: EMI, Paris and Compass Point, Nassau, Bahamas. Producer: The Glimmer Twins, Chris Kimsey. Engineer: Brian McGee, Rod Thear, Steve Lipson, Bobby Cohen, Benji Armbrister.
UK LP UNDERCOVER: 7 November 1983: No 3 – 18 weeks
USA LP UNDERCOVER: 7 November 1983: No 4 – 12 weeks
Rolling Stones with Moustapha Cisse, Brahms Coundoul, Martin Ditcham, Sly Dunbar, Robbie Shakespeare, Chuck Leavell.

One of Mick Jagger's favourites on the album. The lyrics are certainly provocative if taken at face value – Mick sings them in a tough brogue. The guitar solos dropped from *She Was Hot* are laced to good effect on *Tie You Up*. Ron Wood plays bass guitar while Keith Richards delivers the guitar message. After one verse the rhythm simmers down to allow a nifty percussive passage. Charlie Watts' drums are positively featured by Chris Kimsey, making the song's overall sound almost funky. This was certainly a feature of the UNDERCOVER album, helping to make it contemporary, and on this occasion, the disco beat hit its mark.

493. TOO TOUGH (Jagger, Richards)

November 1982–August 1983: EMI, Paris and Compass Point, Nassau, Bahamas. Producer: The Glimmer Twins, Chris Kimsey. Engineer: Brian McGee, Rod Thear, Steve Lipson, Bobby Cohen, Benji Armbrister.
UK LP UNDERCOVER: 7 November 1983: No 3 – 18 weeks
USA LP UNDERCOVER: 7 November 1983: No 4 – 12 weeks
Rolling Stones with Moustapha Cisse, Brahms Coundoul, Martin Ditcham, Sly Dunbar, Robbie Shakespeare.

Too Tough seemed to have the promise of a classic rocker in the mould of a *Brown Sugar*. The guitar riff was certainly a contributory factor to this but alas the song's potential was lost somehow. The necessary raw edge was lacking and it remains as no more than an album filler.

494. IT MUST BE HELL (Jagger, Richards)

November 1982–August 1983: EMI, Paris and Compass Point, Nassau, Bahamas. Producer: The Glimmer Twins, Chris Kimsey. Engineer: Brian McGee, Rod Thear, Steve Lipson, Bobby Cohen, Benji Armbrister.
UK LP UNDERCOVER: 7 November 1983: No 3 – 18 weeks
USA LP UNDERCOVER: 7 November 1983: No 4 – 12 weeks
Rolling Stones with Moustapha Cisse, Brahms Coundoul, Martin Ditcham, Sly Dunbar, Robbie Shakespeare, Chuck Leavell.

Keith Richards rated the lyrics written by Mick Jagger on UNDER-COVER as some of his best since the 1969–72 period. Some, as in *It Must Be Hell*, are full of bleak pessimism. The problems associated with over-dominant, one leadership states are tackled on this track. The British hoped the subject matter was not a hangover from *Hang Fire*. The message is there, however, for everyone. Keith Richards plays a chord sequence reminiscent of *Honky Tonk Women* before it ferments into an archetypal Stones' rocker.

495. TOO MUCH BLOOD (Jagger, Richards)
May 1983–August 1983: EMI, Paris and Compass Point, Nassau, Bahamas and The Hit Factory, New York. Producer: The Glimmer Twins, Chris Kimsey. Engineer: Brian McGee, Rod Thear, Steve Lipson, Bobby Cohen, Benji Armbrister.
UK LP UNDERCOVER: 7 November 1983: No **3** *–* 18 *weeks*
USA LP UNDERCOVER: 7 November 1983: No **4** *–* 12 *weeks*
Rolling Stones with Moustapha Cisse, Brahms Coundoul, Martin Ditcham, Sly Dunbar, Robbie Shakespeare, Chuck Leavell, Jim Barber, Chops.

496. TOO MUCH BLOOD (DANCE VERSION) (Jagger, Richards)
June–August 1983: EMI, Paris and Compass Point, Nassau, Bahamas and The Hit Factory, New York. Producer: The Glimmer Twins. Remix Producer: Arthur Baker. Remix Engineers/Editors: Albert Cabrera, Tony Moran, Chris Lord-Alge, Tom Lord-Alge.
USA twelve-inch single: March 1984
Rolling Stones with Moustapha Cisse, Brahms Coundoul, Martin Ditcham, Sly Dunbar, Robbie Shakespeare, Chuck Leavell, Jim Barber, Chops.

497. TOO MUCH BLOOD (DUB VERSION) (Jagger, Richards)
June–August 1983: EMI, Paris and Compass Point, Nassau, Bahamas, and The Hit Factory New York. Producer: The Glimmer Twins. Remix Engineers/Editors: Albert Cabrera, Tony Moran, Chris Lord-Alge, Tom Lord-Alge.
USA B-side twelve-inch Single: March 1984
Rolling Stones with Moustapha Cisse, Brahms Coundoul, Martin Ditcham, Sly Dunbar, Robbie Shakespeare, Chuck Leavell, Jim Barber, Chops.

The musical and lyrical repertoires of the Stones and their crew of friends culminate on this, the undisputed crown of the UNDERCOVER album, *Too Much Blood*. The riff played on the horns by the Sugarhill brass section, Chops (over-dubbed at a later stage in New York), is inspirational and lifts the track to epic proportions. Mick Jagger's lyrics are uncompromising and savagely vivid; Jagger's tang of humour intertwined therein is first class. The rap sequences, suitably X-rated, are especially good with Mick's vocal delivery quite superb. The track is aided by equipment specialist, Jim Barber, who puts down another guitar line filling out the rhythm of Keith's Jesselli and Ronnie's electric fender. Charlie Watts' drum sound strives at the grandmaster of funk, while even Bill Wyman's short-necked bass delivers a solo passage or two. The late-night movie script conjured up by *Too Much Blood* ensured it could not be officially released as a single without getting savagely edited. Instead, in 1984, at Mick Jagger's instigation, *Too Much Blood* was recut by the Latin Rascals, Albert Cabrera and Tony Moran. Arthur Baker, famous for his mixes on the twelve-inch single format, remixed the track for a release which was principally intended for night clubs. Stones collectors have since fought to get the product in import shops.

The culmination of the project is a gargantuan twenty-minute version, which includes a dance and dub version of the song. The Stones were brought into the computerized technological age by those syncopated control room boys. Arthur Baker's unique production style added a further dimension to *Too Much Blood* but some ideas conflicted with Mick Jagger's. Arthur Baker worked better on a free production rein which Mick was reluctant to give. The Cadets, an American 'fifties rock and roll act, would have been proud of Mick, because while recording further vocal tracks on *Too Much Blood* he used their infamous line: 'Meanwhile, back in the jungle'. Other vocals used in the different mixes by Arthur Baker include a humorous dialogue about Michael Jackson's *Thriller* video: 'How does a werewolf make fucking love anyway?' and Mick calling in desperation to his only mate 'Keith!'. The censors were put to work again in January, 1984. In Mexico, after the recording of the *She Was Hot* video, Julien Temple filmed the Stones for a possible *Too Much Blood* video. The possibility became fact when it was announced in 1984 that a home video-cassette would be released of Stones videos entitled *Rewind*, which would include a gory number *Too Much Blood*. In it Keith and Ron can be seen rampaging with electric saws and there is also the crazed scene of a body in the refrigerator.

The album was complete. It received a lukewarm reception, despite the inevitable radio bannings of certain material, which in itself usually creates interest and curiosity. A decision not to tour so soon after the 1981/82 escapade reduced further sales possibilities. Mick Jagger was beginning to take time out on other projects which included a Michael Jackson collaboration on a single labelled *State of Shock*. He could also be heard on Peter Wolf's solo album on a track titled *Pretty Lady*. A very successful project involved him with Bill Wyman on the Stones' video collection titled *Rewind* featuring videos from the 70s and 80s including the three aforementioned from UNDERCOVER. The videos were interspersed with sketches in a rock and roll museum and rare interview footage. It sold extremely well. Perhaps the most significant event for Mick Jagger was his excursion from the Stones when he first started writing songs for a solo album in March 1984 while relaxing on holiday in the Caribbean.

498. HARLEM SHUFFLE (Relf, Nelson)
February–November 1985: Pathé Marconi Studios, Paris. Producer: Steve Lillywhite, The Glimmer Twins. Engineer: Dave Jordan, Steve

Parker, Tim Crich, Mike Krewick.
*UK Single: 10 March 1986: No **13** – 7 weeks*
*USA Single: 10 March 1986: No **5** – 10 weeks*
*UK LP DIRTY WORK: 24 March 1986: No **4** – 10 weeks*
*USA LP DIRTY WORK: 24 March 1986. No **4** – 15 weeks*
Rolling Stones with Chuck Leavell, Bobby Womack, Don Covay.

499. HARLEM SHUFFLE (NY MIX) (Relf, Nelson)

February–November 1985: Pathé Marconi Studios, Paris. Producer:
Steve Lillywhite, The Glimmer Twins. Engineer: Dave Jordan, Steve
Parker, Tim Crich, Mike Krewick. Remix Engineers: Steve Thompson,
Michael Barbiero.
*UK twelve-inch Single: 17 March 1986: No **13** – 7 weeks*
*USA twelve-inch Single: 17 March 1986: No **5** – 10 weeks*
Rolling Stones with Chuck Leavell, Bobby Womack, Don Covay.

500. HARLEM SHUFFLE (LONDON MIX) (Relf, Nelson)

February–November 1985: Pathé Marconi Studios, Paris. Producer:
Steve Lillywhite, The Glimmer Twins. Engineer: Dave Jordan, Steve
Parker, Tim Crich, Mike Krewick. Remix Engineer: Steve Lillywhite.
UK B-side twelve-inch Harlem Shuffle (NY Mix): 17 March 1986
USA B-side twelve-inch Harlem Shuffle (NY Mix): 17 March 1986
Rolling Stones with Chuck Leavell, Bobby Womack, Don Covay.

In December 1985 after the completion of the new album, Ian Stewart died tragically of a heart attack. The sessionography has always included his contribution within the description, Rolling Stones 'Personnel', since his role had been a major factor to the Stones' over-all groove. The Sixth Stone, Desperate Dan, or plain Stu, was a musicians' musician and one of the greatest exponents of boogie and blues as his own band, Rocket 88, testify. The funeral on 20 December 1985 was attended by the band, Eric Clapton, Astrid Lundstrom (Bill Wyman's ex-wife) and other devotees. Albert Ammons' warm tones of *Boogie Woogie Dream* eclipsed the sad day.

In February 1986 at the 100 Club the band played a private gig as a tribute to the boogie man. It was a night of uncompromising R 'n' B. Celebrity contributions were made by Pete Townshend, Eric Clapton and Jeff Beck, who were all old mates of Ian Stewart. This stage tribute was how he could best be remembered and a good night was had by all.

The time was now March 1986 and not since the recalcitrant days of the early 60s had a non-Jagger/Richards track been released as a studio single. Indeed, ironically it had not been since the Number 1 hit *It's All Over Now* which the Stones had recorded back in 1964. Bobby Womack co-wrote *It's All Over Now* and also performed on *Harlem Shuffle* which had originally been a Top 10 hit in the UK for Bob and Earl during the spring of 1969. Keith Richards, when preparing compilation tapes for his travels, often found that he had included the catchy *Harlem Shuffle*. In anticipation that the Stones might record it, Keith would often copy the song on a tape for Mick Jagger, thinking Mick would be a natural for the vocals. The bait was not taken until one night the band ran through the track in rehearsal for the new album. Mick walked into the sessions, heard the number and put down a vocal track. To enhance the vocals along the lines of the original duo, Bob and Earl, the Stones employed a mate of Ronnie Wood's, Bobby Womack and an old soulster, Don Covay. The opening chords of *Harlem Shuffle* use some deft acoustic strumming, which Keith claimed to have learned from recent trips to Mexico. The technique is lifted from the Mexican fandango guitar players. Chuck Leavell plays synthesized keyboards and it is this instrument that replaces the horns used so predominantly on the Bob and Earl arrangement. The keyboards can be heard much more to the fore on the extended mix versions. The single's success was enhanced by a simple but effective video, which mixed cartoon characters (one of whom resembles a dishevelled Ron Wood) and the band performing on stage at the Kool Kat Club. Keith Richards looks particularly distinguished in gangster trilby, posing ridiculously at the video's end. The Stones were back again in the charts, attaining respectable Top 20 positions.

501. HAD IT WITH YOU (Jagger, Richards, Wood)
February–November 1985: Pathé Marconi Studios, Paris. Producer: Steve Lillywhite, The Glimmer Twins. Engineer: Dave Jordan, Steve Parker, Tim Crich, Mike Krewick.
UK B-side Harlem Shuffle: 10 March 1986
USA B-side Harlem Shuffle: 10 March 1986
UK LP DIRTY WORK: 24 March 1986: No 4 – 10 weeks
USA LP DIRTY WORK: 24 March 1986. No 4 – 15 weeks

The release of Mick Jagger's solo album SHE'S THE BOSS in 1985, although not a surprise to the band since it was a negotiated settlement of the Stones' CBS contract, did prove to be a troublesome element during the recording of DIRTY WORK. Keith Richards openly said that he thought it was a totally inappropriate time to release a solo project – 'it could have at least been an album of Irish folk songs or summat!' Mick's energies were spent in promotion work for his album, leaving the preparatory business for the new Stones' album to Keith. Ron Wood played an important part, teaming up with Keith to start the song-writing process. *Had It With You* is one of the Wood co-compositions. It is a very basic rocker in veritable R 'n' B tradition. Various bass guitars were tried, including an upright bass, but these takes sounded a little too ordinary – 'Oh, it's the Stones at work again'. To avoid this type of sound, the bass was left off so that only Charlie Watts and Keith provided the main instrumentation. It was recorded in just a couple of takes, Mick providing a real live harmonica. In order to fill the song out, at a later date, Ronnie Wood offered a track of whispering tenor sax. On the record, at the track's end, Steve Lillywhite, the production controller, can be heard switching on the studio intercom. Those surprised to find Ronnie on sax may be interested to learn his brass talents were also used on a 1985 Bill Wyman and his All Stars video and album package titled WILLY AND THE POOR BOYS, a charity project in aid of multiple sclerosis. The music was in the good time *Had It With You* style.

502. STRICTLY MEMPHIS (Jagger, Richards)
February–November 1985: Pathé Marconi Studios, Paris. Producer: The Glimmer Twins.
Bootleg only.
Rolling Stones with Bobby Womack.

A great funky duet with Mick Jagger and Bobby Womack on vocals. Other vocalists kept Mick on his toes and this example of a DIRTY WORK out-take proves how useful this tactic could be.

503. DEEP LOVE (Jagger, Richards)
February–November 1985: Pathé Marconi Studios, Paris. Producer: The Glimmer Twins.
Bootleg only.

A rock number on which Keith Richards took the lead vocal. The out-takes from the sessions were essentially Keith's numbers which he worked on prior to the actual recordings with full band line-up. In the summer of 1985, Bob Geldof's 'Live Aid' project was a unique opportunity for the Stones to play live again. Various rumours circulate about their non-appearance but possible explanations include Mick and Keith's split or the intimidating line-up at Wembley. Once the Stones officially declined to appear, Mick Jagger was asked to appear with David Bowie. Instead of a joint performance they decided to record a cover of *Dancing In The Street* and within a 24-hour period also to record a video for world-wide broadcast on 'Live Aid' night. The Martha and The Vandellas hit was later released by Bowie and Jagger – the proceeds went to African famine relief. It became a gigantic hit both sides of the Atlantic entering the British charts immediately at Number 1. Mick Jagger, without full Stones' support, performed in Philadelphia on the American based 'Live Aid' show and played a rousing set backed by the Hall and Oates Band. He was joined by Tina Turner for two memorable numbers. The other Stones remained silent although Keith and Ron Wood made fools of themselves when they accompanied Bob Dylan on a disastrous acoustic set at the 'Live Aid' finale. Keith was cajoled into appearing by Ron Wood; they later blamed the poor result on the atrocious sound quality as can be heard in the States conclusion of *We Are The World.*

504. TOO RUDE (Roberts)
February–November 1985: Pathé Marconi Studios, Paris. Producer: Steve Lillywhite, The Glimmer Twins. Engineer: Dave Jordan, Steve Parker, Tim Crich, Mike Krewick.
*UK LP DIRTY WORK: 24 March 1986: No **4** – 10 weeks*
*USA LP DIRTY WORK: 24 March 1986: No **4** – 15 weeks*
Rolling Stones with Jimmy Cliff.

Steve Lillywhite was the first producer to be used by the Stones since 1973 when Jimmy Miller produced the GOATS HEAD SOUP album. He had an excellent pedigree, his most recent production successes being the Irish rock band, U2. In the mid-'seventies, for Chris Blackwell's Island label, he had produced British reggae artistes Steel Pulse. This experience in the reggae field allowed him to step into the world of dub mixes comfortably and *Too Rude* was tackled. The Stones had attempted the reggae format before but this has got to be their most noteworthy performance. Keith Richards' vocals are used to good effect. Although suitably tempered and layered by Steve Lillywhite, they sound almost too good to be Keith's. Lots of echo tracks are used, particularly the bass, condoning the belief that all good reggae tracks are in the mix. Jimmy Cliff, a well-known reggae artiste, assisted in this respect, having supported Keith on the vocals. *Too Rude* was provisionally a title of the new album, however DIRTY WORK prevailed.

505. **BACK TO ZERO** (Jagger, Richards, Leavell)
February–November 1985: Pathé Marconi Studios, Paris. Producer: Steve Lillywhite, The Glimmer Twins. Engineer: Dave Jordan, Steve Parker, Tim Crich, Mike Krewick.
*UK LP DIRTY WORK: 24 March 1986: No **4** – 10 weeks*
*USA LP DIRTY WORK: 24 March 1986: No **4** – 15 weeks*
Rolling Stones with Chuck Leavell, Jimmy Page.

Chuck Leavell, who worked with Mick Jagger on his solo project, co-wrote this song with Jagger and Richards. This was an honour only previously bestowed to official Stones' members Ron Wood and Mick Taylor. But it signified the adoption of a freer more natural approach to the rigours of collating an album. Guest artists or, more honestly, 'old mates', dropped in; some recorded with the Stones. Jimmy Page was one who performed, which knocked Keith out because he had always admired Page's guitar technique tremendously. *Back To Zero* is a funky number, full of rhythmic guitar passages and, of course, the synthesized organ work of Chuck Leavell. The anti-nuclear lyrics purvey the two-nation race to world destruction. Again, the Stones were singing in an angry pose, determined not to shirk their preordained responsibilities.

506. **WINNING UGLY** (Jagger, Richards)
February–November 1985: Pathé Marconi Studios, Paris. Producer: Steve Lillywhite, The Glimmer Twins. Engineer: Dave Jordan, Steve Parker, Tim Crich, Mike Krewick.
*UK LP DIRTY WORK: 24 March 1986: No **4** – 10 weeks*
*USA LP DIRTY WORK: 24 March 1986: No **4** – 15 weeks*
Rolling Stones with Kirsty MacColl.

The Stones, at work in Paris with new-waver Steve Lillywhite, attracted the modern-day pop stars, including members of Duran Duran. They were startled to find the Stones being recorded ensemble; overdubs and retracking kept to a bare minimum. *Winning Ugly* is essentially a lead guitarist's song, Keith Richards and Ronnie Wood creating an overload of lead solos, which charge in and out of the mix, centred and controlled also by one of Keith's prestigious rock riffs nicked from the Motown catalogue. A USA twelve-inch single of *Winning Ugly* includes extended

'London' and 'New York' mixes. Mick's vocals are enhanced on the track by female backing artistes. Two such vocalists are mentioned on the album sleeve: Kirsty MacColl and Patti Sciafla. Patti was one of Bruce Springsteen's backing vocalists who was then on a European tour. Her contribution to the sessions fuelled wild stories of possible guest guitar appearances by the 'boss' on the album, none of which would be confirmed.

507. FIGHT (Jagger, Richards, Wood)
February–November 1985: Pathé Marconi Studios, Paris. Producer: Steve Lillywhite, The Glimmer Twins. Engineer: Dave Jordan, Steve Parker, Tim Crich, Mike Krewick.
*UK LP DIRTY WORK: 24 March 1986: No **4** – 10 weeks*
*USA LP DIRTY WORK: 24 March 1986: No **4** – 15 weeks*
UK B-side One Hit: May 1986
USA B-side One Hit: May 1986
Rolling Stones with Kirsty MacColl.

Bill Wyman confirmed that Steve Lillywhite was able to add a new recording element particularly to the drum sound without over compli-cating the issue. Charlie Watts' drum sound on *Fight* is testimony to this. The song's tone, as the title suggests, is angry and vitriolic which is conveyed expressively in Mick Jagger's vocals: 'slash you with a razor'. Keith Richards mercilessly attacks the victim with his axe. Keith recalls the circumstances which led to the song's recording. It happened when the band broke up after a less than fruitful day's recording. Keith, frustrat-ed and angry, took hold of his guitar and proceeded to conjure up an instantaneous 'Jumping Jack' lick. Ron Wood joined in on pedal steel and the guitar roadie Alan Rogan plugged in a bass. However, the final version did not include his bass which was rerecorded by Ron Wood. Alan Rogan was 'lent' to the Stones by Pete Townshend during the 1981/82 tour. Alan decided to stay!

508. ONE HIT (TO THE BODY) (Jagger, Richards, Wood)
February–November 1985: Pathé Marconi Studios, Paris. Producer: Steve Lillywhite, The Glimmer Twins. Engineers: Dave Jordan, Steve Parker, Tim Crich, Mike Krewick.
*UK LP DIRTY WORK: 24 March 1986: No **4** – 10 weeks*
*USA LP DIRTY WORK: 24 March 1986: No **4** – 15 weeks*
UK Single: May 1986
*USA Single: May 1986: No **28** – 4 weeks*
Rolling Stones with Kirsty MacColl, Jimmy Page.

509. ONE HIT (TO THE BODY) (LONDON MIX) (Jagger, Richards, Wood)
February–November 1985: Pathé Marconi Studios, Paris. Remix Studio: The Townhouse Studio, London. Producer: Steve Lillywhite, The Glimmer Twins. Re-mix Engineer: Alan Douglas.

UK twelve-inch Single: May 1986: No 28 – 4 weeks
Rolling Stones with Kirsty MacColl, Jimmy Page.

The raw toughness of *Fight* continues on *One Hit*. Again, the artistic direction was controlled, as it was on much of the album, by Keith Richards and Ron Wood. The guitar sound is outstanding. From the opening acoustic patter by Ronnie the song leaps forward to a clash of lead and rhythm thrusts. Jimmy Page is featured on lead guitar, but for contractual reasons was not credited on the sleeve notes. Despite his involvement, lead solos were kept to a minimum. Because of the acoustic guitar, critics were fast to lynch on to the similarity with the anthematic *Street Fighting Man*. The backing vocals give the song a Stateside feel but when released as a single it failed to achieve high chart positions, remaining in the low forties in the UK. An instrumental-only version can be heard via an out-take. A remix by Alan Douglas and Steve Lillywhite for the twelve-inch single market is interesting but not essential. A promotional video to accompany the release failed to assist. Filmed by a young producer, Russell Mulcahy, at London's Elstree Studios, the video is sparse and angry as the guys work out. Mick and Keith can be seen sparring with each other. Images of fights are pushed at the watcher as the Stones explore back street gutter land. Charlie appears bored by it all, a suspicion confirmed by a documentary filmed by BBC TV's 'Old Grey Whistle Test' which captures the shooting of the video on 1 May, 1986. As an epitaph Charlie wisely concludes that the Stones' life has been spent 'five years working, twenty years hanging around'!

510. **WHAT ARE YOU GONNA DO WITH MY LOVE?** (Jagger, Richards)
February–November 1985: Pathé Marconi Studios, Paris. Producer:
The Glimmer Twins.
Bootleg only.
Rolling Stones with Kirsty MacColl, Patti Sciafla.

The band are joined on this gospel track by their guest artists. They perform a vocal-orientated song which is creditable.

511. **YOU'RE TOO MUCH** (Jagger, Richards)
February–November 1985: Pathé Marconi Studios, Paris. Producer:
The Glimmer Twins.
Bootleg only.

Another chance for Keith Richards to show his vocal talents. The DIRTY WORK sessions displayed the freshness and maturity of Keith's song-writing approach. *You're Too Much* uses a gathering of backing vocalists who perform the song in gospel style. This style was to be featured extensively on Keith Richards' solo album released in October 1988 TALK IS CHEAP.

512. **HOLD BACK** (Jagger, Richards)
February–November 1985: Pathé Marconi Studios, Paris. Producer:
Steve Lillywhite, The Glimmer Twins. Engineers: Dave Jordan, Steve

Parker, Tim Crich, Mike Krewick.
*UK LP DIRTY WORK: 24 March 1986: No **4** – 10 weeks*
*USA LP DIRTY WORK: 24 March 1986: No **4** – 15 weeks*
Rolling Stones with Ivan Neville.

One of only three Jagger, Richards compositions on the album, a fact which would set the Glimmer Inc. into a stocks 'n' shares bear market! *Hold Back* was a track originally thought to be nothing better than an out-take. It was salvaged on a play-back when the band decided that the drum sound was too good to waste. To polish it off, Ivan Neville, son of Aaron Neville, was asked to re-do a funky bass line and so the track ended up on the album as a sandwich spread. The message is there in the lyrics; trust your instinct, go for it.

513. **DIRTY WORK** (Jagger, Richards, Wood)
February–November 1985: Pathé Marconi Studios, Paris. Producer: Steve Lillywhite, The Glimmer Twins. Engineers: Dave Jordan, Steve Parker, Tim Crich, Mike Krewick.
*UK LP DIRTY WORK: 24 March 1986: No **4** – 10 weeks*
*USA LP DIRTY WORK: 24 March 1986: No **4** – 15 weeks*
Rolling Stones with Chuck Leavell.

The title track of the album, the sleeve of which for the first time in twenty years showed all of the band photographed on the cover. They were slouching on a sofa in undramatic fashion. The song itself also languishes, not really realizing its own expectations. It is, however, more than a sandwich filler, more a 'brunch'. The track, musically and lyrically, is a grower. The guitars again overdose. Two are understood to be on the original track and then a further two were dubbed on. This enabled solos to continue indefinitely as one solo stepped on another. The rock 'n' roll riffs returned. Chuck Leavell, meanwhile, fed the rhythm. In terms of success, sales were again not aided by the usual album/tour format. Rumours continued to circulate that all was not well with the Jagger, Richards relationship. Keith wanted to go on the road but Mick was definitely not willing. His thoughts were on stepping out of the Stones' mould to concentrate on his solo project.

514. **SLEEP TONIGHT** (Jagger, Richards)
February–November 1985: Pathé Marconi Studios, Paris. Producer: Steve Lillywhite, The Glimmer Twins. Engineers: Dave Jordan, Steve Parker, Tim Crich, Mike Krewick.
*UK LP DIRTY WORK: 24 March 1986: No **4** – 10 weeks*
*USA LP DIRTY WORK: 24 March 1986: No **4** – 15 weeks*
Rolling Stones with Tom Waits.

Keith Richards' repartee with other artists reached a zenith during the DIRTY WORK period. He performed on a Nona Hendryx solo album and also contributed an outstanding three tracks to the new Tom Waits album, 'Rain Dogs'. This particular task was reciprocated by Tom Waits when he, allegedly, performed on *Sleep*. The outcome is a beautiful country rock ballad. Keith uses open Nashville tuning on an acoustic and delivers a sincere passage on electric guitar. Ron Wood supplements the action, playing, for a change, the drums – Charlie Watts was not present at the session but later proffered he could not do better. Keith's vocals grace the track, his second vocal outing on the album. Gospel vocals assist in the background. A seven-minute version recorded at the Right Track Studio, New York where the album was mixed allows a few extra guitar licks. And, then the big sleep began ...

11

STEEL WHEELS ROLLIN' ON

FEBRUARY 1989 – OCTOBER 1989

515. MIXED EMOTIONS (Jagger, Richards)
February–May 1989: Air Studios, Montserrat. Producer: Chris Kimsey, The Glimmer Twins. Engineers: Christopher Marc Potter, Rupert Coulson.
*UK Single: 21 August 1989: No **36** – 5 weeks*
*USA Single: 21 August 1989: No **5** – 12 weeks*
*USA LP STEEL WHEELS: 1 September 1989: No **3** – 20 weeks*
*UK LP STEEL WHEELS: 11 September 1989: No **2** – 8 weeks*
Rolling Stones with Chuck Leavell, Luis Jardin, Sarah Dash, Lisa Fisher, Bernard Fowler, Kick Horns.

In response to Keith Richards' *You Don't Move Me*, Mick Jagger wrote the autobiographical lyrics of *Mixed Emotions*. *Mixed Emotions* heralded a return by the Stones to recording; but more importantly it was a desperately needed antibody to The Glimmer Twins wound which had remained open ever since the release of DIRTY WORK. Keith had been much more involved with the writing process of the DIRTY WORK sessions than Mick had, and he was therefore more prepared to take the work out on tour. Mick was bored, thought the music was not up to scratch and physically thought the band could not sustain a tour. Mick ended 1986 by starting work on his next solo project with the help of Eurythmic, Dave Stewart and guitarist, Jeff Beck – *Primitive Cool* was released in September 1987 to diffident appreciation. Keith was far from idle but a little distraught at not keeping his band together. Steve Jordan, a well known session drummer first took Keith's mind off the Stones when he got him involved with a recording by Aretha Franklin of *Jumpin' Jack Flash*. Keith just about remembered the riff and he produced and played on the track – Ronnie Wood and Chuck Leavell were both present at the sessions. Continuing the Stones connection, *Harlem Shuffle* boys, Steve Thompson and Michael Barbiero produced a great street-cred mix for the twelve-inch format. Keith's collaboration with Steve Jordan continued in October 1986 when they both played and worked on a venture to produce and arrange Chuck Berry for a live concert recording, entitled 'Hail! Hail! Rock 'n' Roll'. This was easier said than done, provoking Keith to say that Chuck was more difficult to work with than even Mick! All-star contributions were made by Bobby Keys, Chuck Leavell (both of Stones fame), Eric Clapton, Robert Cray, Etta James, Julian Lennon, Linda Rondstadt, Joey Spaminato, Ingrid Berry and the legendary Johnnie Johnson who prompted Keith to recall the piano playing of departed mate, Stu. This major project over with, Keith recorded with the Eurythmics in 1987, Feargal Sharkey in 1988, and with Ron Wood he played on an excellent Dirty Strangers R 'n' B album led by Paul Fox of The Ruts fame. Not to be overshadowed by the new crowned kings of rock and roll, U2, he guested with them at a charity concert in 1988. Oh yes, one other thing, in 1988 he recorded and released his first solo album, TALK IS CHEAP – not bad for an out of work guitar player! In May 1988, Mick and Keith began to talk about the possibility of recording again and 1989 was put in the diary as a probable Stones year. Eddie Grant invited Mick and Keith to use his studio in Barbados to write songs. Before Keith departed to Barbados, he told his old lady (Keith's terminology!), Patti, that he would be gone either for a few weeks or for a few days. The old magic was there so they stayed six weeks. About 50 songs were written, most were unfinished but 16 were considered strong enough for the boys to be called in. *Mixed Emotions* was composed by Keith one weekend. It has a strong hook line but lacks a distinctive quality for it to be a huge hit.

516. MIXED EMOTIONS (CHRIS KIMSEY'S TWELVE-INCH) (Jagger, Richards)

February–May 1989: Air Studios, Montserrat. Producer: Chris Kimsey, The Glimmer Twins. Engineers: Christopher Marc Potter, Rupert Coulson, Michael H Brauer. Remix Engineer: Chris Kimsey.
*UK twelve-inch Single: 21 August 1989: No **36** – 5 weeks*
*USA twelve-inch Single: 21 August 1989: No **5** – 12 weeks*
Rolling Stones with Chuck Leavell, Luis Jardin, Sarah Dash, Lisa Fisher, Bernard Fowler, Kick Horns.

Chris Kimsey who had last worked with the Stones on the UNDERCOVER album was asked by Mick Jagger in December 1988 to produce the Stones. Chris agreed cn the condition that the album was recorded in a few months. He did not want it to deteriorate into a lengthy UNDERCOVER type album, at the end of which, he had sworn he would not work again with the protracted amblings of the Stones. This suited Mick down to the ground, and he indicated that the aim was for the album to be released late summer and for a States tour to commence in the autumn; a schedule more reminiscent of the 'sixties. While the Stones wrote songs in Barbados, Chris was working with the band that likes to say Yes, in the guise of Jon Anderson, Bill Bruford, Rick Wakeman and Steve Howe, at George Martin's Air Studios, 300 miles away in Montserrat. This was to be the studio where all the Stones would gather to commence recording and was also, in part, the venue for Keith Richards' solo album. Chris would fly over occasionally to offer comment about the progress of the material and he was pleased to find The Glimmer Twins in such fine fettle – the hatchet had definitely been buried. The album was mixed at Olympic in London in June 1989; the first time these studios had been used by the Stones since December 1970. The twelve-inch version of *Mixed Emotions* was mixed in Olympic by Michael H Brauer and then remixed by Chris Kimsey at the Hit Factory in New York. So sterling did the Stones find his work that the twelve-inch title includes his name in the song title in brackets. Mick plays guitar on *Mixed Emotions* and also performs strongly on vocals. Chuck Leavell is featured on piano and a hammond organ while Luis Jardin whose credits appear with, ABC, Frankie Goes To Hollywood, and Dave Gilmour assists with percussion. Bernard Fowler, Lisa Fisher and Sarah Dash (a former Labelle member who has also performed with Sir Ronald of Wood and on Keith's solo album) contribute backing vocals. Brass is supplied by a four piece entitled Kick Horns. The production is deliberately upfront for single exposure and for once the twelve-inch has a groove which gives it a far more enjoyable edge than the short single version. Chuck's newly revived hammond organ sound is much more visible in the extended mix and the band's guitars jangle effectively. The track especially comes alive towards the end of the six minutes when the horns and vocals are just accompanied by the strong percussive back drop, then the guitar's riff is menacingly introduced. The video to accompany the single release was shot by Jim Signaelli in August 1989 during tour rehearsals at an ex-girls school, Wykeham Rise, near Washington in Connecticut. The video is simply a run through of the song in rehearsal but cuts to black and white film of the Stones relaxing – Ronnie playing pool and a photo session mastered by Dimo Safari.

517. ROCK AND A HARD PLACE (a.k.a. **STEEL WHEELS**) (Jagger, Richards)
February–May 1989: Air Studios, Montserrat. Producer: Chris Kimsey, The Glimmer Twins. Engineers: Christopher Marc Potter, Rupert Coulson, Michael H Brauer.
*USA Single: 13 November 1989: No **23** – 13 weeks*
*USA LP STEEL WHEELS: 1 September 1989: No **3** – 20 weeks*
*UK LP STEEL WHEELS: 11 September 1989: No **2** – 8 weeks*
Rolling Stones with Chuck Leavell, Matt Clifford, Sarah Dash, Lisa Fisher, Bernard Fowler, Kick Horns.

518. ROCK AND A HARD PLACE (DANCE MIX) (Jagger, Richards)
February–May 1989: Air Studios, Montserrat. Producer: Chris Kimsey, The Glimmer Twins. Engineers: Christopher Marc Potter, Rupert Coulson, Michael H Brauer. Remixed by Don Was and Michael Brauer.
*UK twelve-inch Single: 13 November 1989: No **63** – 1 week*

*USA twelve-inch Single: 13 November 1989: No **23** – 13 weeks*
Rolling Stones with Chuck Leavell, Matt Clifford, Sarah Dash, Lisa
Fisher, Bernard Fowler, Kick Horns.

519. ROCK AND A HARD PLACE (BONUS BEATS MIX) (Jagger, Richards)
February–May 1989: Air Studios, Montserrat. Producer: Chris Kimsey,
The Glimmer Twins. Engineers: Christopher Marc Potter, Rupert
Coulson, Michael H Brauer. Remix by Don Was and David McMurray.
UK CD B-side Rock And A Hard Place: 13 November 1989
Rolling Stones with Chuck Leavell, Matt Clifford, Sarah Dash, Lisa
Fisher, Bernard Fowler, Kick Horns.

520. ROCK AND A HARD PLACE (OH-OH HARD DUB MIX) (Jagger, Richards)
February–May 1989: Air Studios, Montserrat. Producer: Chris Kimsey,
The Glimmer Twins. Engineers: Christopher Marc Potter, Rupert
Coulson, Michael H Brauer. Remix by Don Was and Michael Brauer.
UK CD B-side Rock And A Hard Place (Dance Mix): 13 November
1989
USA B-side twelve-inch Rock And A Hard Place (Dance Mix): 13
November 1989
Rolling Stones with Chuck Leavell, Matt Clifford, Sarah Dash, Lisa
Fisher, Bernard Fowler, Kick Horns.

When the songwriting team had completed the ground work on the 16
feasible tunes, Mick and Keith went to Air Studios in March and called in
Charlie Watts first to start work on the drum sound. He was closely
followed by the arrival of Bill Wyman and Ronnie Wood. Ronnie confirmed that they had deliberately left Mick and Keith together to settle
their differences and recreate some of the old magic. At about the same
time, Matt Clifford joined the band – apparently hijacked from the Yes
camp. Matt was a former Gloucestershire choralist who specialized on
the keyboard and synthesizer. He was to play a fundamental part to the
revitalized Stones sound. *Rock And A Hard Place* was one of the first
tracks to be recorded at the sessions, and was known as *Steel Wheels.* It
is a funky, guitar laden song, Bill's Wal bass as peppery and fiery as ever.
Several solos abound and the brass and female vocals are used extensively. The track was released as the second single from the album and it
became a popular favourite on FM stereo radio both sides of the Atlantic.
The single edition was a shortened version of the album cut – the
twelve-inch single and compact disc formats gave the marketing profession plenty of scope for different mixes which were undertaken by Don
Was of Was Not Was, David McMurray and Michael Brauer. They do not
come up to the standard of the *Too Much Blood* dance and dub mixes.

521. ALMOST HEAR YOU SIGH (Jagger, Richards, Jordan)
February–May 1989: Air Studios, Montserrat. Producer: Chris Kimsey,
The Glimmer Twins. Engineers: Christopher Marc Potter, Rupert

Coulson, Michael H Brauer. Literary Editor: Chris Jagger.
USA LP STEEL WHEELS: 1 September 1989: No **3** *– 20 weeks*
UK LP STEEL WHEELS: 11 September 1989: No **2** *– 8 weeks*
Rolling Stones with Chuck Leavell, Matt Clifford, Luis Jardin, Sarah Dash, Lisa Fisher, Bernard Fowler, Kick Horns.

Almost Hear You Sigh, a classic Stones ballad was written by Keith Richards and Steve Jordan during recording for Keith's solo album, TALK IS CHEAP. Keith desperately wanted to avoid recording solo since he felt it was an admission that he had failed to keep the band together. Keith was much more sensitive to the issues of a band break up and it was only after working with Steve Jordan on the Aretha Franklin and Chuck Berry enterprises that he could summon sufficient nerve to record an album. He recorded with Steve Jordan on drums, Charley Drayton on bass (although sometimes Steve and Charley swapped roles), and Waddy Wachtel on guitar. Guest appearances were made by Mick Taylor, Bootsy Collins, Chuck Leavell, Bobby Keys, Ivan Neville, Patti Scialfa, Willie Mitchell, Joey Spaminato, Sarah Dash and others. The main band became known as the Xpensive Winos due to their consumption of expensive Lafite wines. The album was generally cohesive, sometimes soulful, and turned out to be a trump card for getting the Stones back together. Just as Keith was beginning to promote its release, Mick 'phoned him and suggested getting the band back together, Keith jokingly retorted, 'What are you trying to screw me up for?'. In Barbados, Keith told Mick that he had this *Beast Of Burden* type song which would be great for Mick's vocals. Keith used a classical guitar, Matt Clifford and Chuck Leavell played on piano/keyboards, Chuck's contribution overdubbed later. Mick adjusted some of the lyrics, Keith was a little unhappy with the line about feeling your tongue on mine instead of the less seductive lips.

522. SAD SAD SAD (Jagger, Richards)
February–May 1989: Air Studios, Montserrat. Producer: Chris Kimsey, The Glimmer Twins. Engineers: Christopher Marc Potter, Rupert Coulson, Michael H Brauer.
USA LP STEEL WHEELS: 1 September 1989: No **3** *– 20 weeks*
UK LP STEEL WHEELS: 11 September 1989: No **2** *– 8 weeks*
Rolling Stones with Chuck Leavell, Bernard Fowler, Kick Horns, Simon Clarke, Roddy Lorimer, Tim Sanders, Paul Spong.

Sad Sad Sad is a typical Stones belter, it opens with a couple of guitars drawing fire from one to the other, then Mick Jagger spouts the now you're down, then you're up lyrics. Horns were added which immediately allowed parallels to be drawn with other Stones garage tunes, *Bitch,* and *Rocks Off.* The brass was arranged by the troupe Kick Horns and the quad sound of Simon Clarke, Roddy Lorimer, Tim Sanders (all from Dave Gilmour's 1984 band) and Paul Spong who had appeared with pop duo, Wham. *Sad Sad Sad* was written by Mick Jagger with the assistance of Charlie Watts; they wanted to come up with a rocker for the album without it falling into a Stones cliché. Bill Wyman was absent from the session which produced *Sad Sad Sad* – his bass role was taken by Ron Wood. Ron tended to play the bass in a much more frenzied manner, strumming it as opposed to Bill's plucking style. Bill in the meantime, had been sent away by the band to Antigua to speak with the press following the announcement of his engagement to Mandy Smith and planned marriage in June. Bill's association with Mandy had always attracted mass press attention ever since stories circulated of 'underage sexual encounters' with her when she was 13. Mick summed the situation up when he shrugged and said, 'Well that's lurve in the rock and roll world', meanwhile Bill confirmed that Mandy gives him youth and makes him feel younger, prompting men folk to feel just so slightly jealous!

523. HEARTS FOR SALE (Jagger, Richards)
February–May 1989: Air Studios, Montserrat. Producer: Chris Kimsey, The Glimmer Twins. Engineers: Christopher Marc Potter, Rupert Coulson, Michael H Brauer.
*USA LP STEEL WHEELS: 1 September 1989: No **3** – 20 weeks*
*UK LP STEEL WHEELS: 11 September 1989: No **2** – 8 weeks*
Rolling Stones with Matt Clifford, Bernard Fowler.

STEEL WHEELS was acclaimed by the rock press as a very strong album and *Hearts For Sale* typifies the depth the album has, proving it was not the Rolling Stones rehashing the past. The guitar sound is strong from Mick Jagger's opening speaker distorted feedback to the Latin strumming. Mick Jagger plays a burning harmonica and also one of Keith Richards' fenders. Chris Kimsey paid tribute to Mick's harmonica playing when he said that Mick managed to sound like all those old harp players, real breathy, the gaps were just as important as the sound. Similarly, Keith in interviews pointed out that as a musician, your canvas is silence and what you do is play around with silence – that's what rhythm is all about. Mick's contribution was extensive; he played guitar on two thirds of the album which was a significant increase – Woody's lessons had obviously paid off. Ron Wood later cracked, that the STEEL WHEELS sessions had allowed the L plates to be taken off Mick's plectrum. Unlike DIRTY WORK, where Mick was hardly in evidence, STEEL WHEELS was very much a Glimmer Twin production. The location must have helped, it was not so easy to get out of Montserrat as it was Paris – the venue for the last album.

524. HOLD ON TO YOUR HAT (Jagger, Richards)
February–May 1989: Air Studios, Montserrat. Producer: Chris Kimsey, The Glimmer Twins. Engineers: Christopher Marc Potter, Rupert Coulson, Michael H Brauer.
*USA LP STEEL WHEELS: 1 September 1989: No **3** – 20 weeks*
*UK LP STEEL WHEELS: 11 September 1989: No **2** – 8 weeks*

It is surprising that the two out and out rockers on STEEL WHEELS combine the guitar work of Keith Richards and Mick Jagger. Ron Wood was again playing the bass but as such, it loses no power. Guitar licks are traded and meshed as well as on any Richards/Wood outing. The track was written by Charlie Watts and Mick Jagger, confirming that Charlie's low profile belies his actual contribution. Chris Kimsey was worried that recording the band digitally may harm the Stones' furrow, everything might sound too clean, in particular Charlie's drum sound, but these worries were proved to be unfounded. He felt that every nuance of Charlie's playing was perfectly captured. Keith, recalling the sessions, remembers particularly the drive and determination shown by Charlie, 'he was at those sessions working a solid 12 hours a day'. In more ways than one Charlie proved to be a foundation stone to the Stones' reunion. Keith thought that Charlie might have had something to prove to Keith – how dare Keith work with another drummer, alias Steve Jordan!

525. SLIPPING AWAY (Jagger, Richards)
February–May 1989: Air Studios, Montserrat. Producer: Chris Kimsey, The Glimmer Twins. Engineers: Christopher Marc Potter, Rupert Coulson, Michael H Brauer.
*USA LP STEEL WHEELS: 1 September 1989: No **3** – 20 weeks*
*UK LP STEEL WHEELS: 11 September 1989: No **2** – 8 weeks*
Rolling Stones with Chuck Leavell, Matt Clifford, Bernard Fowler, Kick Horns, Sarah Dash, Lisa Fisher.

Keith Richards is featured on vocals on *Slipping Away*. His performance is *à la* Al Green on this plaintive ballad. Matt Clifford provides synthesized strings and also plays an electric piano while Chuck Leavell plays organ and piano. The overall effect is that it is not one of the album's high spots, and it disappointingly concludes the album. Mick Jagger hides away supporting Keith on backing vocals.

526. FOR YOUR PRECIOUS LOVE (Butler)
February–May 1989: Air Studios, Montserrat. Producer: Chris Kimsey, The Glimmer Twins. Engineer: Christopher Marc Potter.
Bootleg only.

A Jerry Butler song which was an original top 20 USA hit for him and Curtis Mayfield's band, The Impressions in 1958. Other lesser known acts who covered the song and attained USA chart positions were Garnet Mimms and The Enchanters and Oscar Toney Junior. The Stones took the opportunity to record it during the sessions and apparently it is one of the 16 tracks to be of a releasable nature.

527. CAN'T BE SEEN (Jagger, Richards)
February–May 1989: Air Studios, Montserrat. Producer: Chris Kimsey, The Glimmer Twins. Engineers: Christopher Marc Potter, Rupert Coulson, Michael H Brauer.
*USA LP STEEL WHEELS: 1 September 1989: No **3** – 20 weeks*
*UK LP STEEL WHEELS: 11 September 1989: No **2** – 8 weeks*
Rolling Stones with Chuck Leavell, Matt Clifford, Bernard Fowler, Luis Jardin.

Can't Be Seen is another vehicle for Keith Richards' vocals – the track is likely to have been a TALK IS CHEAP out-take. The vocals are very un-Stones like – since when did a Stone worry about another woman being married? – their music was indeed growing up. A wurlitzer type organ by Chuck Leavell announces the track's start and then it is immedi-·ately powered forward by Bill Wyman's bass and the percussion work of Charlie Watts and Luis Jardin. Ronnie Wood's guitar work also takes an opportunity to shine. The hitherto unknown Bernard Fowler provides great background vocals, as he does on most of the album helping to give it a consistency. Matt Clifford contributes clavinet on what is musician-wise a good track, but song-wise is a little thin.

528. BREAK THE SPELL (a.k.a. CALL GIRL BLUES) (Jagger, Richards)
February–May 1989: Air Studios, Montserrat. Producer: Chris Kimsey, The Glimmer Twins. Engineers: Christopher Marc Potter, Rupert Coulson, Michael H Brauer.
USA LP STEEL WHEELS: 1 September 1989: No 3 – 20 weeks
UK LP STEEL WHEELS: 11 September 1989: No 2 – 8 weeks
Rolling Stones with Matt Clifford.

Ron Wood stepped into the breach, again substituting for Bill Wyman's bass steps. The track is an adventurous journey into the land of Tom Waits' blues, hence a.k.a. *Call Girl Blues.* It features the Little Walter harp playing of Mick Jagger and Matt Clifford on keyboards. Keith Richards delivers a mean steel guitar while Mick's vocals are suitably affected in a Tom Waits vein by the production team. The lyrics contain some interesting imagery of a lost love.

529. COOK COOK BLUES (Jagger, Richards)
February–May 1989: Air Studios, Montserrat. Producer: Chris Kimsey, The Glimmer Twins. Engineers: Christopher Marc Potter, Rupert Coulson.
UK & USA B-side Rock And A Hard Place: 13 November 1989
Rolling Stones with Matt Clifford, Chuck Leavell.

Cook Cook Blues sounds as though it was used at the beginning of a session to create a mood for subsequent recording. It is a fine boogie and stroll tune which doubtless would have remained on the cutting room floor if it had not been for the flip side of the single requirement. At least the Stones were no longer releasing tracks from the album as the B-side, but surely there was stronger material lurking from the STEEL WHEELS sessions.

530. BLINDED BY LOVE (Jagger, Richards)
February–May 1989: Air Studios, Montserrat. Producer: Chris Kimsey, The Glimmer Twins. Engineers: Christopher Marc Potter, Rupert Coulson: Literary Editor: Chris Jagger.
USA LP STEEL WHEELS: 1 September 1989: No 3 – 20 weeks
UK LP STEEL WHEELS: 11 September 1989: No 2 – 8 weeks

Rolling Stones with Chuck Leavell, Matt Clifford, Bernard Fowler, Phil Beer, Luis Jardin.

The strange marriage of tex-mex, country and western music and the lyrics of women's undoing of men through the centuries is bizarre. The Stones always liked the extraneous works of country but this particular example is contrived. The music sounds like a Mick Jagger solo out-take (Mick is on acoustic!); technically it is good, the use of Phil Beer on fiddle and mandolin is interesting, but over-all it is not a patch on the humorous offerings of *Faraway Eyes.* American representatives, on first hearing it, commented that the lyrics relating to the Prince of Wales giving up his crown might offend, not realizing it was not about the present encumbant! Chris Jagger is puzzlingly credited as literary editor on *Blinded By Love.*

531. TERRIFYING (Jagger, Richards)
February–May 1989: Air Studios, Montserrat. Producer: Chris Kimsey, The Glimmer Twins. Engineer: Christopher Marc Potter, Rupert Coulson, Michael H Brauer.
*USA LP STEEL WHEELS: 1 September 1989: No **3** – 20 weeks*
*UK LP STEEL WHEELS: 11 September 1989: No **2** – 8 weeks*
Rolling Stones with Chuck Leavell, Matt Clifford, Roddy Lorimer, Lisa Fisher.

The whole team hums on this excellent funk number. The rhythm section of Charlie Watts and Bill Wyman provide a great back beat – Charlie tick tacks wonderfully in almost jazz fashion. Chris Kimsey thought that Michael Brauer the mixing engineer really got the best results from Bill's bass – Michael was good at the bottom end. Mick Jagger's vocals are used to terrific effect, the lyrics are full of animal similes; the strange, strange desires, chorus is impressive. Roddy Lorimer provides a bar or two of trumpet and Matt Clifford and Chuck Leavell are again used on keyboards and organ respectively.

532. FANCYMAN BLUES (Jagger, Richards)
February–May 1989: Air Studios, Montserrat. Producer: Chris Kimsey, The Glimmer Twins. Engineer: Christopher Marc Potter.
UK & USA B-side Mixed Emotions: 21 August 1989

As if to prove the Stones were again in fine form, *Fancyman Blues* which was the flip-side of *Mixed Emotions*, is a barnstormer of a blues track. It is played in a strictly pedestrian manner with an atypical blues style piano and the obligatory wailing harmonica. While the Stones toured the States in September 1989, hurricane Hugo swept through the Caribbean and devastated the island of Montserrat. George Martin organized a compilation album to help raise funds for the storm's victims; it was called AFTER THE HURRICANE and the Stones contributed *Fancyman Blues.* It was originally mixed in June 1989, by Chris Kimsey and The Glimmer Twins at Olympic Studios in London. The band remembers they pinned up a cartoon on the wall from an English tabloid newspaper, the *Daily Mirror.* It depicted them fumbling their way down the aisle for Bill Wyman and

Mandy Smith's wedding, the cartoon was doubtless inspired by Spike Milligan's gift to Bill of a walking frame! Eric Clapton bought Bill a pair of silk pyjamas exclaiming that at Bill's age he might need something to keep him warm in bed! Dignity had at last arrived but as Mick Jagger was quick to quip, 'a dignified rock band is a contradiction in terms'.

533. CONTINENTAL DRIFT (Jagger, Richards)
February–May 1989: Air Studios, Montserrat. Producer: Chris Kimsey, The Glimmer Twins. Engineer: Christopher Marc Potter. Arranged by: Mick Jagger, Matt Clifford.
USA LP STEEL WHEELS: 1 September 1989: No 3 – 20 weeks
UK LP STEEL WHEELS: 11 September 1989: No 2 – 8 weeks
Rolling Stones with Matt Clifford, Master Musicians of Jajouka, Bachir Attar, Bernard Fowler, Sarah Dash, Lisa Fisher, Sonia Morgan, Tessa Niles, Farafina.

Experimentation had always been a strength of the Stones' work, but a degree of conservatism had crept into the Stones' sound since the mid 'seventies. *Continental Drift* was an attempt to rescind this feeling; it was written by Mick Jagger as he experimented with a drum machine and a Korg synthesizer. Matt Clifford helped to programme the synthesizer, hence his credit on the album cover as co-arranger. As the song developed it was apparent that it had a North African or Eastern feel to it (*Paint It, Black* revisited). At one stage Mick felt that the Burundi drummers should be approached to add percussion, but a sequence of events where history was about to repeat itself dictated otherwise. Brian Jones had recorded the G'naoua and the Maalimin of Jajouka in 1968. Bachir Attar, the son of the then chief, had now written to the Stones inviting them over to Morocco to record. It seemed a perfect opportunity to take the backing track to Tangier and record the musicians of Jajouka – their music was a rhythmic incantation which featured the ahaita, a high pitched instrument, and the tebel drums. It was not possible to record them at their village due to the lack of amenities such as electricity, so they were brought to the Palace Ben Abbou at the Casbah near Tangier where they enthusiastically contributed their part. A BBC documentary as part of the Rhythms of the World series witnessed the recording process. The musicians were still going full tilt even when the original basis for *Continental Drift* had finished. As Fdall, one of the musicians confirmed, *Continental Drift* is 'big music'; Mick hoped that because of the Moroccan connection the Stones would not be accused of traipsing the New World music made popular by the likes of Peter Gabriel. Charlie Watts later overdubbed drums, Ron Wood an acoustic bass and Keith Richards on acoustic guitar. When the song was originally written in Barbados, Keith had this idea of humanizing the programming of Mick and Matt by incorporating the reverberations of a bicycle wheel. As it span round, Keith hit the spokes with a stick, brush, spoon and knife – the effect is quite audible and can be heard early on in the track. *Speed Of Light* is a masterpiece of recording and will rise to become a Stones classic.

534. 2000 LIGHT YEARS FROM HOME (Jagger, Richard)
28 October 1989: Shea Stadium, New York.
Bootleg only.
Rolling Stones with Matt Clifford, Chuck Leavell, Bernard Fowler, Lisa Fisher.

The STEEL WHEELS tour kicked off ironically at the Veterans Stadium in Philadelphia on 31 August 1989 and trundled its way around the States and Canada until the year end. The set designed by Mark Fisher of 'The Wall' fame was an awe-inspiring catalogue of cat walks, giant orange girders and steel shafts which resembled an urban decay scene of long lost steel factories or abandoned docklands. During the 28 song set Mick Jagger would disappear at one point in *Sympathy* and return at the top of a tower with a precarious vantage point. Giant blow-up dolls were used during *Honky Tonk Woman*. The Stones had always been keen to put on a show and the STEEL WHEELS theatrics were up to scratch. The band themselves were in considerable form. *Start Me Up* opened the show and other standards included *Tumbling Dice*, *Brown Sugar*, and *Miss You*. Recent tunes not played on tour before included *Harlem Shuffle* (the only track from DIRTY WORK), and *Undercover Of The Night* – tracks from STEEL WHEELS were *Rock And A Hard Place*, *Hold On To Your Hat*, *Sad Sad Sad*, and *Mixed Emotions*. Critics and fans especially liked the mid-section of 'sixties oldies including *Play With Fire*, *She's A Rainbow*, *Paint It, Black*, *Ruby Tuesday* and *2000 Light Years From Home* – the latter was mooted to be a tour favourite. The Stones' CBS contact always promised one further album and Michael Cohl's 65-70 million dollar States tour contract was an offer not to be refuted, but Mick Jagger was quick to point our that if money was the sole concern the European tour would have been long since booked. It is likely that the summer of 1990 will see the Stones return to their native land for a tour. Unlike ramblings of The Who, who played in the States and Britain in 1989, the Stones were proving they were not in it for the money alone – a point which even Pete Townshend acknowledged. The Stones have the opportunity to progress this thing called rock and roll from beyond youth and gathered maturity to ...

Sessions in date order

1963

28 JANUARY – 2 FEBRUARY 1963
Regent, IBC, London

1. DIDDLEY DADDY
2. ROAD RUNNER
3. BRIGHT LIGHTS, BIG CITY
4. I WANT TO BE LOVED (1)
5. CRACKIN' UP (1)
6. HONEY WHAT'S WRONG

10 MAY 1963
Olympic, London

7. COME ON (1)
8. I WANT TO BE LOVED (2)

JULY/AUGUST 1963
Decca, London

9. POISON IVY (1)
10. IT SHOULD BE YOU
11. FORTUNE TELLER (1)

14/15 SEPTEMBER 1963
Kingsway, London

12. YOU BETTER MOVE ON (1)
13. BYE BYE JOHNNY (1)
14. MONEY

5 OCTOBER 1963
BBC Radio, London

15. COME ON (2)
16. MEMPHIS TENNESSEE (1)
17. ROLL OVER BEETHOVEN
18. I JUST WANT TO MAKE LOVE TO YOU (1)

7 OCTOBER 1963
Kingsway, London

19. I WANNA BE YOUR MAN
20. STONED

NOVEMBER 1963
Kingsway, London

21. POISON IVY (2)

1964

JANUARY/FEBRUARY 1964
Regent, IBC, London

22. AIN'T THAT LOVIN' YOU BABY
23. ROUTE 66 (1)
24. I JUST WANT TO MAKE LOVE TO YOU (2)
25. HONEST I DO
26. I NEED YOU BABY (MONA) (1)
27. NOW I'VE GOT A WITNESS (LIKE UNCLE PHIL AND UNCLE GENE)
28. I'M A KING BEE
29. CAROL (1)
30. TELL ME (YOU'RE COMING BACK)
31. CAN I GET A WITNESS
32. YOU CAN MAKE IT IF YOU TRY (1)
33. WALKING THE DOG
34. NOT FADE AWAY (1)
35. LITTLE BY LITTLE
36. ANDREW'S BLUES

19 MARCH 1964
Camden Theatre, London

37. COPS AND ROBBERS
38. ROUTE 66 (2)
39. YOU BETTER MOVE ON (2)
40. MONA (2)

MAY 1964
Regent, IBC, London

41. SURPRISE, SURPRISE
42. GOOD TIMES, BAD TIMES
43. OFF THE HOOK (1)
44. CONGRATULATIONS
45. YOU CAN'T CATCH ME
46. TIME IS ON MY SIDE (1)
47. UNDER THE BOARDWALK
48. SUZIE Q
49. GROWN UP WRONG

3 JUNE 1964
Hollywood Palace TV Show, USA

50. NOT FADE AWAY (2)

10/11 JUNE 1964
Chess, Chicago

51. IF YOU NEED ME
52. EMPTY HEART
53. 2120 SOUTH MICHIGAN
     AVENUE
54. CONFESSIN' THE BLUES (1)
55. AROUND AND AROUND (1)
56. STEWED AND KEEFED
57. HIGH HEELED SNEEKERS (1)
58. TELL ME BABY
59. DOWN IN THE BOTTOM (1)
60. DOWN THE ROAD APIECE
     (1)
61. I CAN'T BE SATISFIED
62. DON'T LIE TO ME (1)
63. IT'S ALL OVER NOW (1)
64. LOOK WHAT YOU'VE DONE
65. BYE BYE JOHNNY (2)

11 JULY 1964
Kingsway, London

66. AS TIME GOES BY

JULY 1964
Kingsway, London

67. DA DOO RON RON
68. MEMPHIS TENNESSEE (2)
69. HEART OF STONE (1)
70. SOME THINGS JUST STICK
     IN YOUR MIND
71. SLEEPY CITY

25 OCTOBER 1964
Ed Sullivan TV Show, USA

72. AROUND AND AROUND (2)
73. TIME IS ON MY SIDE (2)

27 OCTOBER 1964
RCA, Hollywood

74. DOWN HOME GIRL (1)
75. EVERYBODY NEEDS
     SOMEBODY TO LOVE (1)
76. EVERYBODY NEEDS
     SOMEBODY TO LOVE (2)
77. PAIN IN MY HEART (1)
78. HEART OF STONE (2)
79. HITCH HIKE
80. OH, BABY (WE GOT A
     GOOD THING GOING)

28/29 OCTOBER 1964
Santa Monica Civic Auditorium

81. AROUND AND AROUND (3)
82. OFF THE HOOK (2)
83. TIME IS ON MY SIDE (3)
84. IT'S ALL OVER NOW (2)
85. I'M ALRIGHT (1)

5/6/8 NOVEMBER 1964
Chess, Chicago

86. WHAT A SHAME
87. I'D MUCH RATHER BE WITH
     THE BOYS
88. WE'RE WASTIN' TIME
89. EACH AND EVERY DAY OF
     THE YEAR
90. LITTLE RED ROOSTER (1)
91. TIME IS ON MY SIDE (4)

DECEMBER 1964
BBC Radio, London

92. YOU CAN MAKE IT IF YOU TRY (2)
93. DOWN IN THE BOTTOM (2)
94. BEAUTIFUL DELILAH
95. HIGH HEELED SNEEKERS (2)

1965

10/11 JANUARY AND 17/18 FEBRUARY 1965
RCA Hollywood.

96. THE LAST TIME (1)
97. PLAY WITH FIRE (1)

5/16 MARCH 1965
Edmonton Regal, Liverpool Empire, Manchester Palace, Greenford Granada.

98. EVERYBODY NEEDS SOMEBODY TO LOVE (3)
99. PAIN IN MY HEART (2)
100. ROUTE 66 (3)
101. I'M MOVING ON
102. I'M ALRIGHT (2)

17/18 APRIL 1965
Olympia, Paris

103. EVERYBODY NEEDS SOMEBODY TO LOVE (4)
104. PLAY WITH FIRE (2)
105. THE LAST TIME (2)
106. LITTLE RED ROOSTER (2)
107. HEY CRAWDADDY

10/11 MAY 1965
Chess, Chicago

108. THE UNDER ASSISTANT WEST COAST PROMOTION MAN (1)
109. MERCY MERCY (1)
110. THAT'S HOW STRONG MY LOVE IS
111. FANNY MAE (1)

12/13 MAY 1965
RCA, Hollywood

112. THE SPIDER AND THE FLY
113. ONE MORE TRY
114. MY GIRL
115. (I CAN'T GET NO) SATISFACTION (1)
116. GOOD TIMES
117. CRY TO ME (1)
118. SHE SAID YEAH (1)
119. GOTTA GET AWAY
120. I'VE BEEN LOVING YOU TOO LONG (1)
121. TALKIN' 'BOUT YOU
122. I'M FREE (1)
123. BLUE TURNS TO GREY

20 MAY 1965
Shindig TV Show, Hollywood

124. (I CAN'T GET NO) SATISFACTION (2)

30 AUGUST 1965
BBC Radio, London

125. MERCY MERCY (2)
126. CRY TO ME (2)
127. EVERYBODY NEEDS SOMEBODY TO LOVE (5)
128. (I CAN'T GET NO) SATISFACTION (3)
129. THE LAST TIME (3)
130. FANNY MAE (2)
131. DOWN THE ROAD APIECE (2)

6/7 SEPTEMBER 1965
RCA, Hollywood

132. GET OFF MY CLOUD (1)
133. THE SINGER NOT THE SONG
134. AS TEARS GO BY (1)

11 NOVEMBER 1965
Hullaballoo TV Show, New York

135. SHE SAID YEAH (2)
136. GET OFF MY CLOUD (2)

3/8 DECEMBER 1965
RCA, Hollywood

137. MOTHER'S LITTLE HELPER
138. DONCHA BOTHER ME
139. GOIN' HOME
140. LOOKING TIRED
141. TRY A LITTLE HARDER
142. TAKE IT OR LEAVE IT
143. THINK
144. RIDE ON BABY
145. SITTIN' ON A FENCE
146. SAD DAY
147. 19TH NERVOUS BREAKDOWN (1)

1966

12 FEBRUARY 1966
Ed Sullivan TV Show, USA

148. (I CAN'T GET NO) SATISFACTION (4)
149. AS TEARS GO BY (2)
150. 19TH NERVOUS BREAKDOWN (2)

3/8 MARCH 1966
RCA, Hollywood

151. OUT OF TIME (1)
152. OUT OF TIME (2)
153. LADY JANE (1)
154. IT'S NOT EASY
155. STUPID GIRL
156. PAINT IT, BLACK (1)
157. LONG LONG WHILE
158. UNDER MY THUMB (1)
159. HIGH AND DRY
160. FLIGHT 505
161. I AM WAITING
162. WHAT TO DO

MAY 1966
BBC TV, London

163. PAINT IT, BLACK (2)

7 AUGUST 1966
RCA, Hollywood

164. HAVE YOU SEEN YOUR MOTHER, BABY, STANDING IN THE SHADOW? (1)
165. WHO'S DRIVING YOUR PLANE?
166. CAN'T BELIEVE

11 SEPTEMBER 1966
Ed Sullivan TV Show, USA

167. PAINT IT, BLACK (3)
168. LADY JANE (2)
169. HAVE YOU SEEN YOUR MOTHER, BABY, STANDING IN THE SHADOW? (2)

23 SEPTEMBER 1966
Royal Albert Hall, London

170. UNDER MY THUMB (2)
171. GET OFF MY CLOUD (3)
172. LADY JANE (3)
173. NOT FADE AWAY (3)
174. I'VE BEEN LOVING YOU TOO LONG (2)
175. FORTUNE TELLER (2)
176. THE LAST TIME (4)
177. 19TH NERVOUS BREAKDOWN (3)
178. TIME IS ON MY SIDE (5)
179. I'M ALRIGHT (3)
180. HAVE YOU SEEN YOUR MOTHER, BABY, STANDING IN THE SHADOW? (3)
181. (I CAN'T GET NO) SATISFACTION (5)

NOVEMBER 1966
Olympic, London

182. RUBY TUESDAY (1)
183. DANDELION
184. LET'S SPEND THE NIGHT TOGETHER (1)

NOVEMBER/DECEMBER 1966
Olympic, London

185. MY OBSESSION
186. ALL SOLD OUT
187. SHE SMILED SWEETLY

188. YESTERDAY'S PAPERS
189. PLEASE GO HOME
190. MISS AMANDA JONES
191. BACK STREET GIRL
192. IF YOU LET ME
193. COOL, CALM AND
COLLECTED
194. SOMETHING HAPPENED
TO ME YESTERDAY
195. WHO'S BEEN SLEEPING
HERE?
196. COMPLICATED
197. CONNECTION

1967

JANUARY 1967
Ed Sullivan TV Show, USA

198. RUBY TUESDAY (2)
199. LET'S SPEND THE NIGHT
TOGETHER (2)

JULY/AUGUST 1967
Olympic, London

200. WE LOVE YOU

JUNE/SEPTEMBER 1967
Olympic Studio and Bell Sound,
London

201. SHE'S A RAINBOW
202. SING THIS ALL TOGETHER
203. SING THIS ALL TOGETHER
(SEE WHAT HAPPENS)
204. 2000 LIGHT YEARS FROM
HOME (1)
205. IN ANOTHER LAND
206. CITADEL
207. 2000 MAN
208. GOMPER
209. THE LANTERN
210. ON WITH THE SHOW
211. SHADES OF ORANGE

1968

MARCH/MAY 1968
Olympic, London

212. JUMPIN' JACK FLASH (1)
213. CHILD OF THE MOON
214. EVERYBODY PAYS THEIR
DUES
215. STREET FIGHTING MAN (1)
216. NO EXPECTATIONS (1)
217. THE DEVIL IS MY NAME
218. SYMPATHY FOR THE
DEVIL (1)

MARCH/JUNE 1968
Olympic, London

219. DEAR DOCTOR
220. DOWNTOWN SUZIE
221. PRODIGAL SON (1)
222. I'M A COUNTRY BOY
223. GIVE ME A HAMBURGER
224. SILVER BLANKET
225. LADY
226. JIGSAW PUZZLE
227. PARACHUTE WOMAN (1)
228. FAMILY
229. SALT OF THE EARTH (1)
230. STRAY CAT BLUES (1)
231. FACTORY GIRL
232. MIDNIGHT RAMBLER (1)
233. YOU GOT THE SILVER
234. YOU CAN'T ALWAYS GET
WHAT YOU WANT (1)

MARCH/OCTOBER 1968
Olympic, London

235. SISTER MORPHINE

JULY 1968
Redlands and Olympic, London

236. STILL A FOOL
237. HIGHWAY CHILD
238. HOLD ON I'M COMING
239. ROCK ME BABY

OCTOBER 1968
Olympic, London

240.   MEMO FROM TURNER (1)
241.   MEMO FROM TURNER (2)

10,11 DECEMBER 1968
BBC, London

242.   YER BLUES
243.   ROUTE 66 (4)
244.   CONFESSIN' THE BLUES (2)
245.   JUMPIN' JACK FLASH (2)
246.   PARACHUTE WOMAN (2)
247.   YOU CAN'T ALWAYS GET
       WHAT YOU WANT (2)
248.   YONDERS WALL
249.   NO EXPECTATIONS (2)
250.   SYMPATHY FOR THE
       DEVIL (2)
251.   SALT OF THE EARTH (2)

1969

MAY 1969
Olympic, London

252.   HONKY TONK WOMEN (1)

JUNE/JULY 1969
Olympic, London

253.   LET IT BLEED (1)
254.   LOVE IN VAIN (1)
255.   I'M GOING DOWN
256.   I DON'T KNOW WHY
257.   MONKEY MAN
258.   JIVING SISTER FANNY

5 JULY 1969
Hyde Park, London

259.   I'M YOURS, AND I'M HERS
260.   JUMPIN' JACK FLASH (3)
261.   MERCY MERCY
262.   STRAY CAT BLUES (2)
263.   NO EXPECTATIONS (3)
264.   I'M FREE (2)
265.   DOWN HOME GIRL (2)
266.   HONKY TONK WOMEN (2)

267.   LOVE IN VAIN (2)
268.   GIVE ME A DRINK
269.   MIDNIGHT RAMBLER (2)
270.   STREET FIGHTING MAN (2)
271.   (I CAN'T GET NO)
       SATISFACTION (6)
272.   SYMPATHY FOR THE
       DEVIL (3)

OCTOBER/NOVEMBER 1969
Elektra, Hollywood

273.   GIMMIE SHELTER (1)
274.   LIVE WITH ME (1)
275.   ALL DOWN THE LINE (1)
276.   COUNTRY HONK
277.   I DON'T KNOW THE
       REASON WHY

NOVEMBER 1969
David Frost TV Show, USA

278.   HONKY TONK WOMEN (3)
279.   YOU CAN'T ALWAYS GET
       WHAT YOU WANT (3)

18/19 NOVEMBER 1969
Ed Sullivan TV Show, USA

280.   GIMMIE SHELTER (2)
281.   LOVE IN VAIN (3)
282.   HONKY TONK WOMEN (4)

27/28 NOVEMBER 1969
Madison Square Gardens, New York

283.   JUMPIN' JACK FLASH (4)
284.   CAROL (2)
285.   STRAY CAT BLUES (3)
286.   LOVE IN VAIN (4)
287.   MIDNIGHT RAMBLER (3)
288.   SYMPATHY FOR THE
       DEVIL (4)
289.   LIVE WITH ME (2)
290.   LITTLE QUEENIE (1)
291.   HONKY TONK WOMEN (5)
292.   STREET FIGHTING MAN (3)

1 DECEMBER 1969
Muscle Shoals, Alabama

293. WILD HORSES
294. YOU GOTTA MOVE (1)
295. BROWN SUGAR (1)

6 DECEMBER 1969
Altamont Speedway, Livermore, California

296. UNDER MY THUMB (3)

1970

JUNE 1970
Olympic, London

297. COCKSUCKER BLUES
298. BITCH
299. MOONLIGHT MILE
300. I GOT THE BLUES (1)
301. SWAY
302. CAN'T YOU HEAR ME KNOCKING?
303. DEAD FLOWERS (1)

17/31 October 1970
Olympic, London

304. AIN'T GONNA LIE
305. GOOD TIME WOMAN

18 DECEMBER 1970
Olympic, London

306. BROWN SUGAR (2)

1971

13 MARCH 1971
Leeds University

307. LET IT ROCK (1)
308. (I CAN'T GET NO) SATISFACTION (7)
309. LITTLE QUEENIE (2)

MAY/SEPTEMBER 1971
Rolling Stones Mobile Unit, Nellcote, France

310. SHAKE YOUR HIPS (1)
311. VENTILATOR BLUES
312. TORN AND FRAYED
313. LOVING CUP
314. LET IT ROCK (2)
315. TURD ON THE RUN
316. ALL DOWN THE LINE (2)
317. TUMBLING DICE (1)
318. SWEET BLACK ANGEL
319. I JUST WANT TO SEE HIS FACE
320. SWEET VIRGINIA
321. RIP THIS JOINT
322. HAPPY (1)
323. SOUL SURVIVOR
324. STOP BREAKING DOWN
325. ROCKS OFF
326. CASINO BOOGIE
327. LET IT LOOSE
328. SHINE A LIGHT
329. EXILE ON MAIN STREET BLUES

1972

APRIL 1972
Rialto Theatre, Montreux, Switzerland

330. TUMBLING DICE (2)
331. BLUEBERRY JAM
332. SHAKE YOUR HIPS (2)

20/21 JULY 1972
Spectrum, Philadelphia

333. DON'T LIE TO ME (2)

NOVEMBER 1972
Elektra, Hollywood

334. BLOOD RED WINE
335. TRAVELLIN' MAN
336. LEATHER JACKET
337. DANCING IN THE LIGHT
338. POTTED SHRIMP

339. ALADDIN STORY
340. TRIDENT JAM

25 NOVEMBER–DECEMBER 1972
Dynamic Sounds, Kingston, Jamaica

341. COMING DOWN AGAIN
342. WINTER
343. SEPARATELY
344. WHO AM I (SEE I LOVE YOU)?
345. CAN YOU HEAR THE MUSIC
346. DANCING WITH MR. D
347. ANGIE
348. SILVER TRAIN
349. 100 YEARS AGO
350. HIDE YOUR LOVE
351. SAVE ME
352. DOO DOO DOO DOO (HEARTBREAKER)
353. STAR STAR (1)
354. THROUGH THE LONELY NIGHTS
355. TOPS

1973

28 SEPTEMBER 1973
Olympiahalle, Munich, West Germany

356. BYE BYE JOHNNY (3)

1974

MARCH-APRIL 1974
Musicland, Munich, West Germany

357. AIN'T TOO PROUD TO BEG
358. DRIFT AWAY
359. IF YOU CAN'T ROCK ME (1)
360. FINGERPRINT FILE (1)
361. TILL THE NEXT GOODBYE
362. IT'S ONLY ROCK 'N' ROLL (BUT I LIKE IT) (1)
363. IF YOU REALLY WANT TO BE MY FRIEND

364. TIME WAITS FOR NO ONE
365. LUXURY
366. LIVING IS A HARDER LOVE
367. DANCE LITTLE SISTER
368. SHORT AND CURLIES

12 DECEMBER 1974
Musicland, Munich, West Germany

369. FOOL TO CRY (1)

15 DECEMBER 1974
Musicland, Munich, West Germany

370. CHERRY OH BABY

1975

DECEMBER 1974–MARCH 1975
Musicland, Munich, West Germany

371. SLAVE
372. WORRIED ABOUT YOU

23 JANUARY 1975
Mobile Studio, Rotterdam, Holland

373. MELODY

MARCH 1975
Musicland, Munich, West Germany

374. SEXY NIGHT
375. COME ON SUGAR

25 MARCH–31 MARCH 1975
Musicland, Munich, West Germany

376. HAND OF FATE
377. CRAZY MAMA
378. HOT STUFF (1)
379. MEMORY MOTEL

2 APRIL 1975
Musicland, Munich, West Germany

380. HEY NEGRITA

6 JUNE 1975
Arrowhead Stadium, Kansas City

381. SURE THE ONE YOU NEED

1976

4/7 JUNE 1976
Avetoire, Paris, France

382. HONKY TONK WOMEN (6)
383. IF YOU CAN'T ROCK ME (2)
384. GET OFF MY CLOUD (4)
385. HAPPY (2)
386. HOT STUFF (2)
387. STAR STAR (2)
388. TUMBLING DICE (3)
389. FINGERPRINT FILE (2)
390. YOU GOTTA MOVE (2)
391. YOU CAN'T ALWAYS GET WHAT YOU WANT (4)
392. IT'S ONLY ROCK 'N' ROLL (2)
393. BROWN SUGAR (3)
394. JUMPIN' JACK FLASH (5)
395. SYMPATHY FOR THE DEVIL (5)

21 AUGUST 1976
Knebworth, England

396. STRAY CAT BLUES (4)

1977

4/5 MARCH 1977
El Mocambo, Toronto, Canada

397. MANNISH BOY
398. CRACKIN' UP (2)
399. LITTLE RED ROOSTER (3)
400. AROUND AND AROUND (4)

12/13 MARCH 1977
Sounds Interchange, Toronto, Canada

401. APARTMENT NO 9
402. WORRIED LIFE BLUES

OCTOBER 1977-MARCH 1978
EMI Pathé Marconi, Paris, France

403. BLACK LIMOUSINE (1)
404. MUNICH HILTON

405. WHEN THE WHIP COMES DOWN (1)
406. RESPECTABLE
407. I NEED YOU
408. HANG FIRE (1)
409. START ME UP (1)
410. YELLOW CAB
411. I THINK I'M GOING MAD
412. BEAST OF BURDEN (1)
413. LIES
414. SHAVED STONE
415. FIJI JIM
416. SOME GIRLS
417. EVERYTHING IS TURNING TO GOLD
418. SHATTERED (1)
419. FAR AWAY EYES
420. CLAUDINE
421. MISTY ROADS
422. MISS YOU (1)
423. MISS YOU (2)
424. JUST MY IMAGINATION (RUNNING AWAY WITH ME) (1)
425. JAH IS NOT DEAD

1978

MARCH 1978
EMI Pathé Marconi, Paris, France

426. BEFORE THEY MAKE ME RUN (1)
427. EVERLASTING IS MY LOVE
428. WHERE THE BOYS GO
429. SUMMER ROMANCE

14 JUNE 1978
Passaic Theatre, New York, USA

430. SWEET LITTLE SIXTEEN
431. WHEN THE WHIP COMES DOWN (LIVE VERSION) (2)

28 JUNE 1978
Memphis, Tennessee, USA

432. HOUND DOG

1979/1980

22 APRIL 1979
Oshawa Civic Auditorium, Toronto, Canada

433. BEFORE THEY MAKE ME RUN (2)
434. PRODIGAL SON (2)

MAY 1979–MAY 1980
Compass Point Studio, Nassau, Bahamas

435. WE HAD IT ALL
436. EMOTIONAL RESCUE
437. GANGSTERS MAUL
438. SWEET HOME CHICAGO
439. DANCE
440. IF I WAS A DANCER (DANCE PART TWO)
441. DOWN IN THE HOLE
442. LONELY AT THE TOP
443. INDIAN GIRL
444. LET'S GO STEADY
445. SEND IT TO ME
446. LET ME GO (1)
447. SHE'S SO COLD (1)
448. ALL ABOUT YOU
449. LINDA LU
450. WHAT'S THE MATTER?
451. BULLDOG
452. LITTLE T & A (1)
453. NO USE IN CRYING

1981

JANUARY-JUNE 1981
Electric Ladyland, Atlantic Studio, New York

454. WAITING ON A FRIEND (1)
455. HEAVEN
456. NEIGHBOURS (1)

AUGUST 1981
Long View Farm. Massachusetts, USA

457. WHOLE LOTTA SHAKIN' GOIN' ON

5 NOVEMBER AND 13 DECEMBER 1981
Meadowlands Arena, New Jersey, New York; Sun Devil Stadium, Tempe, Arizona

458. UNDER MY THUMB (4)
459. LET'S SPEND THE NIGHT TOGETHER (3)
460. SHATTERED (2)
461. NEIGHBOURS (2)
462. BLACK LIMOUSINE (2)
463. JUST MY IMAGINATION (RUNNING AWAY WITH ME) (2)
464. TWENTY FLIGHT ROCK
465. LET ME GO (2)
466. TIME IS ON MY SIDE (6)
467. BEAST OF BURDEN (2)
468. WAITING ON A FRIEND (2)
469. GOING TO A GO-GO
470. YOU CAN'T ALWAYS GET WHAT YOU WANT (5)
471. LITTLE T & A (2)
472. TUMBLING DICE (4)
473. SHE'S SO COLD (2)
474. ALL DOWN THE LINE (3)
475. HANG FIRE (2)
476. MISS YOU (3)
477. LET IT BLEED (2)
478. START ME UP (2)
479. HONKY TONK WOMEN (7)
480. BROWN SUGAR (4)
481. JUMPIN' JACK FLASH (6)
482. (I CAN'T GET NO) SATISFACTION (8)

1982

25 JUNE 1982
Wembley Stadium, London

483. CHANTILLY LACE

1983

NOVEMBER 1982–AUGUST 1983
EMI, Paris, France; Compass Point, Nassau, Bahamas

484. UNDERCOVER OF THE NIGHT (1)
485. UNDERCOVER OF THE NIGHT (DUB VERSION) (2)
486. ALL THE WAY DOWN
487. FEEL ON BABY (1)
488. FEEL ON BABY (INSTRUMENTAL MIX) (2)
489. PRETTY BEAT UP
490. WANNA HOLD YOU
491. SHE WAS HOT
492. TIE YOU UP (THE PAIN OF LOVE)
493. TOO TOUGH
494. IT MUST BE HELL
495. TOO MUCH BLOOD (1)
496. TOO MUCH BLOOD (DANCE VERSION) (2)
497. TOO MUCH BLOOD (DUB VERSION) (3)

1985

FEBRUARY–NOVEMBER 1985
Pathé Marconi Studios, Paris, France

498. HARLEM SHUFFLE (1)
499. HARLEM SHUFFLE (NY MIX) (2)
500. HARLEM SHUFFLE (LONDON MIX) (3)
501. HAD IT WITH YOU
502. STRICTLY MEMPHIS
503. DEEP LOVE
504. TOO RUDE
505. BACK TO ZERO
506. WINNING UGLY
507. FIGHT
508. ONE HIT (TO THE BODY) (1)

509. ONE HIT (TO THE BODY) (LONDON MIX) (2)
510. WHAT ARE YOU GONNA DO WITH MY LOVE?
511. YOU'RE TOO MUCH
512. HOLD BACK
513. DIRTY WORK
514. SLEEP TONIGHT

1989

FEBRUARY–MAY 1989
Air Studios, Montserrat, Leeward Islands

515. MIXED EMOTIONS (1)
516. MIXED EMOTIONS (CHRIS KIMSEY'S 12") (2)
517. ROCK AND A HARD PLACE (1)
518. ROCK AND A HARD PLACE (DANCE MIX) (2)
519. ROCK AND A HARD PLACE (BONUS BEATS MIX) (3)
520. ROCK AND A HARD PLACE (OH-OH HARD DUB MIX) (4)
521. ALMOST HEAR YOU SIGH
522. SAD SAD SAD
523. HEARTS FOR SALE
524. HOLD ON TO YOUR HAT
525. SLIPPING AWAY
526. FOR YOUR PRECIOUS LOVE
527. CAN'T BE SEEN
528. BREAK THE SPELL
529. COOK COOK BLUES
530. BLINDED BY LOVE
531. TERRIFYING
532. FANCYMAN BLUES
533. CONTINENTAL DRIFT

28 OCTOBER 1989
Shea Stadium, New York

534. 2000 LIGHT YEARS FROM HOME (2)

UK and USA Discography

The sessionography and discography only includes compilation albums where significant, i.e. those compilation albums which met with the Stones' official approval or which contain otherwise unreleased material. The release date is given together with catalogue number, chart placing and number of weeks featured in the appropriate chart. The sessionography number is in brackets. Chart positions and number of weeks are quoted until date of going to press.

7 June 1963
UK Single
Decca F 11675
No **21** – 14 weeks
COME ON (7)/I WANT TO BE LOVED (8)

September 1963
UK Compilation Album THANK YOUR LUCKY STARS VOL 2
Decca LK 4554
Other artists but includes *COME ON (7)*

1 November 1963
UK Single
Decca F 11764
No **12** – 16 weeks
I WANNA BE YOUR MAN (19)/ STONED (20)

January 1964
UK Compilation Album READY STEADY GO!
Decca LK 4577
No **20** – 1 week

Other artists but includes *COME ON (7)/I WANNA BE YOUR MAN (19)*

January 1964
UK Compilation Album SATURDAY CLUB
Decca LK 4583
Other artists but includes *POISON IVY (9)/FORTUNE TELLER (11)*

17 January 1964
UK Extended Play Single THE ROLLING STONES
Decca DFE 8560
BYE BYE JOHNNY (13)/MONEY (14)/YOU BETTER MOVE ON (12)/ POISON IVY (21)

21 February 1964
UK Single
Decca F 11845
No **3** – 15 weeks
NOT FADE AWAY (34)/LITTLE BY LITTLE (35)

March 1964

USA Single
London 9657
NOT FADE AWAY (34)/*I WANNA BE YOUR MAN* (19)

26 April 1964

UK Album THE ROLLING STONES
Decca LK 4605
No **1** – 51 weeks
ROUTE 66 (23)/*I JUST WANT TO MAKE LOVE TO YOU* (24)/ *HONEST I DO* (25)/*I NEED YOU BABY (MONA)* (26)/*NOW I'VE GOT A WITNESS* (27)/*LITTLE BY LITTLE* (35)/*I'M A KING BEE* (28)/ *CAROL* (29)/*TELL ME* (30)/*CAN I GET A WITNESS* (31)/*YOU CAN MAKE IT IF YOU TRY* (32)/ *WALKING THE DOG* (33)

May 1964

USA Album ENGLAND'S NEWEST HITMAKERS
London PS 375
No **11** – 12 weeks
NOT FADE AWAY (34)/*ROUTE 66* (23)/*I JUST WANT TO MAKE LOVE TO YOU* (24)/*HONEST I DO* (25)/*NOW I'VE GOT A WITNESS* (27)/*LITTLE BY LITTLE* (35)/*I'M A KING BEE* (28)/*CAROL* (29)/*TELL ME* (30)/*CAN I GET A WITNESS* (31)/*YOU CAN MAKE IT IF YOU TRY* (32)/*WALKING THE DOG* (33)

21 May 1964

UK Compilation Album FOURTEEN
Decca LK 4695
Other artists but includes
SURPRISE, SURPRISE (41)

19 June 1964

USA Single
London 9682
No **24** – 5 weeks
TELL ME (30)/*I JUST WANT TO MAKE LOVE TO YOU* (24)

26 June 1964

UK Single
Decca F 11934
No **1** – 15 weeks
IT'S ALL OVER NOW (63)/*GOOD TIMES, BAD TIMES* (42)

July 1964

USA Single
London 9687
No **26** – 6 weeks
IT'S ALL OVER NOW (63)/*GOOD TIMES, BAD TIMES* (42)

14 August 1964

UK Extended Play Single FIVE BY FIVE
Decca DFE 8590
IF YOU NEED ME (51)/*EMPTY HEART* (52)/*2120 SOUTH MICHIGAN AVENUE* (53)/ *CONFESSIN' THE BLUES* (54)/ *AROUND AND AROUND* (55)

September 1964

USA Single
London 9708
No **6** – 9 weeks
TIME IS ON MY SIDE (46)/ *CONGRATULATIONS* (44)

October 1964

USA Album 12 X 5
London PS 402
No **3** – 20 weeks
AROUND AND AROUND (55)/ *CONFESSIN' THE BLUES* (54)/ *EMPTY HEART* (52)/*TIME IS ON MY SIDE* (46)/*GOOD TIMES, BAD TIMES* (42)/*IT'S ALL OVER NOW* (63)/*2120 SOUTH MICHIGAN AVENUE* (53)/*UNDER THE BOARDWALK* (47)/ *CONGRATULATIONS* (44)/ *GROWN UP WRONG* (49)/*IF YOU NEED ME* (51)/*SUZIE Q* (48)

13 November 1964
UK Single
Decca F 12014
No **1** – 12 weeks
LITTLE RED ROOSTER (90)/*OFF
THE HOOK* (43)

December 1964
USA Single
London 9725
No **19** – 5 weeks
HEART OF STONE (78)/*WHAT A
SHAME* (86)

30 January 1965
UK Album THE ROLLING STONES
NO. 2
Decca LK 4661
No **1** – 37 weeks
*EVERYBODY NEEDS SOMEBODY
TO LOVE* (75)/*DOWN HOME GIRL*
(74)/*YOU CAN'T CATCH ME*
(45)/*TIME IS ON MY SIDE* (91)/
WHAT A SHAME (86)/*GROWN UP
WRONG* (49)/*DOWN THE ROAD
APIECE* (60)/*UNDER THE
BOARDWALK* (47)/*I CAN'T BE
SATISFIED* (61)/*PAIN IN MY
HEART* (77)/*OFF THE HOOK* (43)/
SUZIE Q (48)

February 1965
USA Album THE ROLLING
STONES NOW!
London PS 420
No **5** – 29 weeks
*EVERYBODY NEEDS SOMEBODY
TO LOVE* (76)/*DOWN HOME GIRL*
(74)/*YOU CAN'T CATCH ME*
(45)/*HEART OF STONE* (78)/*WHAT
A SHAME* (86)/*I NEED YOU BABY*
(26)/*DOWN THE ROAD APIECE*
(60)/*OFF THE HOOK* (43)/*PAIN IN
MY HEART* (77)/*OH, BABY(WE
GOT A GOOD THING GOING)*
(80)/*LITTLE RED ROOSTER* (90)/
SURPRISE, SURPRISE (41)

26 February 1965
UK Single
Decca F 12104
No **1** – 13 weeks
THE LAST TIME (96)/*PLAY WITH
FIRE* (97)

March 1965
USA Single
London 9741
No **9** – 8 weeks
THE LAST TIME (96)/*PLAY WITH
FIRE* (97)

May 1965
USA Single
London 9766
No **1** – 12 weeks
(I CAN'T GET NO) SATISFACTION
(115)/*THE UNDER ASSISTANT
WEST COAST PROMOTION MAN*
(108)

11 June 1965
UK Extended Play Single GOT
LIVE IF YOU WANT IT!
Decca DFE 8620
*EVERYBODY NEEDS SOMEBODY
TO LOVE* (98)/*PAIN IN MY HEART*
(99)/*ROUTE 66* (100)/*I'M MOVING
ON* (101)/*I'M ALRIGHT* (102)

July 1965
USA Album OUT OF OUR HEADS
London PS 429
No **1** – 35 weeks
MERCY MERCY (109)/*HITCH
HIKE* (79)/*THE LAST TIME* (96)/
*THAT'S HOW STRONG MY LOVE
IS* (110)/*GOOD TIMES* (116)/*I'M
ALRIGHT* (102)/*(I CAN'T GET NO)
SATISFACTION* (115)/*CRY TO ME*
(117)/*THE UNDER ASSISTANT
WEST COAST PROMOTION MAN*
(108)/*PLAY WITH FIRE* (97)/*THE
SPIDER AND THE FLY* (112)/*ONE
MORE TRY* (113)

20 August 1965
UK Single
Decca F 12220
No **1** – 12 weeks
(I CAN'T GET NO) SATISFACTION
(115)/THE SPIDER AND THE FLY
(112)

September 1965
USA Single
London 9792
No **1** – 11 weeks
GET OFF MY CLOUD (132)/I'M
FREE (122)

6 September 1965
UK Album OUT OF OUR HEADS
Decca LK 4733
No **2** – 24 weeks
SHE SAID YEAH (118)/MERCY
MERCY (109)/HITCH HIKE (79)/
THAT'S HOW STRONG MY LOVE
IS (110)/GOOD TIMES (116)/
GOTTA GET AWAY (119)/TALKIN'
ABOUT YOU (121)/CRY TO ME
(117)/OH BABY (WE GOT A GOOD
THING GOING) (80)/HEART OF
STONE (78)/THE UNDER
ASSISTANT WEST COAST
PROMOTION MAN (108)/I'M FREE
(122)

22 October 1965
UK Single
Decca F 12263
No **1** – 12 weeks
GET OFF MY CLOUD (132)/THE
SINGER NOT THE SONG (133)

November 1965
USA Album DECEMBER'S
CHILDREN
London PS 451
No **4** – 22 weeks
SHE SAID YEAH (118)/TALKIN'
'BOUT YOU (121)/YOU BETTER
MOVE ON (12)/LOOK WHAT
YOU'VE DONE (64)/THE SINGER
NOT THE SONG (133)/ROUTE 66

(23)/GET OFF MY CLOUD (132)/
I'M FREE (122)/AS TEARS GO BY
(134)/GOTTA GET AWAY (119)/
BLUE TURNS TO GREY (123)/I'M
MOVING ON (101)

December 1965
USA Single
London 9808
No **6** – 6 weeks
AS TEARS GO BY (134)/GOTTA
GET AWAY (119)

4 February 1966
UK Single
Decca F 12331
No **2** – 8 weeks
19TH NERVOUS BREAKDOWN
(147)/AS TEARS GO BY (134)

February 1966
USA Single
London 9823
No **2** – 9 weeks
19TH NERVOUS BREAKDOWN
(147)/SAD DAY (146)

March 1966
USA Compilation Album BIG HITS
(HIGH TIDE AND GREEN GRASS)
London NPS 1
No **3** – 35 weeks
THE LAST TIME (96)/AS TEARS
GO BY (134)/TIME IS ON MY SIDE
(73)/IT'S ALL OVER NOW (63)/
TELL ME (30)/19TH NERVOUS
BREAKDOWN (147)/HEART OF
STONE (78)/GET OFF MY CLOUD
(132)/NOT FADE AWAY (34)/
GOOD TIMES, BAD TIMES (42)/
PLAY WITH FIRE (97)

April 1966
UK Album AFTERMATH
Decca SKL 4786
No **1** – 28 weeks
MOTHER'S LITTLE HELPER (137)/
STUPID GIRL (155)/LADY JANE
(153)/UNDER MY THUMB (158)/

DONCHA BOTHER ME (138)/ *GOIN' HOME* (139)/*FLIGHT 505* (160)/*HIGH AND DRY* (159)/*OUT OF TIME* (151)/*IT'S NOT EASY* (154)/*I AM WAITING* (161)/*TAKE IT OR LEAVE IT* (142)/*THINK* (143)/*WHAT TO DO* (162)

April 1966
USA Single
London 901
No **1** – 10 weeks
PAINT IT, BLACK (156)/*STUPID GIRL* (155)

13 May 1966
UK Single
Decca F 12395
No **1** – 10 weeks
PAINT IT, BLACK (156)/*LONG LONG WHILE* (157)

June 1966
USA Album AFTERMATH
London PS 476
No **2** – 26 weeks
PAINT IT, BLACK (156)/*STUPID GIRL* (155)/*LADY JANE* (153)/ *UNDER MY THUMB* (158)/ *DONCHA BOTHER ME* (138)/ *THINK* (143)/*FLIGHT 505* (160)/ *HIGH AND DRY* (159)/*IT'S NOT EASY* (154)/*I AM WAITING* (161)/ *GOIN' HOME* (139)

June 1966
USA Single
London 902
No **8** – 8 weeks
MOTHER'S LITTLE HELPER (137)/ *LADY JANE* (153)

23 September 1966
UK & USA Single
Decca F 12497
No **5** – 8 weeks
London 903
No **9** – 6 weeks
HAVE YOU SEEN YOUR

MOTHER, BABY, STANDING IN THE SHADOW? (164)/*WHO'S DRIVING YOUR PLANE?*(165)

November 1966
USA Album GOT LIVE IF YOU WANT IT!
London PS 493
No **6** – 11 weeks
UNDER MY THUMB (170)/*GET OFF MY CLOUD* (171)/*LADY JANE* (172)/*NOT FADE AWAY* (173)/*I'VE BEEN LOVING YOU TOO LONG* (174)/*FORTUNE TELLER* (175)/*THE LAST TIME* (176)/*19TH NERVOUS BREAKDOWN* (177)/*TIME IS ON MY SIDE* (178)/*I'M ALRIGHT* (179)/ *HAVE YOU SEEN YOUR MOTHER BABY, STANDING IN THE SHADOW?*(180)/*(I CAN'T GET NO) SATISFACTION* (181)

November 1966
UK Compilation Album BIG HITS (HIGH TIDE AND GREEN GRASS)
Decca TXS 101
No **4** – 43 weeks
HAVE YOU SEEN YOUR MOTHER BABY, STANDING IN THE SHADOW? (164)/*PAINT IT, BLACK* (156)/*IT'S ALL OVER NOW* (63)/ *THE LAST TIME* (96)/*HEART OF STONE* (78)/*NOT FADE AWAY* (34)/*COME ON* (7)/*(I CAN'T GET NO) SATISFACTION* (115)/*GET OFF MY CLOUD* (132)/*AS TEARS GO BY* (134)/*19TH NERVOUS BREAKDOWN* (147)/*LADY JANE* (153)/*TIME IS ON MY SIDE* (73)/ *LITTLE RED ROOSTER* (90)

13 January 1967
UK Single
Decca F 12546
No **3** – 10 weeks
LET'S SPEND THE NIGHT TOGETHER (184)/*RUBY TUESDAY* (182)

13 January 1967
USA Single
London 904
No **1** – 9 weeks
RUBY TUESDAY (182)/*LET'S
SPEND THE NIGHT TOGETHER*
(184)

20 January 1967
UK Album BETWEEN THE
BUTTONS
Decca LK 4852
No **3** – 22 weeks
YESTERDAY'S PAPERS (188)/*MY
OBSESSION* (185)/*BACK STREET
GIRL* (191)/*CONNECTION* (197)/
SHE SMILED SWEETLY (187)/
COOL CALM AND COLLECTED
(193)/*ALL SOLD OUT* (186)/
PLEASE GO HOME (189)/*WHO'S
BEEN SLEEPING HERE?* (195)/
COMPLICATED (196)/*MISS
AMANDA JONES* (190)/
*SOMETHING HAPPENED TO ME
YESTERDAY* (194)

20 January 1967
USA Album BETWEEN THE
BUTTONS
London PS 499
No **2** – 19 weeks
*LET'S SPEND THE NIGHT
TOGETHER* (184)/*YESTERDAY'S
PAPERS* (188)/*RUBY TUESDAY*
(182)/*CONNECTION* (197)/*SHE
SMILED SWEETLY* (187)/*COOL
CALM AND COLLECTED* (193)/
ALL SOLD OUT (186)/*MY
OBSESSION* (185)/*WHO'S BEEN
SLEEPING HERE?* (195)/
COMPLICATED (196)/*MISS
AMANDA JONES* (190)/
*SOMETHING HAPPENED TO ME
YESTERDAY* (194)

June 1967
USA Compilation Album FLOWERS
London PS 509
No **3** – 18 weeks

RUBY TUESDAY (182)/*HAVE YOU
SEEN YOUR MOTHER BABY,
STANDING IN THE SHADOW?*
(164)/*LET'S SPEND THE NIGHT
TOGETHER* (184)/*LADY JANE*
(153)/*OUT OF TIME* (151)/*MY GIRL*
(114)/*BACK STREET GIRL* (191)/
PLEASE GO HOME (189)/
MOTHER'S LITTLE HELPER (137)/
TAKE IT OR LEAVE IT (142)/*RIDE
ON BABY* (144)/*SITTIN' ON A
FENCE* (145)

18 August 1967
UK Single
Decca F 12654
No **8** – 8 weeks
WE LOVE YOU (200)/*DANDELION*
(183)

18 August 1967
USA Single
London 905
No **14** – 6 weeks
DANDELION (183)/*WE LOVE YOU*
(200)

November 1967
USA Single
London 906
No **25** – 4 weeks
SHE'S A RAINBOW (201)/*2000
LIGHT YEARS FROM HOME* (204)

November 1967
USA Album THEIR SATANIC
MAJESTIES REQUEST
London NPS 2
No **2** – 13 weeks

December 1967
UK Album THEIR SATANIC
MAJESTIES REQUEST
Decca TXS 103
No **3** – 13 weeks
SING THIS ALL TOGETHER (202)/
CITADEL (206)/*IN ANOTHER
LAND* (205)/*2000 MAN* (207)/*SING
THIS ALL TOGETHER (SEE WHAT*

HAPPENS) (203)/SHE'S A
RAINBOW (201)/THE LANTERN
(209)/GOMPER (208)/2000 LIGHT
YEARS FROM HOME (204)/ON
WITH THE SHOW (210)

December 1967
USA Single
London 907
IN ANOTHER LAND (205)/THE
LANTERN (209)

24 May 1968
UK and USA Single
Decca F 12782
No **1** – 11 weeks
London 908
No **3** – 11 weeks
JUMPIN' JACK FLASH (212)/CHILD
OF THE MOON (213)

August 1968
USA Single
London 909
STREET FIGHTING MAN (215)/NO
EXPECTATIONS (216)

November 1968
USA Album BEGGARS BANQUET
London PS 539
No **5** – 13 weeks

5 December 1968
UK Album BEGGARS BANQUET
Decca SKL 4955
No **3** – 12 weeks
SYMPATHY FOR THE DEVIL
(218)/NO EXPECTATIONS (216)/
DEAR DOCTOR (219)/
PARACHUTE WOMAN (227)/
JIGSAW PUZZLE (226)/STREET
FIGHTING MAN (215)/PRODIGAL
SON (221)/STRAY CAT BLUES
(230)/FACTORY GIRL (231)/SALT
OF THE EARTH (229)

11 July 1969
UK and USA Single
Decca F 12952

No **1** – 17 weeks
London 910
No **1** – 14 weeks
HONKY TONK WOMEN (252)/YOU
CAN'T ALWAYS GET WHAT YOU
WANT (234)

12 September 1969
UK Compilation Album THROUGH
THE PAST DARKLY (BIG HITS
VOL 2)
Decca SKL 5019
No **2** – 37 weeks
JUMPIN' JACK FLASH (212)/
MOTHER'S LITTLE HELPER (137)/
2000 LIGHT YEARS FROM HOME
(204)/LET'S SPEND THE NIGHT
TOGETHER (184)/YOU BETTER
MOVE ON (12)/WE LOVE YOU
(200)/STREET FIGHTING MAN
(215)/SHE'S A RAINBOW (201)/
RUBY TUESDAY (182)/
DANDELION (183)/SITTIN' ON A
FENCE (145)/HONKY TONK
WOMEN (252)

September 1969
USA Compilation Album
THROUGH THE PAST DARKLY
(BIG HITS VOL 2)
London NPS 3
No **2** – 16 weeks
HONKY TONK WOMEN (252)/
PAINT IT, BLACK (156)/STREET
FIGHTING MAN (215)/SHE'S A
RAINBOW (201)/JUMPIN' JACK
FLASH (212)/DANDELION (183)/
RUBY TUESDAY (182)/HAVE YOU
SEEN YOUR MOTHER BABY,
STANDING IN THE SHADOW?
(164)/LET'S SPEND THE NIGHT
TOGETHER (184)/2000 LIGHT
YEARS FROM HOME (204)/
MOTHER'S LITTLE HELPER (137)

October 1969
USA Compilation Album THE
ROLLING STONES –
PROMOTIONAL ALBUM
London RSD-1

ROUTE 66 (23)/ *WALKING THE DOG* (33)/ *AROUND AND AROUND* (55)/ *SUZIE Q* (48)/ *EVERYBODY NEEDS SOMEBODY TO LOVE* (75)/ *OFF THE HOOK* (43)/ *I'M FREE* (122)/ *SHE SAID YEAH* (118)/ *UNDER MY THUMB* (158)/ *STUPID GIRL* (155)/ *2000 MAN* (207)/ *SYMPATHY FOR THE DEVIL* (217)/ *PRODIGAL SON* (221)/ *LOVE IN VAIN* (254)

November 1969
USA Album LET IT BLEED
London NPS 4
No **3** – 19 weeks

December 1969
UK Album LET IT BLEED
Decca SKL 5025
No **1** – 29 weeks
GIMMIE SHELTER (273)/ *LOVE IN VAIN* (254)/ *COUNTRY HONK* (276)/ *LIVE WITH ME* (274)/ *LET IT BLEED* (253)/ *MIDNIGHT RAMBLER* (232)/ *YOU GOT THE SILVER* (233)/ *MONKEY MAN* (257)/ *YOU CAN'T ALWAYS GET WHAT YOU WANT* (234)

20 July 1970
UK Single
Decca F 13203
No **21** – 8 weeks
STREET FIGHTING MAN (215)/ *SURPRISE, SURPRISE* (41)

29 September 1970
UK and USA Album GET YER YA-YA'S OUT
Decca SKL 5065
No **1** – 15 weeks
London NPS 4
No **6** – 10 weeks
JUMPIN' JACK FLASH (283)/ *CAROL* (284)/ *STRAY CAT BLUES* (285)/ *LOVE IN VAIN* (286)/ *MIDNIGHT RAMBLER* (287)/ *SYMPATHY FOR THE DEVIL* (288)/ *LIVE WITH ME* (289)/ *LITTLE QUEENIE* (290)/ *HONKY TONK WOMEN* (291)/ *STREET FIGHTING MAN* (292)

November 1970
UK Single
Decca F 13067
MEMO FROM TURNER (240)/ *NATURAL MAGIC*
NATURAL MAGIC features Jack Nitzsche – single credited to Mick Jagger only.

16 April 1971
UK Single
RS 19100
No **2** – 13 weeks
BROWN SUGAR (295)/ *BITCH* (298)/ *LET IT ROCK* (307)

23 April 1971
UK Compilation Album STONE AGE
Decca SKL 5084
No **4** – 7 weeks
LOOK WHAT YOU'VE DONE (64)/ *IT'S ALL OVER NOW* (63)/ *CONFESSIN' THE BLUES* (54)/ *ONE MORE TRY* (113)/ *AS TEARS GO BY* (134)/ *THE SPIDER AND THE FLY* (112)/ *MY GIRL* (114)/ *PAINT IT, BLACK* (156)/ *IF YOU NEED ME* (51)/ *THE LAST TIME* (96)/ *BLUE TURNS TO GREY* (123)/ *AROUND AND AROUND* (55)
STONE AGE is not an 'official' compilation album.

May 1971
USA Single
RLS 19100
No **1** – 12 weeks
BROWN SUGAR (295)/ *BITCH* (298)

23 April 1971
UK Album STICKY FINGERS
COC 59100
No **1** – 25 weeks

June 1971
USA Album STICKY FINGERS
COC 59100
No **1** – 26 weeks
BROWN SUGAR (295)/SWAY (301)/
WILD HORSES (293)/CAN'T YOU
HEAR ME KNOCKING (302)/YOU
GOTTA MOVE (294)/BITCH (298)/I
GOT THE BLUES (300)/SISTER
MORPHINE (235)/DEAD
FLOWERS (303)/MOONLIGHT
MILE (299)

June 1971
USA Single
RLS 101
No **28** – 5 weeks
WILD HORSES (293)/SWAY (301)

14 April 1972
UK and USA Single
RS 19103 (UK)
No **5** – 8 weeks
RLS 19103 (USA)
USA No **7** – 9 weeks
TUMBLING DICE (317)/SWEET
BLACK ANGEL (318)

12 May 1972
UK and USA Album EXILE ON
MAIN ST.
COC 69100 (UK)
No **1** – 16 weeks
COC 2-2900 (USA)
No **1** – 17 weeks
ROCKS OFF (325)/RIP THIS JOINT
(321)/SHAKE YOUR HIPS (310)/
CASINO BOOGIE (326)/TUMBLING
DICE (317)/SWEET VIRGINIA
(320)/TORN AND FRAYED (312)/
SWEET BLACK ANGEL (318)/
LOVING CUP (313)/HAPPY (322)/
TURD ON THE RUN (315)/
VENTILATOR BLUES (311)/I JUST
WANT TO SEE HIS FACE (319)/
LET IT LOOSE (327)/ALL DOWN
THE LINE (316)/STOP BREAKING
DOWN (324)/SHINE A LIGHT
(328)/SOUL SURVIVOR (323)

June 1972
USA Single
RLS 19104
No **22** – 4 weeks
HAPPY (322)/ALL DOWN THE
LINE (316)

30 June 1972
UK Maxi-Single
Decca 'Maxi-Single' F 13195
EVERYBODY NEEDS SOMEBODY
TO LOVE (75)/STREET FIGHTING
MAN (215)/SURPRISE, SURPRISE
(41)

29 April 1973
UK Single
Decca F 13404
SAD DAY (146)/YOU CAN'T
ALWAYS GET WHAT YOU WANT
(234)

20 August 1973
UK and USA Single
RS 19105 (UK)
No **5** – 10 weeks
RLS 19105 (USA)
No **1** – 13 weeks
ANGIE (347)/SILVER TRAIN (348)

31 August 1973
UK and USA Album GOATS HEAD
SOUP
COC 59101
UK No **1** – 14 weeks
USA No **1** – 19 weeks
DANCING WITH MR. D (346)/100
YEARS AGO (349)/COMING
DOWN AGAIN (341)/DOO DOO
DOO DOO (HEARTBREAKER)
(352)/ANGIE (347)/SILVER TRAIN
(348)/HIDE YOUR LOVE (350)/
WINTER (342)/CAN YOU HEAR
THE MUSIC (345)/STAR STAR (353)

December 1973

USA Single
RS 19109
No **15** – 6 weeks
DOO DOO DOO DOO (HEARTBREAKER) (352)/*DANCING WITH MR. D* (346)

26 July 1974

UK and USA Single
RS 19114 (UK)
No **10** – 7 weeks
RS 19301 (USA)
No **16** – 7 weeks
IT'S ONLY ROCK 'N' ROLL (362)/ *THROUGH THE LONELY NIGHTS* (354)

October 1974

USA Single
RS 19302
No **17** – 7 weeks
AIN'T TOO PROUD TO BEG (357)/ *DANCE LITTLE SISTER* (367)

18 October 1974

UK and USA Album IT'S ONLY ROCK 'N' ROLL
COC 59103 (UK)
No **2** – 9 weeks
COC 79101 (USA)
No **1** – 11 weeks
IF YOU CAN'T ROCK ME (359)/ *AIN'T TOO PROUD TO BEG* (357)/ *IT'S ONLY ROCK 'N' ROLL* (362)/ *TILL THE NEXT GOODBYE* (361)/ *TIME WAITS FOR NO ONE* (364)/ *LUXURY* (365)/*DANCE LITTLE SISTER* (367)/*IF YOU REALLY WANT TO BE MY FRIEND* (363)/ *SHORT AND CURLIES* (368)/ *FINGERPRINT FILE* (360)

23 May 1975

UK and USA Single
Decca F 13584 (UK)
ABKCO 4701 (USA)
I DON'T KNOW WHY (256)/*TRY A LITTLE HARDER* (141)

6 June 1975

UK Album METAMORPHIS
Decca SKL 5212
No **45** – 1 week
OUT OF TIME (152)/*DON'T LIE TO ME* (62)/*SOME THINGS JUST STICK IN YOUR MIND* (70)/*EACH AND EVERY DAY YEAR OF THE YEAR* (89)/*HEART OF STONE* (78)/*I'D MUCH RATHER BE WITH THE BOYS* (87)/*SLEEPY CITY* (71)/ *WE'RE WASTIN' TIME* (88)/*TRY A LITTLE HARDER* (141)/*I DON'T KNOW WHY* (256)/*IF YOU LET ME* (192)/*JIVING SISTER FANNY* (258)/*DOWNTOWN SUZIE* (220)/ *FAMILY* (228)/*MEMO FROM TURNER* (241)/*I'M GOING DOWN* (255)

6 June 1975

USA Album METAMORPHIS
ABKCO ANA 1
No **8** – 8 weeks
OUT OF TIME (152)/*DON'T LIE TO ME* (62)/*EACH AND EVERY DAY OF THE YEAR* (89)/*HEART OF STONE* (78)/*I'D MUCH RATHER BE WITH THE BOYS* (87)/*TRY A LITTLE HARDER* (141)/*I DON'T KNOW WHY* (256)/*IF YOU LET ME* (192)/*JIVING SISTER FANNY* (258)/*DOWNTOWN SUZIE* (220)/ *FAMILY* (228)/*MEMO FROM TURNER* (241)/*I'M GOING DOWN* (255)

6 June 1975

UK and USA Compilation Album MADE IN THE SHADE
COC 59104 (UK)
No **14** – 12 weeks
COC 79101 (USA)
No **6** – 9 weeks
BROWN SUGAR (295)/*TUMBLING DICE* (317)/*HAPPY* (322)/*DANCE LITTLE SISTER* (367)/*WILD HORSES* (293)/*ANGIE* (347)/*BITCH*

(298)/*IT'S ONLY ROCK 'N' ROLL* (362)/*DOO DOO DOO DOO (HEARTBREAKER)* (352)/*RIP THIS JOINT* (321)

5 September 1975
UK and USA Single
Decca F 13597 (UK)
No **45** – 2 weeks
ABKCO 4702 (USA)
OUT OF TIME (152)/*JIVING SISTER FANNY* (258)

20 April 1976
UK Single
RS 19121
No **6** – 10 weeks
FOOL TO CRY (369)/*CRAZY MAMA* (377)

20 April 1976
USA Single
RS 19304
No **10** – 7 weeks
FOOL TO CRY (369)/*HOT STUFF* (378)

20 April 1976
UK and USA Album BLACK AND BLUE
COC 59106 (UK)
No **2** – 14 weeks
COC 79104 (USA)
No **1** – 14 weeks
HOT STUFF (378)/*HAND OF FATE* (376)/*CHERRY OH BABY* (370)/*MEMORY MOTEL* (379)/*HEY NEGRITA* (380)/*MELODY* (373)/*FOOL TO CRY* (369)/*CRAZY MAMA* (377)

September 1977
UK and USA Album LOVE YOU LIVE
COC 89101 (UK)
No **3** – 8 weeks
COC 2-9001 (USA)
No **5** – 7 weeks
HONKY TONK WOMEN (382)/*IF*

YOU CAN'T ROCK ME (383)/*GET OFF MY CLOUD* (384)/*HAPPY* (385)/*HOT STUFF* (386)/*STAR STAR* (387)/*TUMBLING DICE* (388)/*FINGERPRINT FILE* (389)/*YOU GOTTA MOVE* (390)/*YOU CAN'T ALWAYS GET WHAT YOU WANT* (391)/*MANNISH BOY* (397)/*CRACKIN' UP* (398)/*LITTLE RED ROOSTER* (399)/*AROUND AND AROUND* (400)/*IT'S ONLY ROCK 'N' ROLL* (392)/*BROWN SUGAR* (393)/*JUMPIN' JACK FLASH* (394)/*SYMPATHY FOR THE DEVIL* (395)

May 1978
UK Compilation Album TIME WAITS FOR NO ONE – ANTHOLOGY 1971-1977
No chart placing
RSR COC 59107
TIME WAITS FOR NO ONE (364)/*BITCH* (298)/*ALL DOWN THE LINE* (316)/*DANCING WITH MR. D* (346)/*ANGIE* (347)/*STAR STAR* (353)/*IF YOU CAN'T ROCK ME* (383)/*GET OFF MY CLOUD* (384)/*HAND OF FATE* (376)/*CRAZY MAMA* (377)/*FOOL TO CRY* (369)

19 May 1978
UK and USA Single
EMI 2802 (UK)
No **3** – 13 weeks
RS 19306 (USA)
No **1** – 16 weeks
MISS YOU (422)/*FAR AWAY EYES* (419)

2 June 1978
UK and USA twelve-inch Single
12 EMI 2802 (UK)
MISS YOU (423)/*FAR AWAY EYES* (419)

9 June 1978
UK and USA Album SOME GIRLS
RSR CUN 39108
UK No **2** – 25 weeks

USA No **1** – 32 weeks
MISS YOU (423)/*WHEN THE WHIP
COMES DOWN* (405)/*JUST MY
IMAGINATION* (424)/*SOME GIRLS*
(416)/*LIES* (413)/*FAR AWAY EYES*
(419)/*RESPECTABLE* (406)/
BEFORE THEY MAKE ME RUN
(426)/*BEAST OF BURDEN* (412)/
SHATTERED (418)

15 September 1978
UK Single
EMI 2861
No **23** – 9 weeks
RESPECTABLE (406)/*WHEN THE
WHIP COMES DOWN* (405)

September 1978
USA Single
RS 19309
No **8** – 9 weeks
BEAST OF BURDEN (412)/*WHEN
THE WHIP COMES DOWN* (405)

December 1978
USA Single
RS 19310
No **31** – 4 weeks
SHATTERED (418)/*EVERYTHING
IS TURNING TO GOLD* (417)

20 June 1980
UK and USA Single
RSR 105 (UK)
No **9** – 8 weeks
RS 20001 (USA)
No **3** – 14 weeks
EMOTIONAL RESCUE (436)/
DOWN IN THE HOLE (441)

22 June 1980
UK and USA Album EMOTIONAL
RESCUE
RSR CUN 39111
UK No **1** – 18 weeks
USA No **1** – 20 weeks
DANCE (439)/*SUMMER
ROMANCE* (429)/*SEND IT TO ME*
(445)/*LET ME GO* (446)/*INDIAN

GIRL* (443)/*WHERE THE BOYS GO*
(428)/*DOWN IN THE HOLE* (441)/
EMOTIONAL RESCUE (436)/*SHE'S
SO COLD* (447)/*ALL ABOUT YOU*
(448)

September 1980
UK and USA Single
RSR 106 (UK)
No **33** – 6 weeks
RS 21001 (USA)
No **26** – 5 weeks
SHE'S SO COLD (447)/*SEND IT TO
ME* (445)

May 1981
UK and USA Compilation LP
SUCKING IN THE SEVENTIES
RSR CUNS 39112
USA No **15** – 5 weeks
SHATTERED (418)/*EVERYTHING
IS TURNING TO GOLD* (417)/*HOT
STUFF* (378)/*TIME WAITS FOR NO
ONE* (364)/*FOOL TO CRY* (369)/
MANNISH BOY (397)/*WHEN THE
WHIP COMES DOWN* (431)/*IF I
WAS A DANCER (DANCE PART
2)* (440)/*CRAZY MAMA* (377)/
BEAST OF BURDEN (412)

17 August 1981
UK and USA Single
RSR 108 (UK)
No **7** – 9 weeks
RS 21003 (USA)
No **2** – 18 weeks
START ME UP (409)/*NO USE IN
CRYING* (453)

24 August 1981
UK and USA Album TATTOO YOU
RSR CUNS 39114
UK No **2** – 29 weeks
USA No **1** – 30 weeks
START ME UP (409)/*HANG FIRE*
(408)/*SLAVE* (371)/*LITTLE T & A*
(452)/*BLACK LIMOUSINE* (403)/
NEIGHBOURS (456)/*WORRIED
ABOUT YOU* (372)/*TOPS* (355)/

HEAVEN (455)/*NO USE IN CRYING* (453)/*WAITING ON A FRIEND* (454)

30 November 1981
UK and USA Single
RSR 109 (UK)
No **50** – 6 weeks
RS 21004 (USA)
No **13** – 12 weeks
WAITING ON A FRIEND (454)/
LITTLE T & A (452)

April 1982
USA Single
RSR 21300
No **20** – 6 weeks
HANG FIRE (408)/*NEIGHBOURS* (456)

June 1982
UK and USA Single
RSR 110 (UK)
No **26** – 6 weeks
RS 21301 (USA)
No **25** – 5 weeks
GOING TO A GO-GO (469)/*BEAST OF BURDEN* (467)

1 June 1982
UK and USA Album STILL LIFE
(AMERICAN CONCERT 1981)
RSR CUN 39115
UK No **4** – 18 weeks
USA No **5** – 10 weeks
UNDER MY THUMB (458)/*LET'S SPEND THE NIGHT TOGETHER* (459)/*SHATTERED* (460)/*JUST MY IMAGINATION* (463)/*TWENTY FLIGHT ROCK* (464)/*LET ME GO* (465)/*TIME IS ON MY SIDE* (466)/*GOING TO A GO-GO* (469)/*START ME UP* (478)/*(I CAN'T GET NO) SATISFACTION* (482)

September 1982
UK and USA Single
RSR 111
UK No **62** – 2 weeks

TIME IS ON MY SIDE (466)/
TWENTY FLIGHT ROCK (464)

September 1982
UK and USA twelve-inch Single
12 RSR 111
UK No **62** – 2 weeks
TIME IS ON MY SIDE (466)/
TWENTY FLIGHT ROCK (464)/
UNDER MY THUMB (458)

October 1983
UK and USA Single
RSR 113
UK No **11** – 9 weeks
USA No **9** – 10 weeks
UNDERCOVER OF THE NIGHT (484)/*ALL THE WAY DOWN* (486)

October 1983
UK and USA twelve-inch Single
12 RSR 113
UK No **11** – 9 weeks
USA No **9** – 10 weeks
UNDERCOVER OF THE NIGHT (DUB VERSION) (485)/*FEEL ON BABY (INSTRUMENTAL MIX)* (488)

7 November 1983
UK and USA Album
UNDERCOVER
RSR CUN 1654361
UK No **3** – 18 weeks
USA No **4** – 12 weeks
UNDERCOVER OF THE NIGHT (484)/*SHE WAS HOT* (491)/*TIE YOU UP* (492)/*WANNA HOLD YOU* (490)/*FEEL ON BABY* (487)/*TOO MUCH BLOOD* (495)/*PRETTY BEAT UP* (489)/*TOO TOUGH* (493)*ALL THE WAY DOWN* (486)/*IT MUST BE HELL* (494)

February 1984
UK and USA Single
RSR 114
UK No **42** – 4 weeks
SHE WAS HOT (491)/*I THINK I'M GOING MAD* (411)

March 1984
USA twelve-inch Single
RSR 0-96902
TOO MUCH BLOOD (DANCE VERSION) (496)/*TOO MUCH BLOOD (DUB VERSION)* (497)

June 1984
UK Single
SUGAR 1
No **58** – 2 weeks
BROWN SUGAR (295)/*BITCH* (298)

10 March 1986
UK and USA Single
CBS A 6864
UK No **13** – 7 weeks
USA No **5** – 10 weeks
HARLEM SHUFFLE (498)/*HAD IT WITH YOU* (501)

17 March 1986
UK and USA twelve-inch Single
CBS QTA 6864
UK No **13** – 7 weeks
USA No **5** – 10 weeks
HARLEM SHUFFLE (NY MIX) (499)/*HARLEM SHUFFLE (LONDON MIX)* (500)/*HAD IT WITH YOU* (501)

24 March 1986
UK and USA Album DIRTY WORK
CBS 86321
UK No **4** – 10 weeks
USA No **4** – 15 weeks
ONE HIT (TO THE BODY) (508)/*FIGHT* (507)/*HARLEM SHUFFLE* (498)/*HOLD BACK* (512)/*TOO RUDE* (504)/*WINNING UGLY* (506)/*BACK TO ZERO* (505)/*DIRTY WORK* (513)/*HAD IT WITH YOU* (501)/*SLEEP TONIGHT* (514)

May 1986
UK and USA Single
CBS A 7160
USA No **28** – 4 weeks
ONE HIT (TO THE BODY) (508)/*FIGHT* (507)

May 1986
UK and USA twelve-inch Single
CBS TA 7160
USA No **28** – 4 weeks
ONE HIT (TO THE BODY) (LONDON MIX) (509)/*FIGHT* (507)

21 August 1989
UK and USA Single
UK CBS 655193 7
USA Colombia 38-69008
UK No. **36** – 5 weeks
USA No. **5** – 12 *weeks*
MIXED EMOTIONS (515)/*FANCYMAN BLUES* (532)

21 August 1989
UK and USA twelve-inch Single
CBS 655193 8
UK No. **36** – 5 weeks
USA No. **5** – 12 *weeks*
MIXED EMOTIONS (CHRIS KIMSEY'S 12") (516)/*FANCYMAN BLUES* (532)

1 September 1989
USA Album STEEL WHEELS
Columbia 45333
USA No. **3** – 20 *weeks*

11 September 1989
UK Album STEEL WHEELS
CBS 465752-1
UK No. **2** – 8 weeks
SAD SAD SAD (522)/*MIXED EMOTIONS* (515)/*TERRIFYING* (531)/*HOLD ON TO YOUR HAT* (524)/*HEARTS FOR SALE* (523)/*BLINDED BY LOVE* (526)/*ROCK AND A HARD PLACE* (517)/*CAN'T BE SEEN* (527)/*ALMOST HEAR YOU SIGH* (521)/*CONTINENTAL DRIFT* (533)/*BREAK THE SPELL* (528)/*SLIPPING AWAY* (525)

13 November 1989
UK and USA Single
CBS 655422-7

UK No **63** – 1 week
USA No **23** – 13 *weeks*
ROCK AND A HARD PLACE
(517)/COOK COOK BLUES(529)

13 November 1989

UK and USA twelve-inch Single
CBS 655422-8
UK No **63** – 1 week
USA No **23** – 13 *weeks*
ROCK AND A HARD PLACE
(DANCE MIX) (518)/ROCK AND A
HARD PLACE (OH-OH HARD DUB
MIX) (520)

13 November 1989

UK CD Single
CBS 655422-2
UK No **63** – 1 week
ROCK AND A HARD PLACE
(517)/ROCK AND A HARD PLACE
(DANCE MIX) (518)/ROCK AND A
HARD PLACE (BONUS BEATS
MIX) (519)/COOK COOK BLUES
(529)

(The discography does not include reference to Compact Disc releases but the *Rock And A Hard Place* CD issue is significant due to the inclusion of the *Bonus Beats Mix* which is unavailable on vinyl.)

Song Title Index

TITLE   SESSION   NUMBER

Note that the session number is given for each song as recorded – NOT the page number. Refer to the sessions as listed in the main section of this book.

Songwriters' Index

Songwriter	Number of Recordings
Jagger, Richard	252
Jagger, Richards	93
Berry	22
Nanker, Phelge	14
Dixon	9
Jagger, Richards, Wood	9
McDaniel	8
Russell, Burke, Wexler	6
Meade, Norman	5
Payne	4
Troup	4
Covay, Miller	3
Jagger, Richard, Oldham	3
Leiber, Stoller	3
Moore	3
Petty, Hardin	3
Reed	3
Relf, Nelson	3
Alexander	2
Anderson	2
Brown	2
Brown, McShann	2
Higgenbotham	2
Jagger, Richard, Taylor	2
Jarrett	2
Johnson	2
Leiber, Butler	2
Lennon, McCartney	2
McDowell	2
Neville	2
Phelge, Spector	2
Raye	2
Redding, Butler	2
Redding, Walden	2
Roderick, Jackson, Christy	2
Whitfield, Strong	2
Wilkins	2
B and S Womack	2
Wyman	2
Broonzy	1
Butler	1
Clark	1
Cooke	1
Donaldson	1
Fairchild, Cochran	1
Gaye, Stevenson, Paul	1
Gordy Junior, Bradford	1
Gray	1
Hawkins, Lewis, Broadwater	1
Hayes, Porter	1
Holland, Dozier, Holland	1
Jagger, Richard, Wood	1
Jagger, Richards, Jordan	1
Jagger, Richards, Leavell	1
Jamison	1
King, Josea, James, Taub	1
London, McDaniel, Morganfield	1
Merryweather	1
Morganfield	1
Oldham, Richard	1
Ozen	1
Phelge	1
Pickett, Bateman, Sanders	1
Reed, Reed	1
Resnick, Young	1
Richard	1
Richards	1
Richardson	1
Roberts	1
Robinson, Moore, Johnson, Rogers	1
Robinson, White	1
Russell	1
Seal, Fritts	1
Sherrill	1
Snow	1
Spector, Greenwich, Barry	1
Thomas	1
Unknown	1
Waters	1
Whitfield, Holland	1
Williams, David	1
Winter	1
Wonder, Riser, Hunter, Hardaway	1
Wyman, Gosling	1

Surprisingly, it was not until 12-13 May 1965, when the songwriting credits of 'Jagger, Richard' surpassed Chuck Berry's infamous talents!